T0247951

TRIVERGENCE

TRIVERGENCE

Accelerating Innovation with AI, Blockchain, and the Internet of Things

Bob Tapscott

WILEY

To the women in my life: Madison, Marissa, Kathy, and Emma.

Foreword

This book introduces an important and exciting new concept—the "Trivergence" of the three most important technologies of the second era of the digital age. Each of these three is transformational, but together, I believe the Trivergence will drive innovation, competitiveness, and maybe even greater prosperity over the next decade.

The neologism Trivergence arose from a conversation between me and Bob Tapscott several years ago. We were discussing the evolution of the "second era." Bob mused about the "trivergence" of three technologies, and I stopped him in mid-sentence and asked him to repeat the word. As an author and a public figure, I am always looking for formulations and even newly invented words that might help bring clarity to the bewildering developments of the digital age, and it struck me that Bob had come up with a beauty.

I'm delighted that my brother Bob chose to write this book, as Bob has a knack for engaging people with new ideas. Our collaboration began when he was, well, one day old, but it was in the early 1980s when we began to work together professionally. Bob was then the chief technologist at Citibank Canada, and I had left an executive position at Canada's version of Bell Labs—Bell Northern Research (BNR)—where we had been exploring how professional workstations connected to a vast "network of networks" might change the nature of work, management, and competitiveness.

The BNR work was way ahead of its time, and another executive and I left the company in 1982, taking a dozen people with us to set up the first consulting company in this area. A lot of people told me I was nuts. Our company, Trigon Technologies, helped companies develop a strategy for what we called "integrated office systems" at a time when the IBM personal computer had not yet hit the market.

Trigon's first challenge was to get a major corporate client, and Bob stepped up, hiring us to consult for Citi. Then, the corporate real estate division of the bank was open to funding and what emerging technologies might offer to white-collar workers—a radical concept at the time, as only "secretaries" used computers. Bob chose a company called Datapoint, the first commercial networked desktop computer. Using that platform, dozens of executives, including the bank's president, each received a workstation that gave them a spreadsheet program, a word processor, and email.

The team mapped and documented the workflows of complex real estate credits. As a result, Citi developed a system that was part workflow management and part complex loan-analysis tool. It aspired to reduce the time to evaluate the viability of complex multitenant billion-dollar real estate projects from three months down to one. When implemented, to everyone's surprise, the end-to-end analysis and documentation could be done in less than two weeks!

As a result, Citibank Canada crushed its competition, profits soared, and the head of the real estate division was appointed president of the Canadian bank, citing the system as the key factor in the division's success.

Bob described it as "an alternate automated electronic workflow system." Fifteen years later, Michael Hammer and James Champy came up with a more straightforward expression for how technology could impact organizations. They called it "business process reengineering," and their book describing this is one of the best-selling management books of all time. The ideas in the book paralleled the business process design work done at Citi.

The system was eventually installed in the US real estate division, in Europe, and Australia. The story was also important to my first bestseller, *Paradigm Shift: The New Promise of Information Technology*, in 1992.

After his job at Citi, Bob went on to a distinguished career as a CIO for other banks and as an independent consultant. Later, on Wall Street advising JP Morgan about derivatives, he was approached to do some preliminary analysis of a Denver-based company called Jeppesen—the predominant player in offering navigational information, operations planning tools, flight planning products, and software to the commercial aviation industry. If you are a pilot, you know the company.

Their two main products (charts for pilots and directions for the autopilots) were mostly created by human hands. Bob became the chief architect and designer of the system to reengineer and automate these core products. Today, both products are derived from a massive "Jeppesen Aviation Database" containing information for routes around the world, including 2.6 million data records and more than 18,000 airports. The upshot is dramatic improvements in flight safety. The head of the division that was automated went on to become the president of Jeppesen.

I'm sharing this history to let you know that *Trivergence* was not written by someone who is just a dreamer and a visionary but also by a hard-nosed practitioner and executive who has done big technology transformations over four decades. So, when the book describes an opportunity, it's a real one, and when it warns you about a challenge or danger, you would be wise to take heed.

Trivergence is a concept that is big and real. In the early stages, Bob and I had an interesting conversation about what exactly were the three technologies that really mattered. Eventually, we settled on AI, blockchain, and IoT, but there were other candidates. Extended reality—specifically, the metaverse—almost made the cut, but in the end, we concluded that while critical to the future, virtual worlds were more of an application environment than a foundational technology.

Will the word *Trivergence* become one of those neologisms that hits the zeitgeist and becomes part of our vernacular like, say, the singularity? Time will tell, and the winds lifting new concepts to our vocabulary are unpredictable and capricious. Over my history of writing books—18 of them—I am probably batting well under 50 percent. Terms like *paradigm shift*, the *digital economy*, the *digital divide*, *mass collaboration*, *digital capital*, and a few others did stick, although honestly, I'm not sure I was the first to utter such concepts. But there were many more that never caught the right updraft.

Regardless, I believe that Trivergence is a worthy framework to think about our digital future.

Whether you're a technology executive thinking about your company's strategy, an entrepreneur exploring new markets and new product concepts, a government policymaker working on sensible laws and regulations for technology, a business manager in any part of a company, or simply someone curious about the evolution of the digital age, you will find this book helpful and fun to read. So read on, enjoy, take action, prosper, and help us all fulfill the often elusive promise of technological innovation.

— **Don Tapscott, CEO of the Tapscott Group, executive chairman of the Blockchain Research Institute, and author of more than 18 books on business and technology**
October 2023

Contents

1

Introduction to the Era of Trivergence

One day in 2032, Mirai woke in the suburbs to the gentle glow of her smart home. As the sunlight filtered through her windows, the artificial intelligence (AI) embedded in her home adjusted the lighting to mimic the soft hues of dawn. The temperature, too, was attuned to her preferences, providing a cozy atmosphere as she prepared for the day. Her refrigerator, seamlessly integrated with the Internet of Things (IoT) network, sent a notification to her phone, reminding her to order groceries that were running low.

On the streets below, the city's autonomous transportation system flowed like a symphony. The significant reduction in the number of hours in a workweek has ended the rush hour chaos. Self-driving cars glided effortlessly, guided by sensors and algorithms that responded to the ebb and flow of traffic in real time. Public buses navigated routes with uncanny precision, maximizing efficiency and minimizing congestion. Commuters relaxed during their journeys, confident in the reliability of the AI-controlled vehicles.

As Mirai stepped out of her apartment, she securely fastened her digital ID bracelet around her wrist, granting her access to various services throughout the city. With a wave of her hand, she hailed a ride-share pod, which arrived within moments. The blockchain-backed digital ID ensured that her personal information remained encrypted and tamper-proof, safeguarding her privacy while facilitating seamless interactions.

The city's public services had undergone a transformation of their own. Waste management was a well-orchestrated ballet of sensors and algorithms. Smart garbage receptacles alerted the waste management center when they were nearing capacity, ensuring timely pickups that minimized disruptions and maintained the city's cleanliness. Energy consumption was optimized through an intricate network of AI-driven devices that monitored distributed inputs and usage patterns and adjusted accordingly, contributing to sustainability goals.

Further downtown, amidst the city's bustling streets, Amal found himself immersed in a world where work, leisure, and social connection seamlessly converged. As a software engineer, he thrived in the city's tech-driven environment. His hybrid work arrangement provided the autonomy to choose where he would be most productive, whether working remotely or in the sleek office building adorned with solar panels and living greenery—a testament to the city's commitment to sustainable design.

Inside, the open workspace hummed with the sounds of collaboration. Autonomous drones buzzed around, delivering packages and supplies to different teams. As Amal settled into his workspace, AI-assistants offered suggestions and insights as he fine-tuned his algorithms. The blockchain-powered network ensured that his work was securely stored and easily shareable with colleagues across the globe.

During his lunch break, Amal stepped out onto the solar-paneled plaza that doubled as a communal garden. He ordered a freshly prepared meal from a smart vending kiosk, his choices tailored to his dietary preferences and nutritional needs. As he savored his lunch, he couldn't help but marvel at how seamlessly technology had integrated into every facet of his life, enhancing convenience and enriching experiences.

In the heart of the city, Maria worked as a doctor at the advanced medical center. Blockchain, acting as an immutable ledger, maintained secure patient records that could be accessed seamlessly by authorized healthcare providers. Equipped with her AI-driven diagnostics assistant, Maria examined patient cases with a level of accuracy that had once been the stuff of science fiction. The AI processed extensive medical literature, cross-referenced patient data, and provided insights that often eluded even the most seasoned doctors.

Maria's patient, Javier, arrived at the medical center with his health-monitoring wristband displaying irregular readings. The wristband's sensors had detected potential cardiac irregularities, prompting it to notify both Javier and his doctor. Maria reviewed the real-time data, gave Javier a physical examination, and consulted with the AI. Together, they crafted a personalized treatment plan that combined her medical expertise with AI-generated insights.

Within the walls of a city high school, Ella, a spirited and inquisitive student, found herself at the heart of a dynamic environment where face-to-face interactions seamlessly intertwined with digital learning experiences. Her teacher, Ms. Ramirez, understood the delicate balance between harnessing technology's potential and nurturing the essential human connections that enriched learning.

Ms. Ramirez's role extended beyond being a source of knowledge; she was a mentor, a guide, and a source of inspiration. She embraced technology not as a replacement but as a tool that enabled her to focus on what truly mattered. Her warm encouragement and genuine belief in her students' capabilities created an environment where learning flourished. AI-powered tutors were her allies in this quest, providing tailored guidance that adapted to each student's pace, prior experience, and interests.

In her active learning classroom, students engaged in lively discussions, collaborative projects, and thought-provoking debates. These interactions underscored the irreplaceable value of learning alongside peers, developing empathy and communication skills that were essential for the future. Ms. Ramirez carefully curated immersive learning experiences that enabled her students to experience historical events, scientific phenomena, and artistic creations firsthand. These immersive journeys were interwoven with her engaging lessons, enhancing understanding and fostering a thirst for knowledge.

Gone were the days of rigid career paths; instead, citizens were welcomed into a landscape of dynamic job opportunities that adjusted to their unique skills and aspirations. With AI-driven career advisors that analyzed individual strengths and market trends, people found themselves seamlessly transitioning between roles, tapping into their innate potential in ever-changing industries. Blockchain-powered credential verification streamlined job transitions, ensuring that expertise was recognized and valued across various domains. Whether engaging in remote collaborations across the globe or participating in creative think tanks that span continents, the citizens of this city reveled in a work environment that matched their passion and capabilities, fostering a culture of innovation and constant growth.

As the sun dipped below the horizon, the city's lights painted a tapestry of progress and innovation. The symphony of AI, blockchain, and IoT had woven a seamless fabric into the very essence of daily life. Inhabitants moved through a world where technology didn't just coexist; it thrived, guiding their steps, and enhancing their experiences. The convergence of these groundbreaking technologies had sculpted a reality where human potential knew no bounds, opening the door to a future where the union of ingenuity and connectivity set the stage for unparalleled possibilities.

Everyone's privacy was protected, not by government legislation but by the technology itself. By interacting with the world, each player generated massive amounts of data, all which they not only had access to but which they owned.

In this vision, technology contributes to prosperity, health, and quality of life, but no one really noticed technology itself because it was transparent—it was like the air.

Welcome to the Trivergence

A utopian vision? Perhaps. But technology exists today to do everything in this story. It is starting to shake the windows and rattle the walls of companies and governments. Knowledge of these technologies is critical for every manager and anyone who cares about our digital future.

Yes, getting there is fraught with challenges. And to be sure there is a huge dark side for citizens and civilization if we don't do this right.

The digital age has entered a second era. The first era spanned the rise of mainframes, minicomputers, cellphones, the personal computer, fax, the Internet, mobility, the World Wide Web, social media, the mobile Web, the cloud, and big data. We are now entering a second era, where digital technologies permeate every facet of life and business. The unfolding era has been punctuated by innovations such as machine learning, robotics, drones, distributed ledgers, 5G networks, additive manufacturing, virtual reality, and synthetic biology.

Amid this evolution, a trio of technologies has emerged as the foundation for the second era of the digital age: artificial intelligence, blockchain, and the Internet of Things.

Call it the *Trivergence*.

The term is a neologism, invented in a conversation between myself and my brother, Don Tapscott. While many are familiar with AI, blockchain, and the IoT, a brief primer will help put the coming Trivergence into perspective:

Artificial intelligence (AI) refers to the simulation of human intelligence in machines, enabling them to perform tasks that had previously required human cognitive functions. From recognizing patterns in vast datasets to making recommendations for decision-making, AI is transforming industries such as healthcare, finance, and manufacturing. AI-powered virtual assistants, self-driving cars, and personalized content recommendations are just a glimpse of its potential. The significance of AI lies in its ability to automate complex tasks, enhance efficiency, and uncover insights hidden within data. Recent advances in deep learning have expanded beyond focusing on analyzing complex data sets to make predictions to generate entirely new content in data, text, speech, and image. AI is now transitioning from learning from data to beginning to think.

The Internet of Things (IoT) is a vast network of interconnected physical devices, vehicles, buildings, and other items embedded with sensors, software, and connectivity, allowing them to collect and exchange data. The physical world is becoming animated as everyday objects become part of this "web of everything," enabling applications such as smart homes, wearable health devices, climate monitoring, and predictive maintenance in industries. The power of IoT comes from its capacity to bring the digital world into the physical realm, enabling efficient monitoring, analysis, and control of various systems. This interconnectedness enhances convenience, optimizes resource utilization, and opens avenues for new business models and insights.

Blockchains are logs of events that may be implemented as decentralized and distributed ledgers across multiple computers. They achieve trust and transparency by creating a tamper-proof chain of data blocks, ensuring the immutability of records. Beyond cryptocurrencies, blockchain finds applications in supply chain management, identity verification, and secure data sharing. Its significance lies in its potential to eliminate intermediaries, enhance security, and redefine how we establish trust in transactions. By providing a tamper-proof platform, blockchain holds the potential to revolutionize industries, streamline processes, and redefine trust in the digital age. Over the past decade, blockchains have evolved from proprietary, permissioned ledgers to include programmable public networks, with Ethereum currently in the lead.

Each of these foundational technologies is uniquely and individually powerful. However, when taken together, each is transformed. This is a classic case of the whole being greater than the sum of its parts. What happens when we combine the power of AI with blockchain's ability to manage, store, and transact peer to peer, and with the IoT's capability to animate the physical world? What new opportunities will emerge? What new risks will arise?

This book introduces the concept and creates a basic and accessible guide to these complex technologies and their convergence, exploring the difficult decisions that business leaders must make to thrive in this new era. We'll explore how AI's power is exploding from smarter neural networks, multiplied by a new massively parallel architecture whose advances were funded by blockchain mining, manifested as massive arrays of cloud-based parallel processors. After seven decades of failed attempts to get computers to mimic the human brain, the Trivergence of these three factors is bringing thinking machines whose new insights are based on trillions of data points. Historically, Moore's law, which states that the number of transistors on a microchip doubles every two years, has supplied exponential growth to computer speeds. Even then, traditional CPUs are still far too slow to create large AI models. However, in the last decade, first graphics processing, then crypto mining, and now AI has funded NVIDIA[1] and others to produce new architectures with massive parallelism in processing. The result has rendered Moore's law moot. For Intel CPUs, think of a dozen complex parallel processers. For NVIDIA GPUs, think of thousands of simple (but really fast) parallel processors.

We'll learn how blockchain technology is enabling an evolution from an Internet of Information to an Internet of Value and how assets like money, securities, intellectual property, art, music, and even votes can be managed, stored, communicated, and transacted peer to peer. Blockchains increasingly run on the cloud and now—integrating with AI—could bring a new era of smart contracts that could revolutionize many industries and even work itself.

We'll also delve into how the IoT is bringing the physical world to life. Through the integration of these technologies, billions of previously inanimate objects are transforming into "smart" devices capable of conducting transactions and behaving as economic units. As the physical world generates data, today's big data will be replaced by a new generation of "infinite data."

---

[1] https://techhq.com/2023/08/how-is-nvidia-leading-ai-boom-with-chips

The result of this Trivergence will soon make science fiction, science fact. The overall effect may be either utopian or dystopian.

Ultimately, my hope is that *Trivergence* will become a must-read for curious managers or anyone seeking to understand the future of technology and how it will shape our world. Whether you're a business leader looking to stay ahead of the curve, or simply interested in the latest advancements in technology, my hope is that this book will leave you with a deeper understanding of the possibilities—and perils—that lie ahead.

A Glimpse of the Chapters Ahead

The book discusses the three technologies that will define the next era of technology innovation, disruption, and transformation, and what impacts they will have on work, leisure, transportation, education, and other aspects of our daily lives.

The Trivergence Technologies

The book kicks off with a series of chapters about the three big technologies: AI, the blockchain, and the IoT. We begin with AI—a force that's reshaping our world in extraordinary ways. Unless you've been living under a rock, you're likely aware that AI has transformed from being a mere tool into a capable knowledge creator. In Chapter 2, we delve into the evolution and trajectory of AI. From the foundational principles of symbolic systems to the breakthroughs of neural networks, we trace the development of AI's fundamental components that have paved the way for current advancements in large language models (such as ChatGPT), generative image tools (like DALL-E, Midjourney, and Stable Diffusion), and much more.

This brings us to some fundamental questions: When will AI surpass human-level intelligence? How will AI transform society and the economy? Can we control this technology moving forward, and what steps should we take now to prevent or mitigate the potential harm that AI systems could cause?

The question of when AI might reach human-level intelligence prompts us to delve into the concept of artificial general intelligence (AGI). We investigate the strides AI has made in tasks such as gameplay, image recognition, and natural language processing, all the while contemplating the significant impacts that will arise when AI converges with human cognition. As we traverse the realm of AI's impact, we uncover the potential for heightened productivity, accuracy, safety, personalization, and decision-making.

We'll explore how industries such as healthcare, transportation, finance, and education stand on the precipice of radical transformation, propelled by the inventive solutions and immense possibilities brought forth by AI. We'll see how governments are at the threshold of reimagining their roles through digital technologies and AI, redefining interactions with citizens and stakeholders to deliver unparalleled public value. In the transportation industry, we'll explore the path toward autonomous vehicles, including the complex tapestry of safety concerns, ethical considerations, and transformative impacts on urban living. We'll then confront the delicate interplay between human creativity and AI-driven imitation in the arts and entertainment industry, prompting us to reflect on the very essence of artistic expression.

Chapter 3 takes us to the Internet of Things—a world where the physical and digital realms merge. The IoT is about more than just smart gadgets. It's about creating an intelligent fabric that links everything—transforming industries, landscapes, and even how we understand the planet.

Our journey begins with a dive into IoT's evolution from isolated gadgets to interconnected ecosystems where devices, platforms, and applications interact on a massive scale. We'll witness IoT's impact on conservation, planetary monitoring, and ocean exploration. From tracking deforestation and illegal logging to safeguarding marine environments, the IoT is driving vital changes. It's also reshaping urban life, promising to redefine smart cities with real-time sensing and reporting capabilities. And when it comes to robotics—from factories humming with automation to a future where robots assist in daily tasks—the impact of the IoT is undeniable.

As the IoT connects everything from homes to natural environments, new challenges arise. How do billions of sensors and devices work together? How do we balance the benefits of the IoT with personal privacy? The chapter sheds light on these questions and more, hinting at how blockchain, AI, and the IoT are converging to provide solutions that shape our connected world.

In Chapter 4, we turn our attention toward blockchain—a technology born from the ambition to establish a secure, peer-to-peer electronic cash system that transcends conventional financial structures. We'll explore how blockchain has evolved from its origins in cryptocurrency to transform industries and redefine how we interact with information and create value.

As hyper-transparency becomes paramount, blockchain emerges as the key to unlocking insights into global supply chains, offering a solution for the ever-present need to trace products from source to destination. Yet the application of blockchain doesn't stop at commerce; it extends its hand to the public good. We'll discover how governments around the world are leveraging blockchain to streamline processes, modernize recordkeeping, and uphold the integrity of vital functions such as voting, healthcare, and identification. From land registries to Estonia's digital identity revolution, we'll explore how blockchain breathes life into public administration, ensuring efficient and secure interactions.

The term Web3, popularized in Alex Tapscott's book *Web3: Charting the Internet's Next Economic and Cultural Frontier*, is emerging as a useful moniker for the next generation of blockchains. Web3 aims to establish a decentralized and user-centric online ecosystem, leveraging the capabilities of blockchain technology. As we venture into the world of Web3, we'll witness the aspiration of an internet that breaks free from the confines of Web1 (characterized by static websites) and Web2 (defined by interactive websites and social media platforms). Web3 envisions an Internet that is open, secure, and devoid of permission limitations—a decentralized infrastructure that redefines the digital landscape. It's often referred to as the "read-write-own" web, with a central goal of granting users' greater control and ownership over their digital assets.

Peering ahead, we'll uncover blockchain's immense potential to reshape industries, economies, and societies. As technical barriers crumble and fresh applications emerge, the influence of blockchain continues to evolve, offering the promise of unlocking unparalleled levels of innovation, collaboration, and decentralized power. Subsequent chapters will unveil the ongoing ripple effect of blockchain across industries, economies, and society—ushering in a future where decentralization, transparency, and boundless possibilities intersect.

Key Enablers of the Era of Trivergence

The next few chapters focus on some of the key enablers of the era of Trivergence. In a world driven by digitized knowledge, the cloud emerges as an unseen driving force. From user-generated content to vast archives, the cloud silently curates and grants access to enormous datasets with a simple click. Chapter 5 guides us through the transformative realm of cloud computing—a catalyst for innovation, collaboration, and the integration of advanced tools like AI, IoT, and blockchain. We'll explore how the cloud has reshaped enterprise capacity planning, once a complex task, into a streamlined process. Empowering organizations with scalability, cost efficiency, data security, and innovation, cloud computing redesigns the framework of modern businesses.

We'll meet the trailblazers of the cloud—Amazon, Google, and Microsoft—and discover their unique contributions to this landscape. We'll also uncover the three pillars of cloud computing—infrastructure as a service (IaaS), platform as a service (PaaS), and software as a service (SaaS)—that underpin the modern digital ecosystem.

As our journey continues, we'll witness that the cloud is not just a technological feat; it's a dynamic influence shaping interconnectivity in our digital world. The cloud offers instant access to high-performance computing, AI, middleware, database software, and even quantum computing. This dynamic capacity fuels innovation, enabling businesses to embrace new services, enhance productivity, and create novel applications.

As the Internet and the number of devices connected to it multiplies, so does the amount of data we generate. In Chapter 6, we explore the shift from big data to something even bigger—what we call *infinite data*. We'll see how this change is affecting everything from science to our personal privacy.

We begin by understanding the rise of big data—ignited by the Internet's expansion and the surge of unstructured data. This lays the groundwork for infinite data, where data from AI, the IoT, and blockchain combine. But how does this data explosion truly influence our world, and what awaits us in the era of infinite data?

Witness how infinite data fuels AI's evolution, offering the essential fuel for training, predictions, and uncanny insights across diverse domains. As the ocean of data grows, AI models flourish, adapting to new challenges and enriching industries with unprecedented capabilities. We'll see how high-speed transmissions, massive storage capabilities, and computational prowess have joined forces to power generative AI—an engine driving rapid advancements in our understanding of language, culture, and complex queries.

Infinite data is not just about improving technology; it's changing how we do science. We'll examine how infinite data is transforming research and discoveries in fields such as astronomy and genomics, revolutionizing methodologies, and leading to unprecedented collaboration across domains.

While infinite data has its advantages, it raises concerns about privacy. How do we ensure our digital identities remain in our control amidst data's tidal waves? In a world where corporations and governments hold vast amounts of our personal information, the notion of self-sovereign identity emerges—a beacon of hope for reclaiming control over our personal data and fostering greater privacy and inclusivity in the digital economy.

Applications and Implications

So far in our Trivergence journey, we've witnessed the remarkable evolution of AI, blockchain, and IoT—each making significant strides in their own right. But what happens when these forces converge, when their combined potential surpasses the sum of their individual parts? In Chapter 7, we look at the Trivergence in action across various sectors, including healthcare, agriculture, and transportation.

Imagine a world where healthcare doesn't use a one-size-fits-all approach and where the fusion of genomics with AI offers personalized medicine, aligning treatments with individual genetic codes. AI assists doctors with data-driven insights, revolutionizing not only diagnostics but the search for cures. Meanwhile, IoT generates a vast stream of health data that AI mines to detect patterns and correlations. Blockchain steps in to secure this data-sharing ecosystem, fostering a community-driven Internet of health data—a hub for wellness promotion and medical research, where patients retain control and ownership over their own data.

In agriculture, the complexity of modern supply chains often obscures the origin and journey of our food. We'll learn how the Trivergence comes to the rescue and how giants like Walmart and Nestlé have collaborated with companies like IBM to create blockchain and IoT-powered solutions for food provenance from farm to fork. This technology doesn't just trace our food's location; it radically improves supply chain transparency, making the complete history of any food product available instantaneously. These innovations improve the efficiency and sustainability of the global food system, reducing waste, and elevating productivity.

We'll also take a look at how the Trivergence is propelling the transportation industry, with autonomous vehicles emerging as a powerful illustration of its capabilities. In the journey toward self-driving cars, we'll explore how AI and IoT play a vital role in optimizing traffic, predicting maintenance needs, and even creating a whole new economy of movement. We'll see how organizations such as the Mobility Open Blockchain Initiative (MOBI) are pioneering secure blockchain-based standards, transforming how vehicles communicate and transact in our evolving mobility landscape.

Embracing Trivergence technologies demands more than mere adoption. It requires a deep understanding of the challenges and implications that lie ahead. In Chapter 8, we'll dive into the challenges of the era of Trivergence. These aren't considered showstoppers, but rather implementation challenges to be overcome. We'll explore two types of challenges: technological challenges and social challenges.

Technological challenges involve the complexities of the technologies themselves and the trade-offs that need to be made for them to function effectively. To begin, amid the proliferation of devices generating vast amounts of data, concerns arise around the integrity, reliability, and authenticity of this data. Maintaining data integrity becomes increasingly daunting as the sheer volume of data amplifies the risk of errors, data inconsistencies, and tampering.

As we move into the era of modern distributed networks, with blockchain being a key example, Vitalik Buterin wrote about what he called the "blockchain trilemma." This trilemma suggests that public blockchains, which aim to be secure, decentralized, and scalable, must make trade-offs among these three factors. We'll explore how concepts rooted in the blockchain trilemma continue to hold significance in the era of Trivergence, where the convergence of the IoT, blockchain, and AI technologies demands innovative solutions that strike the right balance between data consistency, system reliability, and establishing trust in the digital realm.

Interoperability poses another complex technological challenge, requiring AI, the IoT, and blockchain to communicate and work together seamlessly. Yet each technology comes with its own unique data formats, models, and interfaces, complicating integration. Alongside these technological challenges, we'll also uncover some of today's software limitations of AI, blockchain, and the IoT, and what can be done to overcome them.

The Trivergence isn't just about technology—it's about how people use it and the impact it has on society. Our look at social and economic challenges invites us to consider the complex dynamics that come into play when society adopts these technologies.

We begin with the challenge of speculation and hype, where media sensationalism and misinformation fuel exaggerated expectations. Next, we'll examine the challenge of regulation, including how policy tends to lag behind technological advancements, opening the door to privacy, security, and ethical issues. Worse uncontrolled, this time around, it may pose an "existential threat." We'll look at the challenge of governance, and the crucial role of governance frameworks in guiding the responsible and ethical use of these technologies, aligning with societal values, and managing risks effectively. Finally, we'll look at the challenge of access and inclusivity, requiring supportive environments for diverse individuals to harness the potential of the era of Trivergence.

The future isn't something to be predicted, but something to be achieved. As the era of Trivergence unfolds, how will these challenges be addressed, and who will shoulder the responsibility of architecting this future?

Chapter 9 serves as an executive guide to the era of Trivergence, offering practical insights and crucial considerations for business leaders. This guide helps you evaluate your organization's readiness, vision, and strategy in the face of AI, the IoT, and blockchain integration. By engaging with these insights, you'll position your business to tap into the vast potential of these technologies, driving growth, innovation, and sustained competitive advantage.

First, we'll delve into the strategic integration of Trivergence into your business framework. This involves assessing your organization's readiness to fully embrace these transformative technologies, considering factors like business case clarity, resource availability, and capacity to leverage AI, blockchain, and IoT effectively. From there, we'll delve into crucial considerations for Trivergence implementation, covering potential risks, costs, and benefits. Armed with this understanding, you'll be able to make informed decisions, define mitigation strategies, and ensure seamless integration.

Next, we'll emphasize the establishment of a phased implementation roadmap. This involves delineating phases, milestones, resource allocation, and timelines. We'll also discuss how regular evaluation of key performance indicators (KPIs) guides the iterative refinement of Trivergence initiatives, ensuring optimal performance at every step.

The importance of collaborating with industry peers and stakeholders cannot be overstated. We'll introduce a concept called *coopetition*—a strategic approach fostering collaboration among business competitors, driving mutual benefits while upholding individual competitive positions. In the context of Trivergence adoption, this approach takes on renewed significance, emphasizing partnerships and data sharing as catalysts for success.

Finally, we'll underscore the importance of creating a culture of innovation within your organization, encouraging continuous learning, experimentation, and employee empowerment. The aim is to cultivate an environment where new ideas are embraced, calculated risks are encouraged, and innovative thinking is celebrated.

The era of Trivergence presents both an opportunity and a responsibility for business leaders. Merely being a spectator to change without active engagement can result in stagnation and skepticism. Effective leadership in the era of Trivergence holds immense importance. We'll conclude Chapter 9 by looking at the vital role of leadership in maneuvering the Trivergence era—capitalizing on the opportunities it presents and steering your business toward growth and success.

The book closes with some frank and sobering thoughts on the dangers to each of us and civilization as a whole. Chapter 10 shows how the impact of AI, the IoT, and blockchain transcends individual industries, touching the very essence of how we live, interact, and shape the world around us. As we explore the big picture, we uncover the potential consequences and opportunities that lie ahead.

How will the era of Trivergence redefine privacy and identity management? In a world where AI algorithms learn from your behaviors and IoT devices capture your daily routines, we unravel the intricate balance between the convenience of interconnectedness and the need to safeguard personal information. Ethics take center stage as Trivergence technologies become an integral part of our lives. How do we navigate the ethical dilemmas posed by AI bias, pervasive IoT monitoring, and blockchain's transparency and immutability? We explore the intricacies of ethical considerations in a world where machines make choices and infinite data shapes decisions.

But that's just the beginning. We'll also peer into the future of work, calling for a new paradigm for amplifying human potential while preserving the values that make us inherently human. AI should augment human abilities, not replace them, fostering a symbiotic relationship for problem-solving and innovation. Furthermore, using new technologies, we can fundamentally alter how we create wealth. Consider a world where creativity knows no bounds, where the protection of our ideas is seamlessly integrated into the digital realm. How might blockchain revolutionize the ways we understand and interact with intellectual property? From rights management and royalties to patent protection, we'll dive into the exciting opportunities for value creation in the digital age.

As democracy evolves, how might blockchain empower citizens to play an active role in shaping policy decisions? We'll uncover the potential for increased transparency and security in voting systems, redefining how we participate in governance. But the era of Trivergence doesn't stop there. With environmental concerns at the forefront, how can AI, IoT, and blockchain join forces to create a more sustainable planet? We delve into the ways these technologies could drive positive ecological impact, transforming the relationship between technology and the environment.

As we navigate this whirlwind of potential impacts, one thing becomes clear—the Divergence era requires a collaborative effort. Governments, industries, and individuals must come together to harness the benefits of AI, the IoT, and blockchain while minimizing any unintended consequences. Our journey through this final chapter guides us toward a future where innovation harmonizes with our values, and where we all play a role in shaping a civilization powered by the forces of the era of Trivergence. We must do nothing less than reimagine our social contract—the basic expectations between business, government, labor, and civil society for a new digital age and develop a set of strategic initiatives to achieve it. This will not be easy.

The book closes with a challenge to you, gentle reader. Trivergence represents a new paradigm of the digital age. As Don Tapscott said in his seminal 1993 book *Paradigm Shift*, new paradigms cause disruption and uncertainty. They are often received with coolness or, worse, mockery and hostility. Legacy interests, fight against change, and leaders of all paradigms have great difficulty embracing the future. This time, the change will be far broader, deeper, and faster than those imagined in his book. It will be a shock as well as a shift.

What will be your role in bringing in this new paradigm and the new business and social opportunities it creates? Can you participate in ensuring the promises are fulfilled and the dark side is avoided?

My experience has shown that the best ideas often come from people who are not in the corner offices. In technology, the traditional approach has been to outline in a specification document what you want and expect a computer system to do prior to management approval, funding, and project launch. This approach is now outdated and will lead to suboptimal results. Given the cloud enables very low-cost proof of concepts, bottom-up experimentation may create more value than top-down dictates. Many traditional concepts of management will not survive this paradigm shift.

My experience has shown that leadership is not just the responsibility of the CXOs and that it, in fact, typically does not start at the top. Rather, anyone can be a leader if they will it.

This is your opportunity. Read on!

2 Artificial Intelligence

Imagine a not-too-distant future in which AI had transformed society in unimaginable ways. One remarkable example was its profound impact on education—a sector that had long been seeking innovative approaches to cater to diverse learning needs and enable lifelong learning.

In this transformed society, a young girl named Maya embarked on her educational journey. Maya's personalized education experience began before she stepped foot in a traditional classroom. AI algorithms had analyzed vast amounts of data about her cognitive abilities, learning styles, and interests. Armed with this knowledge, the AI-powered learning system tailored a unique curriculum to maximize her potential and foster her love for knowledge.

As Maya entered her AI-enhanced classroom, she found a vibrant and collaborative environment. Schools replaced the traditional rows of desks with interactive learning pods, where students engaged in hands-on activities and problem-solving exercises. Their AI-powered virtual assistant, AIVA, provided immediate feedback, answered questions, and offered guidance personalized to each student's needs.

In this transformed education landscape, Maya's teachers had become facilitators and mentors, working in tandem with AI technologies. The teachers leveraged AI-powered tools to gather real-time insights into student progress, identifying areas where students needed additional support. By analyzing the data, AI algorithms helped teachers identify specific concepts or skills that required reinforcement, allowing them to effectively tailor their instruction to individual students.

Beyond the classroom, AI extended Maya's educational opportunities. Virtual reality simulations allowed her to explore historical events, visit distant places, and experience scientific phenomena firsthand.

AIVA's language translation capabilities enabled her to connect with students from diverse backgrounds and learn from global perspectives. AI-powered recommendation systems suggested personalized reading materials and educational resources, opening doors to new subjects and areas of interest.

Maya's story was not unique. Across society, AI democratized education, making quality learning accessible to all, regardless of geographical location or socioeconomic background. Along the way, educators, parents, and other stakeholders pulled together to address several concerns about the pervasive presence of AI in education. Educators worried that insufficient human interaction in the classroom could undermine students' social and emotional development and limit their critical thinking skills. Social justice advocates voiced concerns about the potential for bias and lack of diversity in AI algorithms to perpetuate existing inequalities. Fiscal conservatives demanded much higher student-faculty ratios. Parents and students feared that AI systems might collect and store profoundly personal information about students and redeploy it in hyper-targeted marketing campaigns.

In this stylized reality, AI did not replace human teachers but elevated their roles, enabling them to focus on fostering creativity, critical thinking, and emotional intelligence. Developers honed their systems by training AI models on diverse datasets, drawing on the educational experiences of a broad and inclusive population of learners. Strict privacy safeguards ensured that students and parents retained full custody of and control over their personal data. Most stakeholders saw AI as an indispensable ally, augmenting human abilities and revolutionizing the way knowledge was acquired, shared, and applied.

Sound far-fetched? Not really, because AI's growing impact on education is already evident today. Edtech companies such as Eightfold, Gloat, Docebo, Squirrel AI, Cognii, and Degreed are currently incorporating advanced AI capabilities to accurately identify content that matches skill requirements, offer personalized tutoring and coaching, and provide learners at all levels with highly targeted educational materials and experiences. Whether educational institutions are ready or not, AI will quickly redefine the very nature of teaching and learning. And yet, education is just one domain where artificial intelligence is shaking up the world as we know it.

Sped by the exponential rate of technological progress, powerful artificial intelligence systems are creating a new era of superintelligence that will reshape the social and economic landscape. From robotic surgery to autonomous vehicles, from revolutionary biotech research to reading cat scans, the applications for increasingly smart machines will span healthcare, legal and financial services, transportation, construction, agriculture, manufacturing, and much more. With companies such as Facebook, Google, Amazon, Microsoft, Alibaba, and others in and outside the software industry making multibillion-dollar investments in talent and research, state-of-the-art AI capabilities will advance even more rapidly in the years to come, opening up new possibilities and applications that we can scarcely imagine today.

The Evolution of AI

Artificial intelligence (AI) can be defined as the ability of computers to perform tasks that had previously required human intelligence, such as perception, learning, reasoning, complex problem-solving, and decision-making. It is a broad field that encompasses a wide range of techniques and approaches, including machine learning, natural language processing, computer vision, robotics, and expert systems.

The notion that computers can "think" as we do is a concept originally envisioned in the 1950s, and is rooted in the work of computing pioneers like Alan Turing and John McCarthy. Early AI research focused on developing algorithms and symbolic logic to simulate human intelligence. By the middle of that decade, Arthur Samuelson had programmed a computer to play a reasonable game of checkers. He simply defined artificial intelligence as the "field of study that gives computers the ability to learn without being explicitly programmed."[1]

Realistically, computers were far too slow to deliver on the dream that someday computers would think. The only remaining question was when?

In the 1960s and 1970s, computerized AI development efforts began in earnest with rules-based systems, game theory, and mathematical methods where if-then-else statements were used to mimic human decision-making processes. Expert systems, such as DENDRAL for chemistry and MYCIN for medical diagnosis, were notable achievements during this period.

In the 1980s, AI researchers focused on knowledge-based systems, which utilized large knowledge bases to solve complex problems. These systems used inference engines to reason and draw conclusions based on available knowledge. For many, the aspiration that computers could use neural networks to reason was tried and failed and re-tried and re-failed. To most, it was clearly time to pronounce them dead.

The 1990s witnessed a resurgence of interest in AI with the rise of machine learning. Another attempt at getting ever-larger neural networks to think was tried and failed again. Using different AI approaches, researchers explored various algorithms and approaches that allowed computers to learn from data and make predictions or decisions (see the sidebar "The Five Tribes of AI").

THE FIVE TRIBES OF AI

In his paper "A Few Useful Things to Know About Machine Learning," Professor Pedro Domingos identifies five main "tribes" or approaches within machine learning.[2] These "tribes" represent different perspectives and methodologies within the field of machine learning, each with its own strengths, weaknesses, and areas of application.

Symbolists/rule-based learners: Symbolists focus on representing knowledge in explicit rules or logical formulas. They emphasize the interpretability and understandability of the learned models. In symbolic reasoning, the logic is analyzed and then hard-coded into a static program. Its roots are in logic and philosophy. Symbolic AI systems use knowledge representation, reasoning, and inference to make decisions. Examples include classical expert systems that are still used today to provide advice in specific domains, such as medicine or law. This approach was first successfully implemented in the 1970s.

Evolutionaries/genetic programmers: Evolutionary algorithms are inspired by the process of natural evolution. They use techniques like genetic algorithms to evolve populations of models over generations. The fittest models survive and reproduce, gradually improving their performance through selection, crossover, and mutation. Defined by the research of John Holland at the University of Michigan in 1960, useful implementations became popular in the 1990s.

Bayesians/probabilistic learners: Bayesians approach machine learning from a probabilistic perspective. They use probability theory and statistical inference to model uncertainty and make predictions. Bayesian methods incorporate prior knowledge and update beliefs based on observed data, enabling the calculation of posterior probabilities for different outcomes. This method was first published by Thomas Bayes in 1763. It was first computerized in late 1950s to early 1960s. A modern example today is political polling.

Analogizers/instance-based learners: Analogizers learn by identifying similarities between new instances and instances encountered during training. They rely on measures of similarity and distance to make predictions or decisions. Instance-based learning methods, such as k-nearest neighbors (KNN), store and retrieve instances to make predictions based on the similarity to the nearest neighbors. Discussed in the 1950s, it was first published by Thomas Cover and Peter Hart in 1967.[3]

Connectionists/neural network learners: Connectionists, also known as neural network learners, are inspired by the human brain's neural networks. They learn patterns and relationships by constructing interconnected layers of artificial neurons. Deep learning, a subset of connectionist methods, involves training neural networks with multiple hidden layers to handle complex tasks. The critical point is that the AI of the 1960s was hard-coded and composed of if-then-else statements, whereas the neural networks researchers deploy today learn to recognize patterns and perform tasks, such as image and speech recognition, by "observing" massive quantities of data. As an approach, it was first envisioned by Walter Pitts and Warren McCulloch in 1943.[4] It was half a century later before advances in the technique and much faster computers started to demonstrate somewhat credible results.

In the early 2000s, after most data scientists and mathematicians had abandoned the tedious and then unsuccessful approach of neural networks, a few plodded on—notably Geoffrey Hinton, a professor emeritus at the University of Toronto (U of T), and his students. Using modified techniques for deep learning algorithms on these networks, they achieved breakthroughs in areas such as natural language processing and computer vision. Not surprisingly, Hinton was soon hired to spend 25 percent of his efforts for Google. He is often described as "the father of machine learning." Given that efforts in this field dated back 70 years, the more appropriate description for Hinton would probably be an "unusually gifted great-grandson." In early 2023, concerned about the release of immature yet powerful AI offerings, Hinton, Yoshua Bengio (the most published author on AI, from the University of Montreal), and many other domain experts wrote an open letter about "the risk of extinction from AI."[5] Among other things, experts have warned that AI could lead to pervasive disinformation, economic disruption, mass surveillance, and even the extinction of humanity itself if self-replicating smart machines spiral out of control.

In the 2010s and beyond, advancements in neural networks for natural language processing allowed AI systems to understand and generate human language more accurately (see Figure 2.1). Conversational AI, chatbots, and virtual assistants have significantly improved, enabling more interactive and intuitive human-computer interactions. In recent years, AI has become increasingly integrated into our daily lives. AI-powered applications and services, such as voice assistants, recommendation systems, and personalized advertisements, even personalized billboards, have become commonplace. What is fascinating about deep learning approaches to a problem is you don't have to program the logic. Give a neural network enough relevant data and spend the time to properly train it, and the network may derive conclusions that humans have never thought of.

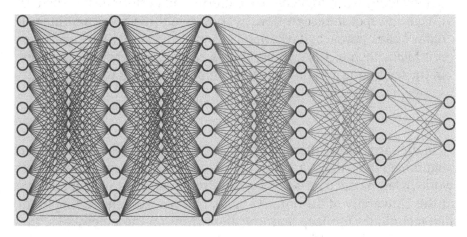

Figure 2.1 Sample neural network

Today, there are a plethora of AI initiatives being launched by such companies as Google, Facebook, Microsoft, IBM, Tencent, Alibaba,

AWS, and most major corporations with access to massive datasets and computing power. The International Data Corporation (IDC) predicts a 26 percent compound growth rate of AI expenditures for the foreseeable future. Maintained for a decade, this snowballing investment would result in more than a tenfold increase. It is not just software companies. In mid-2023, about 40 percent of all JPMorgan open positions were AI-related, be it for data engineers and quants, as well as ethics and governance roles.[6] For the foreseeable future, demand for neural network talent will far exceed the supply.

As breakthroughs with AI gather pace, people are asking three critical (if not existential) questions.

- When will AI surpass human-level intelligence?
- How will AI transform society and the economy?
- Can we control this technology moving forward, and what steps should we take now to prevent or mitigate the potential harm that AI systems could cause?

I elaborate on and answer the first two questions throughout the remainder of the chapter. The third question is discussed in Chapter 10.

When Will AI Surpass Human-Level Intelligence?

In 1996 and 1997, a now infamous chess match series unfolded between Gary Kasparov and Deep Blue, a supercomputer built by IBM. The IBM supercomputer's software relied on a seemingly unbeatable combination of rules and heuristics developed by grandmasters, such as Joel Benjamin, and coded by students from Cornell. Think of traditional programs written with if-then-else statements. Deep Blue analyzed the potential outcomes of possible moves at about 100,000 positions per second, something (one would suspect) far beyond the capabilities of any human brain. Yet, when put to the task, Kasparov crushed Deep Blue four games to two.

Stunned that a mere mortal had defeated its supercomputer, IBM doubled the size of the computer and spent another year programming even more subtleties of the game into its software. In 1997, it was finally able to beat Kasparov narrowly in three-and-a-half games to two-and-a-half games. The chess experts evaluated Kasparov's strategy between games. As a result, the programmers tweaked the code to give the IBM supercomputer a better chance of victory. We can debate the fairness of such mid-game tweaking. Some experts have argued, however, that Deep Blue's most surprising and smartest move was actually a bug. When the logic in the code malfunctioned, it picked a surprisingly smart move at random.[7]

Over the next few decades, hard-coded chess programs improved their skills and heuristics. The current open-source chess program Stockfish was considered nearly unbeatable because of input from many grandmasters, a massive experience database of millions of more games, and the dramatic increase in hardware speeds. Trying a new approach, leveraging the advances in neural networks, Google AI's subsidiary DeepMind introduced just the basic rules of chess to its AlphaZero deep learning program without any history, advice, or expertise.[8] AlphaZero achieved a superhuman level of skill within a few hours simply by competing with itself. In a 100-game matchup with Stockfish, it never lost a game. Within a day, it was demonstrating winning strategies never seen before in 1,000 years of recorded chess history.[9] More surprisingly, to clobber Stockfish, it needed to evaluate only 80,000 positions per move compared to its competitors' 70 million. DeepMind was not programmed to play chess. It was simply given the basic rules and designed to learn from its own experiences and those of countless other players. Computers were starting to "think."

What many people in computer science were convinced would stump computers indefinitely was a 2,500-year-old game called Go. The game is that complex. The board has 19×19 squares (about five times more than chess) and typically takes about 150 moves or more than four times the number of moves as found in a typical game of championship chess. *Scientific American* estimates that in Go there are about 250^{150} possible moves dwarfing the relative complexity of chess. Most experts assumed that even the most powerful AI systems would need to evaluate far too many possibilities to devise winning strategies in a timely manner. In practice, computer programs were only able to play, at best, a mediocre amateur game.

Then, in the 2010s, neural-networks-based AlphaGo taught itself to play without any expertise. In March 2016, with more than 200 million people watching online, AlphaGo played the visionary Lee Sedol, then considered to be the greatest player of the decade because Sedol had won 18 world titles. The Go world was stunned as AlphaGo emerged as a surprise four-to-one victor. Most experts saw this breakthrough as a "decade ahead of its time."[10] And with the Trivergence, it is. AlphaGo won by playing highly innovative moves that contradicted centuries of unquestioned Go strategy and expertise. It thought for itself.

AI's recent, rapid advances have overturned a number of deeply held convictions about the limitations of AI. When AI will truly master non-rule-based areas of expertise has yet to be seen. However, the emergence of large language models such as ChatGPT has many experts believing it will happen much sooner than previously expected as a result of three factors.

- Revolutionary advances and disruptive breakthroughs in neural networks and deep learning methods that are continuously improving and are now implemented on the cloud.
- A cornucopia of deep learning's new food: the explosion of data supplied by computers, humans web surfing, and now the Internet of Things (IoT).
- A recent revolution in hardware design where massive arrays of parallel simple processors (called reduced instruction set computers, or RISC, chips) originally designed for image rendering (on your display) were morphed and then heavily funded for crypto mining, which were again morphed for AI. The result is an effective throughput for neural networks that is a billion times faster than Moore's law anticipated. Thanks to the blockchain, the power to build massive AI models is suddenly here.

These rapid advances were, for many in the field, unforeseen. AI's capabilities have suddenly become a decade or two ahead of where many expected. I examine the latter two developments more extensively in Chapter 6. The bottom line? Very few are prepared for the rapid advances in AI that are coming thanks to the explosion of new data and parallel processing power.

Already there is much to appreciate about the rapidly increasing size of the neural networks of today. Open AI's ChatGPT, for example, had 117 million parameters in its first release in 2018; then GPT-2 followed in 2019 with 1.5 billion parameters; GPT-3 in 2020 had 175 billion parameters; and GPT-4 released in 2023 is rumored to be close to 100 trillion. GPT-3 and GPT-4 are rumored to have read much of the data from the Internet, including Wikipedia, WebText (which separates the wheat from the chaff of URLs by the number of Reddit links), books, and other sources.

It is worth noting that there is not necessarily a correlation between the number of parameters and the intelligence of the system.[11] Garbage in will produce garbage out. AI's well-documented potential to "hallucinate" or produce factually incorrect information at this stage is not surprising given that the Internet—the primary source material for ChatGPT and Google's Bard—is riddled with untruths. For example, on the launch day of Google's Bard, the new chatbot famously claimed that the James Webb Space Telescope was the first to capture images of a planet outside our solar system, which turned out to be false. Today's AI has been caught lying again and again in a fashion that has unnerved many. OpenAI's ChatGPT can demonstrate some uncanny reasoning, but it can also be incredibly naïve on some relatively simple questions. Though it will know Albert Einstein's formula for how gravity affects space and time ($G\mu\nu = 8\pi G\ T\mu\nu$) and can apply it, its actual understanding of these two basic concepts is less than that of a three-year-old.[12]

Despite these imperfections, it is evident that AI systems are ever more rapidly trending toward greater intelligence. OpenAI asserts that GPT-4 is 40 percent more likely to produce factual results than GPT-3, a staggering improvement over a 33-month period.[13] These deep learning models have advanced dramatically in the last few years and have demonstrated remarkable proficiency in a wide range of tasks. For example, GPT-4 can pass both the bar and medical licensing exams with significantly above-average results.[14] As for the SATs, GPT-4 can ace them. Users with little to no coding experience have used GPT-4 to re-create iconic video games such as Tetris and Pong. OpenAI even demonstrated how GPT-4 could turn a drawing into a functional website within minutes. In another intriguing demonstration of AI's potential, the New York Times showed GPT-4 the contents of a refrigerator and prompted it to propose dinner recipes based on the available ingredients. With emerging robotic aids, it will not be long before smart robots will not only propose what to cook but actually prepare your dinner for you.

Still, the question of when AI will surpass human-level intelligence—often referred to as artificial general intelligence (AGI)—remains uncertain. In some areas, it already has. While AI has made significant advancements in specific tasks such as image recognition, natural language processing, and game playing, achieving AGI requires the development of a system that can understand, learn, and apply knowledge across a wide range of domains. However, with recent advances, the question is now more about when, not if.

There are several challenges that need to be overcome to reach AGI. These challenges include developing algorithms that can generalize from limited data, understand context, exhibit common sense reasoning, engage in creative problem-solving, and demonstrate social and emotional intelligence. The timeline for achieving AGI is influenced by factors such as advancements in computing power, breakthroughs in AI research, availability of quality training data, and progress in related fields like neuroscience and cognitive science. The toughest of these challenges for AGI is now the quality of the data.

As of now, AI systems, including the most advanced ones, are based on algorithms and computational processes that do not possess subjective experiences or consciousness. While AI can mimic human-like behavior and perform tasks with impressive proficiency, it does not demonstrate the same level of awareness and subjective experience that humans possess. The field of AI primarily focuses on creating systems that can process and analyze data, learn patterns, and make decisions based on programmed rules and statistical models, or simply derive associations and thoughts from the data itself. These systems lack the subjective, qualitative nature of human consciousness.

The question of whether AI systems can become sentient in the future is speculative and depends on scientific advancements and our understanding and definition of consciousness. Some theories suggest that consciousness might emerge from complex computational systems, while others argue that it may require biological or physical substrates that are yet to be fully replicated in AI systems. In simpler terms, to become human, AI needs to live in our four-dimensional world. With robotics, it soon will.

Of course, the possibility of AI becoming sentient raises profound ethical and philosophical questions. If we were to develop AI systems that exhibit signs of sentience, considerations about their rights, moral status, and treatment would need to be carefully addressed. Moreover, the ultimate impact and implications of sentient AGIs will (ideally) depend on how such systems are designed, deployed, and governed by ethical and regulatory considerations.

At present, AI systems are tools created by humans, and any potential for sentience or consciousness in AI would require significant advancements and a deeper understanding of the nature of conscious-ness itself. Given the current state of AI research and the complexity of achieving AGI, it is challenging to imagine when such advancements will materialize.

How Will AI Transform Society?

AI will perform an ever-increasing array of tasks that today require human intelligence, such as learning, reasoning, problem-solving, per-ception, and decision-making. Across these various domains, some of the key promises of AI include the following:

- **Improved productivity:** AI can automate repetitive tasks and decision-making processes, freeing up time for humans to focus on more complex and creative tasks.
- **Enhanced accuracy and precision:** AI algorithms can process vast amounts of data and identify patterns that humans might miss, leading to more accurate predictions.
- **Increased safety:** AI can be used to monitor and control complex systems, such as self-driving cars, reducing the risk of accidents.
- **Personalization:** AI can analyze individual preferences and behaviors to deliver tailored recommendations and experiences.
- **Better decision-making:** AI can provide insights and recom-mendations that humans might not have considered, leading to better decision-making in many fields.
- **Enhanced security:** AI can improve safety and security in both the physical and digital worlds through AI-powered surveillance and threat detection.
- **Increased efficiency:** AI-powered optimization and automation can reduce costs in industries such as manufacturing, logistics, and transportation.
- **Improved communication:** Natural language processing and speech recognition technologies can speed up the production of complex texts and reduce language barriers.

Given these attributes, it's easy to imagine how AI will rapidly trans-form numerous industries and fields by providing innovative solutions to complex problems and improving efficiency and accuracy. Already, ground-breaking applications are evident in domains such as healthcare, transportation, public administration, finance, education, and entertainment. For illustration purposes, let's examine the applications of AI in government, transportation, and entertainment.

Artificially Intelligent Government

Like other institutions in society, digital technologies have created a historic opportunity for governments to fundamentally rethink and redesign how they operate, how and what the public service provides, and, ultimately, how the public institutions interact with citizens and other stakeholders to create public value. In the first wave of Internet-enabled transformation, governments around the world harnessed the Internet to deliver some important benefits. They made government information and services more accessible to citizens while creating administrative and operational efficiencies. But too many of these initiatives focused on automating existing processes and moving existing government services online. In other words, so-called e-government strategies added a new channel for service delivery and citizen engagement but did not fundamentally challenge or disrupt the existing structures, processes, or competencies of government. Nor did it set a very high bar for the digital experience (think static information portals and one-size-fits-all solutions).

Today, the e-government strategies of the past are no longer good enough. For most people, the Internet is now an inextricable part of everyday life. The increasing connectivity brings heightened public expectations and pressure on governments to be much more innovative and attuned to digital trends and capabilities. Indeed, as the commercial digital experience continues to improve, the bar for governments keeps getting higher. Meanwhile, the gap between what citizens expect and what government delivers grows alarmingly wide.

Given the mixed record of governments in leveraging technology to improve public services, it would be prudent to remain somewhat skeptical of the promise of AI to revolutionize public administration. And yet, there is an emerging body of public sector use cases for AI, suggesting that forward-thinking administrations could leverage the power of new technologies, such as big data and artificial intelligence, to bring heightened levels of innovation and productivity to the many functions and permutations of government.

Broadly speaking, I see five clear advantages to using AI in public service. First, as governments make headway in transitioning their service delivery to digital platforms, AI holds the potential to add a new layer of functionality that will improve user experiences and create operational efficiencies. In leading jurisdictions, such as Singapore, artificially intelligent software agents or so-called chatbots serve as frontline interfaces for citizens and businesses, allowing people to access a service or accomplish a task with verbal or text-based conversations using their phones or computers. Some worry that chatbots and other automation efforts could lead to depersonalized service and hinder the ability of governments to address more nuanced and complex service needs. However, the quality and timeliness of service will improve if AI systems are used to augment rather than outright replace human workers. And, of course, when AI augments a human being delivering a service, it will learn to be more human itself. Unlike us, AI can perform its tasks 24/7 without the need for meal breaks, sleep, or vacations. Today, AI-powered translation tools can help break language barriers and improve accessibility for diverse communities by providing multilingual services, translating official documents, and ensuring information reaches a broader audience. In fact, AI has reduced the time to dub a movie into a foreign language from months to days.

Second, like in private companies, process automation can help the public sector achieve operational improvements by assigning administrative and data management tasks to AI systems, making many government operations more effective and less costly. For example, AI's immense capacity to process data could easily make onerous information submission and process processing, like tax filing, for instance, a thing of the past. In Estonia, corporate balance sheets are on a government-hosted cloud where AI files monthly returns and adjusts tax rates accordingly. Opportunities for automation will extend to routine administrative processes, such as issuing permits, licenses, or processing applications. Deloitte's Center for Government Insights estimates that simply automating tasks that computers already routinely do could potentially save the U.S. federal government $3.3 billion.

Third, AI holds great potential to analyze historical data and predict future trends, enabling proactive resource allocation and enforcement of regulations and policies. As an example, Canada's Office of the Superintendent of Bankruptcy (OSB) is using debtor data, along with the results of past examinations, to train an ML algorithm to accurately choose debtors for examination along with a confidence rating. The project is helping the OSB identify debtors who may warrant investigation. AI can also detect fraudulent activities, such as tax evasion or benefit fraud, by analyzing patterns and anomalies within large datasets.

Fourth, recent advances in data analytics capabilities have improved the ability of policymakers to craft public policies and regulations that deliver the desired outcomes effectively, with a minimal margin of error and reduced risk of unintended consequences. AI systems could take evidence-based decision-making efforts to new levels of timeliness and sophistication, improving the analysis of complex information, improving the accuracy of budget projections, and handling many other tasks humans can't easily do, such as running complex models and simulations or sifting through millions of documents in real time for the most relevant content.

Finally, AI can enhance public safety by analyzing large volumes of data from various sources, such as surveillance cameras, social media, and sensor networks. It can identify potential security threats, aid in emergency response planning, and assist in predicting and preventing criminal activities. Many schools in the United States have AI routines examining video surveillance in real time to look for guns in schools. Though the results to date have been underwhelming, these systems do learn from their own experiences.[15] Of course, such capabilities border on the Orwellian and would need to be deployed with appropriate safeguards.

AI-Powered Transportation

The dream of fully autonomous and intelligent transportation has long captured the imagination of technologists and science-fiction enthusiasts, and it's easy to see why. The potential benefits of self-driving vehicles are numerous. In a perfect world, you could turn your garage into a spare bedroom while your self-driving car is out making money as an Uber. It could make the blind mobile and safely drive inebriated partiers home.

Even more impressive, a combination of self-driving cars and smart-centralized software could enable just-in-time ride sharing. It could eliminate half the cars on the road and dramatically decrease rush-hour traffic, reducing everyone's commute time. Downtown parking garages could be redeployed for badly needed downtown housing.

Despite the obvious potential, delays in bringing fully autonomous vehicles to market illustrate some of the challenges and limitations of today's AI-powered systems. For example, in December 2017, General Motors (GM) announced plans to launch an autonomous car for commercial fleets beginning in 2019.[16] GM further elaborated that there would be no steering wheel, pedals, or manual controls. Well, it seemed a little more difficult than it first appeared.

Despite the wondrous possibilities, it turns out a safe self-driving car is far more complicated than originally envisioned. In 2016, some predicted driverless cars were five years out. Today's cynics expect that they will remain that way.[17] Bloomberg reports that after a $100 billion investment by Google, Tesla, GM, and others, "self-driving cars are going nowhere."[18] Automotive News estimates it to be closer to $160 billion. In San Francisco, the bizarre behavior of self-driving cars is often reported.[19] Simple cones have been known to confuse them.

Surprisingly, Tesla has abandoned previous efforts to use lidar (short for light detection and ranging, a remote sensing method used to examine the surface of Earth).[20] Without it, it is difficult to tell leaves blowing across the road from a truck painted with autumn leaves crossing the road. Simply put, there are some things that the human mind recognizes instantly that AI is befuddled by. If a prankster on a road with whitewash drew lines to lead you into a tree, a human would know to ignore it and stay on the road. When and if AI will be that smart is still many years away.

Shortly before the pandemic, I spoke in Detroit at a convention. The speaker ahead of me was the chief information officer (CIO) of "North America's largest car-seat manufacturer." I was surprised he did not mention the inevitable impact of AI on seat design—for it will be profound. Front seats could very well face backward in the future with a table in between (similar to train cars). Instead of waking up at 4:30 a.m. to take that 7:00 a.m. red-eye, sleeping in the car on an overnight drive may be cheaper and far more pleasant. And realistically, on longer drives, what used to happen in the back seat of a stationary 1957 Chevy will inevitably happen in the new seat design of future cars on longer drives.

Fully autonomous vehicles may be years off, but how about self-driven planes? Years ago, I had the honor at Jeppesen (now a Boeing subsidiary) of being the chief architect for the system that supplies the flight instructions (AIRINC data) to the computers that fly the majority of the world's commercial aircraft. Relatively speaking, flying an airplane by computer is far simpler than driving a car by computer. It is merely a matter of directing it through radio beacon or GPS-defined waypoints at a particular altitude. With instrument landing systems, an aircraft with a CAT III guidance system can follow various electronic beams to the runway to land itself. These systems were in production and available more than 25 years ago.

At Jeppesen, it was described to me then that being a pilot is 99 percent boredom and 1 percent terror—terror being when the unexpected occurs. It is not an easy job. John Kasten, then Jeppesen's chief domain expert, anticipated that one day the cockpit would have one pilot (to ease passenger concerns) and a Doberman Pinscher as the copilot to ensure the human did not touch the controls. Given that air traffic control is verbal and with engine noise often difficult to hear, clearly the aspiration of pilotless aircraft back then was but a dream.

Beginning in 2016, the Federal Aviation Administration (FAA) started building systems to digitize that once verbal process, sending instructions as text. It is hard to believe that it took until 2016 to realize that re-readable text message instructions are far less confusing than verbal instructions listened to over the background noise of an aircraft.[21] The largest civilian aircraft disaster occurred when a pilot misheard "report when runway clear" to believe that the runway was cleared. That change is a pre-requisite to pilotless aircraft. Safely managing them when on the ground is yet another matter.

Though pilotless commercial aircraft seem inevitable, I would expect them to move freight a decade before they ever move people. Then again, for a short-haul passenger-carrying drone, the weight of a pilot would be prohibitive. Expect to see pilotless short-distance taxis flown by AI in a neighborhood near you sooner than you may expect. They are already flying today![22] Counterintuitively for a computer, flying in three dimensions is a lot easier than driving in two.

AI-Enabled Entertainment and the Arts

Over the decades, I have heard multiple counterarguments that technology will never be creative, computers will never learn on their own, computers will never develop independent thinking, and robots will never replace anything other than repetitive manual labor.

In the last decade, all of these arguments have fallen by the wayside. Using software from tools such as DALL-E, Midjourney, and Stable Diffusion, you can now request very realistic portraits of, say, your kids in the style of Rembrandt or Vincent van Gogh. Whether or not that will make them roll over in their graves is debatable, but when (for a few dollars) AI can generate a painting of your cottage in the style of a living artist (instead of commissioning that artist for thousands of dollars), who should be the beneficiary?

In June 2023, Indiana Jones V was released with a super young Harrison Ford.[23] Earlier in April 2023, the German artist Boris Eldagsen won the prestigious Sony world photography award using an AI-generated image. Eldagsen ultimately declined the award, noting that the entry was a cheeky attempt to gauge whether the photography world is ready for AI-generated entries.[24] Meanwhile, musical artist Grimes has suggested that anyone can use her AI-generated voice and will split the artistic portion of the sales 50/50.[25] For other artists, I anticipate the results will be litigious.[26] Then again, if AI-generated art in the style of a living artist is hung on your living room wall, how is the original artist ever to know?

I think it is only a matter of time before an AI-generated song tops the charts or an AI-generated thriller makes the best-seller list. Today publishers are inundated with (for now) terrible AI-generated stories.[27] AI has entered another seemingly subjective field, assisting musicians in generating music. The Beatles were originally successful in generating hit after hit in three chords. With the help of AI, what you lack in harmonizing can be solved by a computer. Now, there's an entire industry built around AI services for creating music, including Flow Machines, IBM Watson Beat, Google Magenta's NSynth Super, Jukedeck, Melodrive, Spotify's Creator Technology Research Lab, and Amper Music.[28] The source for this, of course, is a mountain of other music and computer-generated insights that we like a beat that is similar in timing to our own heartbeats.

When an AI-generated song wins a Grammy, there will be humans in the development process who accept the award. In the longer view, there may not be. AI poses many challenges, how to award it anything from a Grammy to an Oscar to a Noble Peace prize being among the least of our concerns. In less than a decade, I suspect you will be able to give an AI routine the seeds of a plot and the (younger) age of your favorite actors and watch a full-motion picture personalized to your tastes in just a few hours. So many people have been conned by deep fakes it is now recognized as a national security threat.[29] The day you get a fake Zoom call from your child asking for money is not that far off. With both video and audio, ever more realistic images generated, we must adapt to the adage that "seeing is no longer believing."[30] There is little doubt that AI will be the basis of billions in fraud.[31] As technology advances, it has been and always will be a double-edged sword.

Notes

1. www.incompleteideas.net/book/ebook/node109.html
2. www.astro.caltech.edu/~george/ay122/cacm12.pdf
3. Cover, T., and P. Hart. "Nearest Neighbor Pattern Classification." IEEE Transactions on Information Theory 13, no. 1 (January 1967): 21–27. https://doi.org/10.1109/TIT.1967.1053964.
4. McCulloch, Warren S., and Walter Pitts. "A Logical Calculus of the Ideas Immanent in Nervous Activity." The Bulletin of Mathematical Biophysics 5, no. 4 (December 1, 1943): 115–33. https://doi.org/10.1007/BF02478259.
5. www.usatoday.com/story/news/politics/2023/05/31/ai-extinction-risk-expert-warning/70270171007
6. www.bloomberg.com/news/features/2023-05-31/jpmorgan-s-push-into-finance-ai-has-wall-street-rushing-to-catch-up?re_source=boa_mustread
7. www.wired.com/2012/09/deep-blue-computer-bug
8. www.theguardian.com/technology/2017/dec/07/alphazero-google-deepmind-ai-beats-champion-program-teaching-itself-to-play-four-hours
9. www.scientificamerican.com/article/20-years-after-deep-blue-how-ai-has-advanced-since-conquering-chess
10. www.deepmind.com/research/highlighted-research/alphago/the-challenge-match
11. www.theatlantic.com/technology/archive/2023/03/openai-gpt-4-parameters-power-debate/673290
12. www.cmswire.com/digital-experience/gpt-3-is-impressive-but-it-isnt-artificial-general-intelligence
13. www.bloomberg.com/opinion/articles/2023-03-16/chatgpt-google-s-breakthroughs-are-much-bigger-than-ai
14. https://relevantmagazine.com/culture/tech-gaming/chatgpt-just-passed-the-bar-and-med-school-exams

15. Though the results to date have been underwhelming, these systems do learn from their own experience.

16. www.greencarreports.com/news/1114096_commercial-tests-of-self-driving-chevy-bolt-ev-to-launch-in-many-cities-in-2019

17. www.kitsapdailynews.com/opinion/self-driving-cars-are-always-5-years-away

18. www.bloomberg.com/news/features/2022-10-06/even-after-100-billion-self-driving-cars-are-going-nowhere

19. www.digitaltrends.com/cars/weird-thing-happened-with-fleet-of-autonomous-cars

20. oceanservice.noaa.gov/facts/lidar.html

21. www.npr.org/sections/alltechconsidered/2016/10/03/496393787/air-traffic-controllers-and-pilots-can-now-communicate-electronically

22. www.thefirstnews.com/article/is-it-a-bird-is-it-a-plane-no-its-a-jetson-one-europes-first-passenger-drone-takes-to-the-skies-27156

23. www.foxnews.com/entertainment/how-new-indiana-jones-film-features-super-young-harrison-ford

24. www.theguardian.com/technology/2023/apr/17/photographer-admits-prize-winning-image-was-ai-generated

25. https://decrypt.co/137649/grimes-offers-50-royalties-on-ai-generated-music-using-her-voice

26. www.voanews.com/a/ai-tools-can-create-new-images-but-who-is-the-real-artist-/6925658.html

27. www.businessinsider.com/chatgpt-ai-written-stories-publisher-clarkesworld-forced-close-submissions-2023-2

28. www.theverge.com/2018/8/31/17777008/artificial-intelligence-taryn-southern-amper-music

29. www.dhs.gov/sites/default/files/publications/increasing_threats_of_deepfake_identities_0.pdf

30. www.brookings.edu/research/is-seeing-still-believing-the-deepfake-challenge-to-truth-in-politics

31. www.thedailybeast.com/romance-scammer-used-deepfakes-to-impersonate-a-navy-admiral-and-bilk-widow-out-of-nearly-dollar300000and

3

Animating the Physical World

Technologists and science-fiction writers have long envisioned a world where a seamless global network of Internet-connected sensors could capture every event, action, and change on Earth. Not long ago, the notion that a world of inanimate objects imbued with intelligence could reshape the very foundation of society might have seemed fanciful. Yet, today, that vision of a seamless and intelligent fabric of interconnected devices and objects is edging closer and closer to reality.

The origins of the so-called Internet of Things (IoT) can be traced back to the early 1980s when researchers started exploring the idea of connecting devices to communication networks. At this stage, IoT pioneers focused primarily on machine-to-machine (M2M) communication and industrial applications. Simple devices like sensors and actuators were connected to internal networks, enabling data collection and remote control.

The 1990s marked a significant milestone with the proliferation of Internet connectivity. The development of protocols such as TCP/IP and the growth of wireless communication technologies, including Wi-Fi and 5G, laid the foundation for IoT expansion. This era saw the emergence of consumer-oriented IoT devices, including home automation systems, smart appliances, and the first generation of wearable devices.

The early 2000s witnessed massive growth in data generation and storage capabilities. Cloud computing platforms offered scalable storage and computing resources on demand, enabling organizations to manage and process the vast amount of data generated by a growing array of devices. Cloud-based solutions facilitated data analytics, real-time monitoring, and remote device management, expanding the capabilities and potential of pervasive computing.

As sensor technologies and networks evolved over the next decade, we gained the ability to capture increasingly diverse and granular data streams. Sensors became smaller, more affordable, and energy-efficient, leading to the proliferation of IoT devices in various domains. Industries such as agriculture, healthcare, transportation, and energy management embraced the IoT for applications such as precision farming, remote patient monitoring, smart transportation systems, and energy efficiency optimization.

Today, we are witnessing the convergence of the IoT with artificial intelligence (AI), blockchain, big data analytics, edge computing, and 5G connectivity. AI algorithms and machine learning models enabled intelligent data processing, predictive analytics, and automation. Edge computing empowered real-time decision-making at the device level, reducing latency and enabling faster responses. The rollout of 5G networks enhanced connectivity, enabling seamless communication among devices and supporting IoT deployment at a larger scale. It offers order-of-magnitude increases in speed and much-reduced latency over 4G. This decade, 6G will do it again.

The upshot of the Trivergence is that the IoT has transcended individual devices and expanded into interconnected ecosystems. Devices, platforms, and applications can now seamlessly interact, exchange data, and collaborate on a mass scale. This interconnectivity has transformed many industries, creating innovative solutions and unlocking new business models. For example, we now have unprecedented access to new data streams that can help business leaders manage the world of physical assets, from auto parts in manufacturing supply chains to infrastructure assets like roadways, pipelines, bridges, and buildings—all in real time. Distributed sensors can monitor just about anything from hospital equipment to international cargo shipments to air pollutants, sniff out pesticides and pathogens in food, or even "'recognize'" the person using them and adapt accordingly. Scientists and environmentalists are using distributed sensor networks and the data these tools generate to revolutionize our ability to model the world and its ecological systems, giving us new insights into social and natural phenomena and the ability to forecast trends such as climate change with greater accuracy.

The Trivergence is making cities smarter too. As I document later in this chapter, skyscrapers laden with sensors and AI-enabled building automation solutions can regulate lighting and indoor temperatures in accordance with external conditions. Additional sensors can curtail water flow to your lawn and garden as a result of sensing recent rain. Smart traffic lights can reduce road congestion by adjusting the light cadence to real-time traffic conditions. Connected parking meters and EV charging docks can broadcast their availability to nearby drivers, while smart garbage receptacles notify waste management companies that a pickup is required, eliminating the need for routine schedules.

Autonomous robots empowered by AI are the ultimate manifestation of a world with seamless interconnectivity among inanimate objects. Indeed, the integration of robotics and IoT technologies creates a powerful synergy that enhances automation, data exchange, and intelligent decision-making. For example, robots equipped with sensors and actuators can contribute to the broader IoT data ecosystem, providing real-time insights and enabling intelligent decision-making based on information about environmental conditions, object detection, or movement patterns. At the same time, IoT connectivity enables robots to seamlessly integrate into existing infrastructures, collaborate with other devices, and adapt to changing environments. This flexibility is driving the deployment of robotic systems in various domains, such as manufacturing, healthcare, agriculture, or transportation, enabling automation and efficiency at a larger scale. Increased automation, in turn, will lead to profound workforce transformations, ideally shifting human workers toward more complex and creative roles.

In short, IoT has evolved from a concept of interconnected devices to a powerful network of intelligent systems, including growing swarms of ever-more capable robots. IoT's importance lies in its ability to enhance efficiency; enable real-time, data-driven decision-making; drive automation and innovation; promote sustainability; improve quality of life; and contribute to economic growth. As I argue in this chapter, the IoT's impact on society, industries, and the way we live and work will be nothing short of revolutionary.

A Global Network for Planetary Monitoring and Conservation

Throughout most of human history, humans lived in relative harmony with the natural environment, deeply interconnected with the ecosystems that sustained their livelihoods. However, the advent of industrialization marked a turning point, as humanity's impact on the environment rapidly escalated, leading to a significant disruption of the delicate balance that existed for millennia.

The industrial revolution fueled unprecedented economic growth, technological advancements, and population expansion. With the rise of skyscrapers, factories, mass production, and the combustion of fossil fuels, human activities began to exert an unprecedented impact on the environment. The need for raw materials to fuel industrial production led to the large-scale extraction of resources from Earth's ecosystems.

Industrial processes released vast amounts of pollutants into the air, water, and soil. Factories emitted toxic gases and particulate matter, contaminating the air and contributing to respiratory diseases. Chemical waste from industries found its way into water bodies, impairing aquatic ecosystems and endangering human health. Forty-five percent of the water supply in the United States is contaminated with human-made "forever chemicals."[1] The production of nonbiodegradable materials, and the generation of large volumes of waste has strained the planet's capacity to absorb and recycle materials.

Industrialization also facilitated the rapid growth of cities and the migration of populations from rural areas to urban centers. As cities expanded, natural habitats were destroyed to make way for infrastructure, leading to the loss of biodiversity and fragmentation of ecosystems. This loss of biodiversity has not only affected plant and animal populations but also disrupted vital ecosystem services such as pollination, water purification, and nutrient cycling.

Meanwhile, the burning of fossil fuels released significant amounts of carbon dioxide and other greenhouse gases into the atmosphere. A rapid warming of the planet has altered weather patterns, increased the frequency and intensity of extreme weather events, melted glaciers and polar ice caps, and further disrupted natural ecosystems.

Most of these environmental challenges are ongoing and will continue to have far-reaching consequences for both natural systems and human societies unless we implement proactive measures to manage and mitigate their impacts. Information technologies are by no means a silver bullet for curing an ailing planet. However, the Internet of Things is revolutionizing the way we monitor the natural environment and can provide crucial insights into air and water quality, biodiversity, climate change, and other issues. IoT devices communicating through satellites can give us real-time data from the most remote locations.

Several IoT-enabled projects are demonstrating that empowering individuals, communities, and policymakers with actionable information can contribute to sustainable decision-making, resource optimization, and the preservation of vital ecosystems.

Tackling Deforestation with the IoT

Take deforestation, a critical global problem that contributes to biodiversity loss and is a significant driver of climate change. For example, we now know that the loss of carbon capture from tropical deforestation is comparable to the emissions of the European Union and greater than those of all the cars, trucks, planes, ships, and trains on the planet.[2] Scientists hoping to uncover the location and rates of deforestation around the world used to conduct expensive field studies that might involve traversing through vast tracks of the jungle in Indonesia or Brazil. Today, many rely on tools like Global Forest Watch, which are available to anyone with a PC and an Internet connection.

Launched in 2014 by the World Resources Institute (WRI), Global Forest Watch (GFW) improves transparency and accountability in forest management decisions by increasing the public's access to information on forestry developments around the world. The underlying principle is that increasingly powerful information technologies make transparency one of our most potent mechanisms for strengthening the incentives for responsible industry practices and building the capacity for sustainable forest management. The site provides access to a wealth of information about threats to forests and the entities behind those threats. Within minutes, an interested researcher can see the location and duration of a company's logging concessions, look up local forestry laws and regulations, and check whether the logging companies have paid their taxes. Most information can be easily navigated using a visual map interface that taps into a combination of satellite imagery, national forest datasets, and "on-the-ground" reports. More advanced users can download geographical data from their warehouse and manipulate it for their own analyses using third-party apps like Google Earth.

According to Crystal Hamilton, formerly the WRI's senior manager for Global Forest Watch, the technology for forest monitoring has improved dramatically. In the past, data on forest cover in countries with advanced regulatory regimes was updated annually, while data for developing nations was updated much less frequently, if at all. Regardless of the source, Hamilton called the data unreliable and noted that assessing the rates of deforestation was extraordinarily difficult and labor-intensive. "Someone would need to go through the data to compare past and present satellite imagery," she said. "It required a lot of technical expertise and a lot of time."[3]

Today, Global Forest Watch taps into NASA's satellite imagery and an advanced analytics platform called FORMA that was developed by computer scientists at the Center for Global Development. The new system analyzes the entire planet every 16 days at a resolution of 250 meters. FORMA's built-in algorithms can automatically detect changes in forest cover, allowing researchers, policymakers, industry, and communities to respond to issues immediately. Hamilton calls the new system "exceptionally powerful and a vast improvement in the tools available to communities, policymakers, scientists, and companies."[4]

While Global Forest Watch relies principally on satellite observation, another group called Rainforest Connection uses IoT-enabled sensors deployed in tropical rainforests to detect illegal logging and wildlife poaching. The heart of the real-time monitoring system is what Rainforest Connection calls its "Guardian device"—a solar-powered acoustic streaming device that it mounts in tree-top canopies.[5] The device's primary purpose is to gather a continuous stream of data on the surrounding environment for processing and storage. When connected via GSM or via satellite, the Guardian device uploads a real-time recording of the surrounding soundscape to the cloud for instant analysis. Rainforest Connection's data platform uses AI and machine learning to identify potentially harmful behavior and help rangers and conservationists pinpoint and stop destructive activities as they occur. Similar sensor-based systems have been deployed to identify and track species, map habitats, and monitor endangered or elusive species.

Water scarcity is another urgent issue where pervasive computing technologies could make a crucial difference. Currently, the world's lack of fresh water is shaping up to be a catastrophe for humanity; 2.8 billion (or 44 percent) of the world's population lives in regions where freshwater resources are under severe stress. This troubling figure is set to rise to 3.9 billion by 2030.[6] As yet, nobody has determined exactly how the world's long-term need for fresh water will be met. But in the meantime, advanced informatics solutions such as remote sensing and geospatial mapping are helping policymakers and affected communities better understand the implications of the current demands being placed on regional water systems.

Consider, for example, that about one-third of the world's population depends to some degree on freshwater within the High Asia hydrological system, including the populations of Bhutan, Nepal, China, India, Pakistan, Afghanistan, Kazakhstan, Uzbekistan, Kyrgyzstan, and Tajikistan. At present, not enough data exists on river and stream flows, and the contribution of seasonal snow and glacier melt to paint an accurate picture of the water resources there. But thanks to a combination of satellite monitoring and remote sensing, the University of Colorado Boulder and a network of local communities and Asian research institutes are working together to supply more accurate data on how much water there actually is and how demand and supply are changing as increased development and climate change place new strains on the region's water resources.[7] The data will enable water management officials to forecast the future availability and vulnerability of water resources in the region and make sound decisions with regard to how to manage resources, assess flood risks, and understand variations in seasonal flow.

The IoT and Final Frontier of Ocean Exploration

Policymakers, scientists, and technologists have understandably focused considerable attention on monitoring the health of inland freshwater resources in the face of accelerating climate change. However, another critical opportunity for resolving environmental challenges lies at the intersection of the IoT and the world's ocean. The ocean covers some 71 percent of the world's surface and holds an estimated 97 percent of the world's water. The ocean significantly impacts climate, the global food supply, and an estimated $1.5 trillion in economic activity, from tourism to shipping to fishing.[8] Despite its size and impact, more than 80 percent of the ocean has never been mapped, explored, or even seen by humans.[9] Given how little is known, the ocean's potential seems almost limitless.

Growing efforts to understand and harness the ocean's potential have given rise to a diverse constellation of ocean technologies with far-reaching applications, including proven technologies available today and new technologies still in development. From autonomous robotic vehicles to distributed ocean sensor networks, powerful scientific instruments are powering quantum leaps in the volume and diversity of data about the marine environment and its inhabitants. One estimate suggests the amount of ocean observation data collected each year is already greater than that gathered in the 100 years prior.[10]

The plethora of data raises both new challenges and new opportunities. Novel protocols, infrastructure, and tools will be required to manage and explore massive datasets. Advances in artificial intelligence will help transform data into knowledge that end users can deploy to build commercial applications and shape policy. Marine transport, fisheries, and offshore energy production, for example, are all reliant on detailed observations of ocean conditions. So, too, is the scientific community's capacity to accurately model and forecast the interaction between climate change and the health of ocean ecosystems.

With its unique coastal location, the Canadian city of Halifax has emerged as a natural hub for ocean science, innovation, and new venture creation in the ocean-tech space. Proximity to the Atlantic Ocean provides competitive advantages for companies providing ocean-sensing technologies and advanced maritime transportation and logistics solutions. So, too, does the wealth of Halifax-based scientists and ocean technology ventures working full-time to accelerate ocean R&D and develop the platforms, equipment, and information services to deliver the ocean observations, measurements, analyses, and forecasts enabling the broader Ocean Economy.[11]

The Centre for Ocean Ventures and Entrepreneurship (COVE) is one of several Halifax-based organizations working on translating promising AI and IoT technologies into viable products and services that address sustainability challenges and help traditional industries operate more efficiently in the ocean environment. In May 2021, COVE launched a multisensor subsea data collection platform called the Stella Maris to accelerate the development of new ocean informatics solutions.[12] The platform hosts acoustic sensors, undersea cameras, and a high-precision infrared imaging system. "Technology demonstrations are very expensive for individual companies," said COVE's CEO, Melanie Nadeau. "Our platform provides opportunities to significantly lower the cost of testing, refining and validating new ocean-based sensors and instruments and new data-based applications."

Dartmouth-based Marecomms, for example, recently demonstrated that its Robust Acoustic Modem (ROAM) can send sonar images and photos through a 2 kilometer channel in the busy waters of the Halifax harbor. According to Marecomms's CEO, Ulaş Güntürkün, the test demonstrates an improvement of three orders of magnitude (i.e., 1,000x) over off-the-shelf technologies.[13] The undersea modem, which uses sound waves to send data through water, could be deployed to monitor subsea pipelines and infrastructure or enable communication between autonomous undersea vehicles. Other applications include IoT-powered buoys equipped with sensors to monitor water quality indicators, such as salinity, pH, and oxygen levels. These buoys provide valuable insights into the health of coastal ecosystems, aiding in the protection of marine biodiversity.

As in other application areas, ocean technology ventures are highlighting the power of converging technologies. For example, the data collected by IoT devices in the ocean can be encoded on a blockchain and transmitted in real time to data centers or cloud platforms for analysis. Advanced analytics, machine learning algorithms, and AI-based models can process this data, providing valuable insights into oceanographic phenomena, biodiversity patterns, and ecosystem health. These insights, in turn, can inform conservation strategies, help identify vulnerable species, and enable early detection of environmental changes or threats, such as pollution, habitat degradation, or the effects of climate change.

Halifax and other coastal cities have long recognized the paramount importance of the world's oceans for economic prosperity and the broader health of our planet. Now, with a powerful new generation of IoT technologies, they are equipped with a powerful toolset to contribute to the preservation and sustainable use of marine environments. Harnessing the potential of IoT in the oceans will be critical to gathering the information necessary to safeguard their invaluable ecological role and ensure a healthier and more prosperous future for coastal communities.

The IoT Meets the Urban Environment

If a global biosphere laden with sensors can provide real-time information about the health of the planet, could the Internet of Things help us monitor our built environments, including the essential infrastructures that sustain our cities—from electrical grids to roadways to water and sanitation systems? Many believe that the quality of life in today's urban environment fundamentally depends on it.

In recent history, the world has witnessed a significant shift in population from rural to urban areas, leading to the rapid growth of cities. This trend of urbanization has been driven by various factors, including wide-scale distribution of electricity, economic opportunities, improved infrastructure, access to better healthcare and education, and social and cultural attractions.

Over the past few decades, urbanization has accelerated, particularly in developing regions such as Asia, Africa, and Latin America. Mega-cities such as Tokyo, Delhi, Shanghai, and Sao Paulo have experienced unprecedented population growth, resulting in the emergence of sprawling urban landscapes and the development of diverse urban cultures.

Though slowed by the pandemic, the trend of urbanization is expected to persist, with the global urban population projected to increase significantly. By 2050, it is estimated that nearly 70 percent of the world's population will reside in cities, leading to the emergence of new mega-cities and the expansion of existing urban areas.

Sustainability and resilience will be critical considerations in urban planning and development. Cities need to focus on reducing carbon emissions, implementing renewable energy systems, adopting eco-friendly infrastructure, and enhancing climate resilience to mitigate the impacts of climate change. Affordable housing, accessible infrastructure, inclusive public spaces, and opportunities for social and economic mobility are also increasingly critical. Across all these domains, technological advancements such as the IoT, data analytics, and artificial intelligence will play a vital role in enhancing the efficiency of urban services, improving sustainability, and creating more livable cities.

The rise of digital connectivity, the Internet, and mobile technologies has already profoundly transformed the way cities function and how people interact within urban environments. However, a new generation of IoT technologies promises to take the whole notion of the smart city to a new level. For example, motion and vibration detectors are some of the most common among this next generation of sensors. More accurately called accelerometers, they are found in today's smartphones. The kind you find in an iPhone is sensitive enough to "feel" a heartbeat. But the most exquisitely sensitive accelerometer today can now detect a

10-femtometer change in position. At less than one-billionth the width of a human hair, it's exceptionally sensitive. Such accelerometers have been broadly deployed to detect earthquakes in real time and to monitor the structural integrity and resilience of civil infrastructure such as bridges, buildings, and tunnels.[14]

Accelerometers are merely the tip of the iceberg, though. There are sensors for light, temperature, barometric pressure, airflow, and humidity. And around the corner, are sensors that can "taste and smell." Researchers are using nanomaterials to boost a standard chemical and biological detection technology (Raman spectroscopy) to 100 million times its usual sensitivity rates. As sensitivity rises, sensor size can shrink. That could lead to detectors small enough to clip onto a mobile phone. With a wave over produce, the sensor might warn consumers of salmonella on spinach leaves or pesticides present in "organic" produce.

This plethora of new sensing capabilities will unleash countless new monitoring and real-time reporting opportunities. Indeed, the potential to make dumb infrastructure intelligent has companies like Cisco, IBM, and HP hastily staking claims and developing intelligent infrastructures to measure everything from water and natural gas flows to urban infrastructure, transportation networks, and office buildings.

Urban planners think that equipping entire cities with such capabilities could have a massive impact on utility usage, as well as a wide range of other benefits. As a test of this proposition, the coastal city of Santander in Spain recently won a multimillion-dollar grant from the European Commission to become one of Europe's "smartest" cities. The city has deployed tens of thousands of sensors to monitor everything from garbage collection to crime to air quality.[15] Some of these sensors conserve energy by optimizing street lighting—dimming the lights when there is no one on the street and emitting less light during a full moon than on a rainy night. Sensors in parking spaces direct drivers to available spaces and enable a time-based metering system that matches prices to demand. City buses transmit their position, mileage, and speed, as well as data from the ambient environment, such as ozone or nitric oxide pollution levels. Taxis and police cars do the same. Back at the University of Cantabria, which houses the data and the city's central dashboard, researchers and city officials can observe where the traffic jams are and where the air is bad. Citizens can access all of the same data on their smartphones with a few clicks on Santander's Pulse of the City app.

Santander is just one of many smart city hubs around the world. In Copenhagen, the EnergyLab Nordhavn project utilizes IoT sensors and energy management systems to integrate renewable energy sources, storage, and demand response mechanisms.[16] The lab's pioneering work enables Copenhagen to balance energy supply and demand, reduce greenhouse gas emissions, and promote a sustainable energy ecosystem. Meanwhile, the Edge building in Amsterdam, considered one of the smartest buildings globally, utilizes IoT systems to monitor occupancy, adjust lighting and temperature based on real-time data, and optimize energy consumption.[17] The Edge, and other buildings like it, provide occupants with a comfortable environment while minimizing energy waste.

In Barcelona, the municipality employs IoT-enabled waste management systems that use fill-level sensors in containers, optimizing waste collection routes and minimizing costs. Barcelona also uses IoT-based sensors to monitor water quality in real time across the city's water distribution network. The data the city collects helps detect leaks, identify areas with water quality issues, and optimize water resource management.[18]

Across the Atlantic, the City of Chicago is addressing local air quality concerns with IoT sensors to monitor carbon monoxide, nitrogen dioxide, sulfur dioxide, ozone, ambient sound pressure, and vehicle traffic. Researchers involved with Chicago's Array of Things project hope the data will help residents make informed decisions about the healthiest and unhealthiest walking times and routes through the city.[19]

In smart cities around the world, the drive to make all things "intelligent" by connecting inanimate objects to the Internet will result in a flood of new data that can be aggregated and analyzed, providing a powerful engine for infrastructure management dashboards that provide a real-time view of how assets across the system are faring. Reaching that kind of scale, however, will take some work. IBM, a leading provider of smart city solutions, estimates it takes a million or so sensors for a big business application, such as cargo shipping; and at least a trillion sensors will be required to "informate" the entire planet. At that rate, sensor nodes must cost next to nothing yet measure everything. They soon will. Currently, there are about three IoT sensors per person, increasing to about four in 2026.[20]

The recent history of urbanization has seen an unprecedented rise in global urban populations driven by economic, social, and technological factors. Looking to the future, the most vibrant, resilient, and prosperous cities will embrace sustainability, connectivity, and inclusivity. The Internet of Things has already provided a catalyst for transforming urban environments and improving the quality of life in today's cities by helping city administrators and residents address urban challenges, such as mobility, energy consumption, waste management, and public safety. As cities continue to evolve, the potential of IoT converging with AI and blockchain to reshape urban landscapes and improve the lives of residents remains one of the most promising and vital manifestations of the Trivergence.

The Robotic Future: From Industrial Automation to Robot Swarms

It is impossible to talk of Trivergence or animating the physical world without exploring the accelerating impact of robotics. It is not a huge leap to envision a world where robots will live among us, make our beds, drop off and pick up our dry cleaning, walk our dogs, drive our kids to school, run our factories, and build everything from new homes to wind turbines. The question is how quickly and how efficiently millions (or possibly billions) of robots can be built to perform these tasks. Because robots are now building robots, which can then build far more robots, which will build a massive number of robots, it may be sooner than we think.[21]

Robotics has a long history rooted in computer science and industrial automation. For decades, the adoption of industrial robotics has been proceeding at a breakneck pace. The International Federation of Robotics estimates that a fleet of 3.5 million industrial robots is currently operating in factories around the world, with China accounting for nearly one-third of all industrial robots installed worldwide.[22]

One key indicator for gauging the current degree of automation within the international markets is robotic density: the ratio of robots to human employees. As of 2021, the average global robotic density in producing industries lies at 141 robot units per 10,000 employees—more than double the rate of six years ago. However, the density among leading countries is significantly higher.[23] As the current global leader in industrial robotic automation, South Korea's robotic density exceeds the global average by a good sevenfold (1,000 units), followed by Singapore (670 units), Japan (399 units), (Germany (397 units), and China (322).[24]

Advanced economies as a whole may be some distance from fully automated manufacturing. But for many high-tech manufacturers, that reality is here today. Companies like Flextronics, for example, can compete with the Chinese in the production of solar panels with a plant in Mexico because most of the production process is fully automated. In its state-of-the-art plant—where the assembly line runs 24 hours a day, 7 days a week—there are robots everywhere and few human workers. Robots do all the heavy lifting and almost all of the precise work involved in stringing together solar cells and sealing them under glass panels. As machines do more work and humans do less, the outsourcing advantages of labor arbitrage are now fading. Nearshoring is replacing outsourcing. Expect more manufacturing to occur closer to their markets. Also, expect the plants built in North America to be highly labor efficient.

While robots have long been a part of manufacturing, the cost and competency of those robots continue to advance at a rapid pace. The establishment of robust theoretical frameworks augmented by AI learning from the IoT, empowered by the cloud, has yielded remarkable successes in foundational tasks, such as speech recognition, image classification, autonomous vehicles, machine translation, legged locomotion, and question-answering systems.

An inventory of recent advances makes today's robots function more like humans every day. For example, AI algorithms and machine learning techniques allow robots to learn from data, recognize patterns, make decisions, and adapt their behavior. In other words, robots on a continuous feedback loop will be able to handle ever more complex tasks, learn from their experiences, and improve performance over time.

Advanced sensor technologies, including depth sensors and tactile sensors, enable robots to navigate autonomously, recognize objects, detect obstacles, and interact with their environment. Adding computer vision techniques takes robotic perception capabilities to a whole new level. Now robots can analyze and interpret visual information from cameras or other imaging devices, allowing these smart machines to recognize objects, track motion, and perform tasks that require visual understanding. Computers can now feel as well as see.

Some of the most intriguing advancements include human-robot interaction technologies that aim to make robots more intuitive and user-friendly. Improvements in natural language processing are permitting robots to understand and process human language, which means they can respond to voice commands and read written instructions.

Beyond speech, there have been advances in gesture recognition, haptic interfaces, and augmented reality, enabling more natural and seamless interactions between humans and robots.

Connecting robots to the cloud allows robots to leverage vast computational resources and access large datasets. The ability to handle computationally intensive tasks will further enhance the capacity of robots to continuously learn and update their capabilities. Meanwhile, a combination of cloud connectivity and AI will give rise to what researchers call "robotic swarms," where multiple robots collaborate to accomplish tasks collectively. Just like humans, teams of robots will work together, share information, and exhibit emergent behaviors that enhance their problem-solving capabilities. And through "preventative maintenance," robots will be able to repair robots on the assembly lines.

While most people envision large industrial machines or humanoid robots with rigid body mechanics, there is a trend toward robots getting smaller and more organic in nature. The miniaturization of components and the emergence of bio-inspired soft robotics is allowing for the creation of smaller, more flexible, and versatile robots. Soft robotics, for example, leverage materials that mimic the properties of living organisms, enabling robots to interact safely and more naturally with humans and delicate environments.

These technical developments are continually pushing the boundaries of what robots can achieve, allowing them to perform increasingly complex tasks, adapt to different environments, and interact more seamlessly with humans. The upshot is that robots that were once consigned to carefully controlled tasks and segregated work environments can now work alongside people and perform many tasks in unpredictable environments. And because of ever-cheaper sensors and chips, increasingly intelligent robots are much more powerful per dollar, year after year.

At the same time, robots of various sorts are making forays into new domains, driven by advancements in technology and increased demand for automation in diverse sectors. For example, medical professionals are using surgical robots to perform minimally invasive procedures with increased precision, control, and reduced invasiveness. Rehabilitation robots are being used to facilitate physical therapy and recovery, while robotic exoskeletons can assist individuals with mobility impairments. Soon, a growing field force of robotic companions and care aids will provide social and emotional support to patients, especially in eldercare.

At the Knollwood Military Retirement Community in Washington, D.C., a 4-foot, 7-inch humanoid-like robot called Stevie has been leading karaoke sessions, taking meal orders, and facilitating video-conferencing sessions between elder residents and their doctors and family members.[25] Stevie's presence in Knollwood is part of a long-term effort by researchers at Trinity College Dublin to determine how AI and robots could help address the growing disparity between the increasing number of aging Americans requiring care and the limited number of professionals available to attend to them. In the United States alone, there will be an estimated shortfall of 151,000 paid care workers by 2030.[26] By 2040, the gap could more than double, creating an acute need for socially assistive robots that can cater to the social, emotional, and physical requirements of elderly individuals while upholding their dignity and privacy with unwavering reliability.

Excellence in the broader service and hospitality sectors has long been synonymous with the grace and poise of human attendants. However, staffing shortages and a drive to cut costs have a growing number of establishments looking to robots to automate routine tasks and enhance customer experiences. In Japan, Hong Kong, and Singapore, robotic receptionists, concierge assistants, and waiters are popping up in hotels, airports, and sushi bars. In some domains of customer service, robots are arguably superior. For example, at the Henn-na Hotel in Nagasaki, Japan—the world's first robot-staffed hotel—advanced androids can respond to guests' queries in English, Japanese, Chinese, and even sign language.[27]

Like manufacturing, the mass grunt labor required for industrial agriculture and construction is ripe for increased automation. For example, agricultural robots can perform activities such as planting, harvesting, crop monitoring, and pesticide application. Most modern farm machinery has largely swapped out human operators for a combination of computer vision, AI, and GPS. Combined with ubiquitous sensors and improved analytics, these advances in agricultural automation can optimize resource utilization, reduce environmental impacts, and increase crop yields.[28] Meanwhile, construction robots can lay bricks, pour concrete, weld steel beams, and safely demolish unwanted structures with unrivalled efficiency. In addition to increasing productivity, automating these repetitive and dangerous tasks significantly improves worksite safety.[29]

In the outer reaches of space, robotics is playing a vital role in exploration and research. Robotic rovers, such as NASA's Mars rovers, have been deployed to explore extraterrestrial environments and collect scientific data. Robotic systems are also widely used in satellite assembly, maintenance, and repair tasks. Closer to home, the field of personal and domestic robotics is evolving rapidly. Robotic vacuum cleaners, lawnmowers, and window cleaners have become increasingly common. Social robots for entertainment, companionship, and education purposes are also gaining popularity.

The growing use of robots in defense and security is arguably the most controversial of applications. Using robots to dispose of bombs or to conduct surveillance and reconnaissance missions is routine and seems harmless enough. However, lethal autonomous weapons are increasingly commonplace, with AI-enabled drones routinely demolishing infrastructure and hunting down high-value targets on battlefields ranging from Ukraine to Ethiopia. AI-powered robotic guns have also been used by the United States in Iraq, by Israel in the West Bank, and even by comparatively low-tech Syrian rebels.[30]

In theory, autonomous weapons enhance the accuracy of firing by ensuring they hit the "right targets." Today, Israel's AI-powered weapons fire tear gas, stun grenades, and sponge-tipped bullets. But arming robotic guns with far more lethal outputs is trivial and sadly inevitable.[31] Human rights activists are surprisingly not concerned about "the digital dehumanization of weapons systems" and see their use as "a powder keg for human rights."[32]

The prospect of digital armies of killer robots "manning" the battlefields of future conflicts is alarming to many. In such a scenario, killer robots, once activated, would likely operate without direct human control or intervention. The lack of human oversight raises concerns about the ability to determine responsibility and accountability for their actions, potentially leading to unintended consequences or violations of international humanitarian law. After all, the willingness to die for your country is no longer a consideration for killer robots. Moreover, autonomous weapons may not possess the ability to distinguish between combatants and civilians accurately, increasing the risk of indiscriminate attacks. A war with massive civilian and few military casualties seems a disturbing possibility.

Some fear that developing and deploying autonomous weapons would inevitably lead to an arms race among nations, escalating tensions and increasing the risk of armed conflicts. The widespread adoption of such weapons may also lower the barriers for nonstate actors to acquire and use them, further destabilizing global security. Imagine killing flying machines under the control of even the lowest-tech nonstate actors. For higher-tech countries, one of today's design limitations for fighter jets is the g-forces a human body can sustain. With AI, the next generation of fighter jets will have eliminated the pilots and their physical limitations.

Much of what I have described is either happening today or on the near-term horizon. Over the medium-to-long term, ever-more intelligent robots will profoundly reshape our world and give rise to significant socioeconomic shifts. Robotic automation will unavoidably result in job displacement, requiring the retraining and reskilling of workers on a mass scale. A recent Oxford study predicts that more than 1.5 million jobs will be lost to robots in the United States by 2030. In China, that number will exceed 11 million. Across EU member states, almost 2 million people will lose out on employment because of automation.[33]

On the upside, the rise of robots could give rise to entirely new industries and services. For example, there will be increased demand for robot design, manufacturing, programming, and maintenance services. Additionally, new service sectors may emerge, catering to the needs of robots and their users, such as robot training, customization, and specialized support. McKinsey optimistically argues that robotic automation will lead to innovation and thus create more jobs while delivering a GDP growth of 7 percent. Whether the net effect will be positive is anyone's guess.

While robots have already played a vital role in space exploration, their prevalence may enable further advancements in this domain. Robots can be instrumental in conducting complex tasks in extreme environments, enabling human exploration and colonization of other celestial bodies. As robots become more advanced and capable, we will witness deeper integration between humans and machines. This could involve the development of brain-computer interfaces, enabling direct communication and control between the human brain and robots. Such integration could lead to new possibilities in areas such as cybernetics, cognitive enhancement, and human-machine collaboration.

Finally, fusing robotics with the developments in artificial intelligence described in Chapter 2 will surely result in the most far-reaching and unsettling implications for society. For example, the realization of artificial general intelligence will imbue robots with the capacity for complex reasoning, creativity, and problem-solving. When these abilities surpass those of humans, the very nature of humanity as we know it today will be called into question.

Managing the IoT

In the data-poor world, the devices we used to capture and process data were sparsely distributed and intermittently connected. The result was an incomplete and often outdated snapshot of the real world.

But distribute billions and perhaps trillions of connected sensors around the planet—just as we are doing today—and virtually every animate and inanimate object on Earth could be generating and transmitting data, including our homes, our cars, our natural and man-made environments, and, yes, even our bodies.

It's not just that the sensors are getting smaller and faster, as Moore's law predicts they will. The absolute number of sensors is exploding as more and more applications emerge. In other words, it's a double exponential in terms of the amount of data being generated.

The deluge of data generated by transactions, medical and legal records, videos, and social technologies—not to mention the sensors, cameras, bar codes, and transmitters embedded in the world around us—has enormous economic potential, especially as advances in blockchain, computational power, and AI help organizations transform this sea of data into new services, new innovations, and new opportunities for significant operational efficiencies.

However, the copious amount of new data also raises new questions. For example, how will these distributed devices and assets interoperate? Where should the data reside? Can organizations exploit IoT data while also safeguarding personal privacy? And how can organizations securely access, analyze, and share massive datasets? Many see the convergence of blockchain, AI, and IoT as providing practical solutions for these challenges.

■ **Interoperability:** On a technical level, one of the key challenges with the IoT is ensuring interoperability among the distributed devices and assets within an ecosystem. IoT devices come from different manufacturers, use diverse communication protocols, and serve various purposes, so ensuring seamless connectivity and interoperability is crucial. Standardization efforts, such as the development of common communication protocols (e.g., MQTT, CoAP), interoperability frameworks (e.g., OCF, oneM2M), and industry alliances, aim to address these challenges. These initiatives enable devices to communicate and share data effectively, allowing for interoperability and the creation of integrated IoT solutions.

- **Privacy:** The widespread adoption of the IoT has raised significant privacy concerns because of the nature of the data collected, transmitted, and analyzed by IoT devices. In many instances, IoT devices continuously collect and transmit data about users' behaviors, preferences, and activities. This constant monitoring raises concerns about privacy invasion and surveillance. For example, smart home devices, wearables, and even public infrastructure sensors can gather highly personal information, such as daily routines, health data, our associations, and location information. The aggregation of this data from multiple sources can create detailed profiles and insights about individuals, potentially leading to privacy breaches or misuse of personal information. Users may not fully understand or have visibility into the data being collected, how it is used, or with whom it is shared. This lack of transparency and control limits individual autonomy and undermines the ability of users to make informed decisions about their privacy.

  I will have much more to say about privacy and user control in Chapter 6, where I discuss the implications of a world with seemingly infinite data. For IoT-specific applications, devices and systems should be designed with privacy considerations from the outset. Privacy-enhancing technologies, such as data anonymization, encryption, and access control mechanisms, should be integrated into IoT architectures to protect personal information and minimize privacy risks. IoT providers should be transparent about data collection practices, data usage, and sharing policies. For example, a best practice is giving users clear visibility into the data collected, the purposes for which it is used, and options for managing and controlling their data. Technologies such as blockchain can also facilitate secure and traceable data sharing while maintaining data integrity and provenance.

- **Data residency:** Closely related to privacy considerations is the issue of data residency. Determining where IoT data should reside raises questions related to data privacy, security, and legal compliance. As noted, IoT devices generate data that can be sensitive or personally identifiable, necessitating careful consideration of data residency and storage. Factors such as data sovereignty laws, privacy regulations, and the nature of the data itself influence decisions regarding data residency. In some cases, data may need to reside locally to comply with legal requirements, while in other instances, cloud-based storage solutions or edge computing approaches may be appropriate. Organizations need to assess the regulatory landscape and consider the trade-offs between local storage and centralized data repositories to ensure compliance, data protection, and efficient data processing. The design of these systems must take into consideration future legislation, such as the EU's "right to be forgotten."

- **Analytics:** Managing and deriving insights from the massive datasets generated by IoT devices present additional challenges related to data aggregation and analysis. In the aggregation phase, organizations should deploy encryption, authentication mechanisms, and secure communication protocols that are essential to safeguard sensitive IoT data. Access control mechanisms, such as identity and access management systems, help ensure that only authorized individuals or systems can access and analyze the data. Furthermore, organizations can employ techniques such as data anonymization or aggregation to balance the need for data analysis with privacy concerns.

  To effectively analyze massive datasets, organizations can leverage big data analytics techniques, including machine learning and artificial intelligence algorithms. Edge computing enables data processing at the edge of the network, reducing latency and improving real-time insights. Cloud-based platforms offer scalable computing resources and data storage capabilities, enabling efficient analysis of IoT data.

Successfully navigating these challenges will ensure the benefits of an IoT-enabled world are fully realized. We have already seen evidence of improved resource management, enhanced convenience, personalized experiences, and increased efficiency in everything from healthcare to global supply chains. Expanding the IoT ecosystem by connecting more devices, systems, and people holds the potential to fuel radical innovation, groundbreaking discoveries, and solutions to complex problems. In a world where technology seamlessly integrates with everyday life, individuals, organizations, and communities will have almost limitless potential to harness the vast socioeconomic potential of an era of unprecedented connectivity and intelligence.

Notes

1. United States Geological Survey. "Tap Water Study Detects PFAS 'forever Chemicals' across the US," July 5, 2023. www.usgs.gov/news/national-news-release/tap-water-study-detects-pfas-forever-chemicals-across-us.
2. www.edf.org/news/scientists-and-ngos-deforestation-and-degradation-responsible-approximately-15-percent-global-w
3. Interview with Crystal Hamilton, senior manager, Global Forest Watch, World Resources Institute.
4. Ibid.
5. https://rfcx.org/guardian
6. Geoffrey Lean, "Water scarcity 'now bigger threat than financial crisis'," The Independent (March 15, 2013).
7. www.colorado.edu/asmagazine/2011/12/01/cu-researchers-examine-water-asia
8. www.oecd.org/sti/science-technology-innovation-outlook/ocean-economy-and-innovation
9. www.nationalgeographic.org/encyclopedia/ocean
10. www.frontiersin.org/articles/10.3389/fmars.2019.00440/full
11. https://coveocean.com/wp-content/uploads/2021/10/COVE_Whitepaper_8.5x11_Oct5_2021_DIGITAL.pdf
12. www.covestellamaris.com
13. entrevestor.com/home/entry/marecomms-moves-into-commercialization-phase
14. eos.org/science-updates/tiny-accelerometers-create-europes-first-urban-seismic-network
15. www.spiegel.de/international/world/santander-a-digital-smart-city-prototype-in-spain-a-888480.html
16. www.energylabnordhavn.com
17. www.bloomberg.com/features/2015-the-edge-the-worlds-greenest-building

18. https://ec.europa.eu/digital-single-market/en/success-stories/smart-water-management-barcelona
19. https://arrayofthings.github.io
20. Lueth, Knud Lasse. "State of IoT 2023: Number of Connected IoT Devices Growing 16% to 16.7 Billion Globally." IoT Analytics, May 24, 2023. iot-analytics.com/number-connected-iot-devices.
21. https://techcrunch.com/2022/11/22/researchers-are-building-robots-that-can-build-themselves
22. https://ifr.org/img/worldrobotics/Executive_Summary_WR_Industrial_Robots_2022.pdf
23. https://ifr.org/downloads/press/Executive_Summary_WR_2017_Industrial_Robots.pdf
24. https://ifr.org/ifr-press-releases/news/china-overtakes-usa-in-robot-density
25. https://time.com/longform/senior-care-robot
26. www.reuters.com/article/us-column-miller-caregivers-idUSKBN1AJ1JQ
27. https://group.hennnahotel.com
28. www.mckinsey.com/industries/agriculture/our-insights/agricultures-connected-future-how-technology-can-yield-new-growth
29. https://dozr.com/blog/5-robots-that-are-changing-construction
30. www.euronews.com/next/2022/10/17/israel-deploys-ai-powered-robot-guns-that-can-track-targets-in-the-west-bank
31. www.euronews.com/next/2022/10/17/israel-deploys-ai-powered-robot-guns-that-can-track-targets-in-the-west-bank
32. https://humanrightsclinic.law.harvard.edu/stop-killer-robots-global-meeting-showcases-campaigns-strength
33. www.cnbc.com/2019/06/26/robots-could-take-over-20-million-jobs-by-2030-study-claims.html

4 Blockchain

I n 2008, a mysterious figure named Satoshi Nakamoto published a whitepaper titled "Bitcoin: A Peer-to-Peer Electronic Cash System." This paper introduced the concept of *blockchain*—a decentralized ledger that could securely record and verify transactions without the need for intermediaries. Nakamoto's creation, Bitcoin, became the first successful implementation of blockchain technology.

As Bitcoin gained popularity, developers and visionaries began to explore the potential of blockchain beyond cryptocurrency. They realized that the underlying technology could be applied to various sectors, providing transparency, security, and immutability. In essence, a blockchain is an encoded digital ledger stored on multiple computers in a public or private network. It consists of data records, or *blocks*, aggregated into time-stamped chains that cannot be changed or deleted by a single actor; instead, they are verified and managed through automation and shared governance protocols. As a result, blockchain provides an unassailable, immutable transparent record.

Blockchain's potential was soon realized beyond the financial realm. Entrepreneurs and innovators began to develop new blockchain-based platforms. Ethereum, introduced in 2015 by Vitalik Buterin, allowed for the creation of smart contracts and decentralized applications (DApps). This opened doors for a new wave of innovation and experimentation.

In their best-selling book *Blockchain Revolution*, Don and Alex Tapscott described blockchains as nothing less than an Internet of Value. They argued that the Internet today connects billions of people around the world, and certainly, it's great for communicating and collaborating online. But because it's built for moving and storing information and not *value*, they argue that it has done little to change the way we do business. When you send information to someone, like an email, Word document, PDF, or PowerPoint presentation, you're really sending a copy, not the original. It's OK (and indeed advantageous) for people to print a copy of their PowerPoint file but not OK to print, say, money. So with the "Internet of information," as they dub it, we have to rely on powerful intermediaries to establish trust. Banks, governments, and even social media companies like Facebook all do the work of establishing our identity and helping us own and transfer assets and settle transactions.

Overall, they've done a pretty good job, but there are limitations. They use centralized servers, which can be hacked. They take a piece of the value for performing this service—say 10 percent to send some money internationally. They capture our data, not just preventing us from using it for our own benefit but often undermining our privacy. They are sometimes unreliable and often slow. They exclude 2 billion people who don't have enough money to justify a bank account. Most problematic, they are capturing the benefits of the digital age asymmetrically—and today.

Don and Alex Tapscott posed the question: what if there were an Internet of Value—a global, distributed, highly secure platform, ledger, or database where value could be stored and exchanged, and we could all trust each other without powerful intermediaries? Collective self-interest, hard-coded into this new native digital medium for value, could ensure the safety, security, and reliability of commerce online.

In supply chain management, blockchain enabled end-to-end visibility, ensures transparency and traceability of goods. It also disrupted the healthcare sector, facilitating secure and interoperable sharing of patient records. Governments have begun exploring blockchain for voting systems, land registries, and identity verification.

As blockchain matured, different variations emerged to cater to specific needs. Private blockchains, permissioned by selected participants, gained popularity among and between enterprises seeking to harness the benefits of blockchain while maintaining control. Consortium blockchains formed collaborations between multiple organizations, pooling resources for shared infrastructures. The early trend to use private, permissioned blockchains paralleled the creation of "intranets" 30 years earlier. Enterprises, concerned that the Internet was not secure, robust, safe, and reliable, built their own proprietary intranets. Over time as the public Internet infrastructure became more capable, these were abandoned, and companies adopted the public infrastructure. A similar process is happening today.

As blockchain adoption grew in size and complexity, the need for interoperability and scalability became apparent. Solutions like Cosmos, Polkadot, and ICON emerged to bridge different blockchain networks, enabling seamless communication and data transfer between them. Layer 2 solutions, such as Lightning Network for Bitcoin and state channels for Ethereum, alleviated scalability concerns by conducting transactions off-chain.

Blockchain technology has also faced challenges related to energy consumption and scalability. Innovators began exploring alternative consensus mechanisms, moving away from the energy-intensive proof-of-work (PoW) used by Bitcoin. By 2020, proof-of-stake (PoS), delegated proof-of-stake (DPoS), and other more energy-efficient algorithms were gaining traction and reducing somewhat the carbon footprint of blockchain networks.

How will this powerful technology evolve and reshape the future? In this chapter, I examine how blockchain is not only changing how we collect, manage, and record information but also surfacing powerful new opportunities for organizational transformation. Starting with the automotive sector, I look at how blockchain is enabling a complex supply chain traceability solution for the critical minerals required for lithium-powered EV batteries. Turning to government and the broader public sector, I examine how blockchain is streamlining public services, creating trusted and secure repositories of data, and introducing new opportunities to leverage complementary technologies such as smart contracts and artificial intelligence. Finally, I document the rise of Web3—a fully decentralized and user-centric model of the Internet that could shift the locus of power from big tech companies to individuals.

What these and other examples suggest is that the opportunities for blockchain-enabled innovation and transformation are limited only by our imagination. When combined with artificial intelligence, the Internet of Things, and other emerging technologies, the applications for trivergence across sectors will be profound, even mind-boggling, in their potential.

How Blockchain Is Powering Transparent Global Supply Chains

If there is a killer app for blockchain, it is arguably providing the information ledger for the far-flung supply chains of modern business ecosystems. In an age of hyper-transparency, brand-conscious companies are turning to blockchain for better visibility into the business practices of distant suppliers. Whether eliminating conflict stones from the global trade in rough diamonds or tracking the offshore manufacturing processes used to assemble iPhones and luxury apparel items, enterprises need secure infrastructures for supply chain traceability.

Along with complimentary Internet of Things technologies like sensors and RFID, blockchain is helping answer these concerns by providing immutable ledgers for tracking goods across extended supply chains, ensuring that what occurs at each point in the chain can be chronologically recorded on a distributed ledger. Companies can use the immutable record encoded on a blockchain, in turn, to reassure consumers, regulators, and other stakeholders that their end products have been ethically sourced.

Consider the automotive sector, where UK-based company Circulor has developed a suite of blockchain-enabled tools to help its customers address the environmental and human rights challenges surrounding the production, use, and disposal of EV batteries. While EVs are often positioned as an environmentally responsible transportation option, there are also serious environmental costs associated with the production and disposal of EV batteries. The mineral extraction process is energy and water intensive and produces toxic by-products that can contaminate groundwater and local waterways.[1] Batteries are also costly and extremely difficult to recycle, often resulting in the disposal of spent but still toxic batteries in local landfills.[2] The estimated rate of battery recycling is 5 percent in Europe and North America and less in other jurisdictions. Industry analysts predict that the volume of spent lithium-ion batteries will hit two million metric tons per year by 2030.[3]

To compound matters, most of the world's known reserves of cobalt—a critical component in the lithium-ion batteries that power electric vehicles—are contained in the copper belt in the Democratic Republic of the Congo (DRC) and Zambia. In 2022, the DRC alone accounted for 70 percent of global production, which makes the cobalt supply chain especially precarious.[4] The DRC is among the poorest, most corrupt, and most coercive countries on Earth. In 2020, it ranked 151st out of 162 countries in the Cato Institute's Human Freedom Index, 161st out of 180 countries in the Transparency International's Corruption Perceptions Index, and 175th out of 189 countries on the UN's 2020 Human Development Index with a GDP per capita ($796).[5]

According to the DRC's own estimates, 20 percent of the cobalt production comes from artisanal miners—independent workers who work alongside larger industrial mining operations but dig holes and extract ore with picks and shovels. Amnesty International estimates that there are approximately 110,000 to 150,000 artisanal miners in the DRC, and UNICEF alleges that up to 40,000 of those are children.[6] Children involved in the cobalt trade work up to 12 hours a day, can be as young as seven years old, and can receive as little as two dollars a day for their efforts.[7]

Many industry heavyweights, including Panasonic, Tesla, BMW, and Honda, are working on new batteries that will alter the cathode chemistry to lessen the reliance on cobalt. However, there is no clear timeline for delivering next-generation batteries, and most observers are skeptical that cobalt can be eliminated completely without causing performance issues.[8]

The bottom line is that neither cobalt-free batteries nor alternative sources of cobalt supply outside the DRC will provide a realistic short-term solution to the industry's woes. Major electronics and car manufacturers have vowed, in the meantime, not to tolerate child labor and other abuses in their supply chains. Apple, Samsung, Sony, and several brand-name companies have joined the Responsible Cobalt Initiative, which was established in 2016 under the China Chamber of Commerce of Metals, Minerals, and Chemicals Importers and Exporters to establish a code of conduct for an ethical cobalt supply chain.[9] However, the need to operationalize these commitments quickly to source cobalt ethically has presented major OEMs in the electronics and EV market with a daunting challenge.

The cobalt supply chain is complex, with many stakeholders and production stages involved in transforming raw ore into end products. While extracted in places like the DRC, cobalt undergoes a complex metamorphosis through multiple processing steps in different countries before it is installed as batteries inside cars, mobile phones, and other electronics. Here is where Circulor's blockchain-enabled solution shines because it enables lithium suppliers like Vulcan Energy and brand-name OEMs such as BMW, Polestar, and Volvo to follow raw materials through the EV battery production process, creating an immutable audit trail with a nearly real-time view of the supply chain. Indeed, Circulor has invented a series of techniques to resolve complex challenges in tracing cobalt, from digitizing raw cobalt at the point of extraction, tracking its movement, and automating the compliance and contractual paperwork in each hand-off.

Tracking a raw material through a supply chain boils down to solving two core problems: reliably digitizing the commodity at the source and connecting the input materials to the output product at any step in the supply chain. While blockchain technology is part of the solution, blockchain alone is not enough. As Johnson-Poensgen explains, "A blockchain will record an immutable record of custody of a material, the locations it's traveled through, its composition over time, and all that, but if you're trying to make sure the wrong material never enters the system in the first place, you need processes to make this work." Accordingly, Circulor's approach to supply chain traceability combines technology with rigorous protocols, third-party audits, and on-the-ground due diligence.

The technology component of Circulor's solution is built on the distributed, permissioned ledger written on Hyperledger Fabric and hosted on the Oracle Blockchain Platform. The Circulor platform also provides the infrastructure for scanning and tracking the EV battery components at each location and stage of the process, from the mines and aggregation sites through to the cobalt refineries and cathode manufacturing plants. While blockchain technology serves as the secure ledger for recording data, Circulor uses other technologies to flesh out the solution. For example, the company developed mobile scanning applications to enable midstream refiners, recyclers, and cathode manufacturers to track the flow of materials through their operations. "Many of the midstream supply chain participants in China don't have scan-in scan-out technologies or sophisticated quality management systems," said Johnson-Poensgen. "Almost everything still gets done on paper."

The processes that complement this technology platform are vital to ensuring that Circulor is tracking only cobalt from legitimate and well-managed mining concessions through its platform. To begin with, Circulor allows only accredited mining sites to access the platform. To be accredited, these sites must have perimeter fencing, security details, and measures that prevent pregnant women and children from working in their mines. Most also have safety protocols in place that limit the depth of the pits that miners can work in, with working conditions that more closely resemble EU standards. To vet the mining sites, Circulor partnered with Kumi Consulting, a specialist in responsible sourcing and the sole auditor for EU conflict minerals regulations. In other words, Kumi performs the litmus test on whether a mining location is operating responsibly and whether the cobalt from these sites has been extracted ethically.

Vetting participants is the first step in establishing an ethical cobalt supply chain. The second step is digitizing the cobalt at source, which effectively initiates the chain of custody in Circulor's system. The digitization process starts at the aggregation sites where cobalt from vetted industrial mines is placed in secure bags, tagged with a QR code, and recorded on Circulor's blockchain. Extra precautions, including use of a facial recognition app to tighten security, are taken to ensure that the on-site person inputting data into the system is a trusted source.

"We focus on reliably capturing four things: who's bringing the material; who's recording the data to our system for the first time; where are they; and, finally, we assign an identity to a bagged quantity of raw cobalt in order to track it through the supply chain," explains Johnson-Poensgen. The identity tags issued by Circulor's system include attributes about how, where, when, and by whom the materials are going to be used at various stages of the production process. "What that means is that there's no black market for these materials because 'used anywhere else by anyone else' immediately flags the material as an anomaly."[10]

Circulor's ability to instill confidence in these processes with blockchain makes it a valuable partner to brands like BMW and Volvo. "The combination of physical audit plus the integrity of the blockchain-enabled process is what gives us that reliable chain of custody," said Douglas Johnson-Poensgen, the company's founder. "To create absolute certainty for companies like Volvo requires a segregated process all the way through the supply chain, which is enforced by our blockchain solution."[11]

While the founders established the company to address the environmental and human rights challenges surrounding cobalt production, clients are using the platform to track the provenance of a variety of materials, from palm oil to beef.[12] Johnson-Poensgen sees the potential to expand its client group to include companies from the aerospace, consumer electronics, and other mining sectors in the near future. After all, the provenance of the cobalt in EV batteries is just one in a wide range of things that go into manufacturing cars and electronics that could have ethical sourcing implications. In fact, the European Commission recently published a report identifying 18 materials around which they would like to see the industry implement responsible sourcing practices.[13] Beyond cobalt and the EV market, there are sustainability concerns surrounding most natural resources. "Deforestation, industrial farming, flooding, chemical contamination, and dislocation of communities are just some of the issues that both manufacturers and consumers need to be aware of," said Johnson-Poensgen.[14]

Blockchain for Public Good

While commercial enterprises have shown the highest levels of interest and investment in blockchain, government agencies and other public-sector organizations have just as much to gain from deploying with this technology to digitize existing records and manage them within a secure infrastructure. Indeed, the algorithmic techniques used in digital ledger technologies hold the potential to streamline and enhance government processes for registering voters, identifying recipients of healthcare, financial support, and emergency aid; issuing passports and visas; registering patents and trademarks; recording marriage, birth, and death certificates; and maintaining the integrity of government records.

Putting Land Registries on the Blockchain

With the abundance of potential use cases, governments around the world are either adopting or exploring blockchain applications for a variety of purposes. Take something as seemingly straightforward as a government land registry. For most countries, tracking land ownership remains a manual and outdated affair, involving extensive paperwork, hand-signed documents, and reliance on couriers and lawyers. That is if a country is fortunate enough to have a modern land registry. According to the World Bank, 70 percent of the world's population lacks access to modern land titling.[15] Achieving unanimous agreement at every stage of a property transaction and maintaining a permanent, tamper-proof record requires a combination of security, coordination, and trust that many countries lack.

Sweden is one of several countries experimenting with putting land registries on a blockchain. Since June 2016, the Swedish land registry authority (called the Lantmäteriet) has been testing a way to use blockchain to record property transactions. According to the consultancy Kairos Future, which is involved in the project, eliminating paperwork, reducing fraud, and speeding up transactions with a blockchain-based system could save the Swedish taxpayer more than €100 million ($106 million) a year.[16]

Whereas the first phase of the pilot demonstrated the technology's potential, a second pilot phase initiated in 2017 also involved the phone company Telia and two Swedish banks. This latest phase involved the creation of a pilot blockchain registry and a series of smart contract templates that automate transactions. Each property registered on the blockchain is uniquely coded and linked to a smart key held only by the owner. When ownership changes hands, the blockchain verifies and records each step of the transaction. And instead of signing a bill of sale at a lawyer's office, the pilot project demonstrated how digital signatures from the buyers and sellers could be verified automatically.

While Sweden's land registry is out in front, arguably, the most significant benefits of blockchain-based systems are likely to be enjoyed by counties where ownership of land holdings is less certain and fraud is more common. Although blockchain will not remove the issue of incorrect data and the requirement for trusted inputs, countries with limited, centralized land recording will see blockchain registries as effective in making property ownership more transparent, reliable, and secure. For example, the World Bank estimates that a digital land registry could be the most cost-efficient and fastest way to increase GDP in the medium term. The bank's analysis suggests efficient land registries serve as a foundation for better investments in land, enable the development of a mortgage market and a credit market in general, and become an institution for trust in one of the most fundamental parts of an economy: land and real estate.[17]

Estonia's Blockchain Revolution

Registering land titles is ultimately just one in a long list of services provided by the government. In nearby Estonia, nearly all government functions—legislation, voting, education, justice, healthcare, banking, taxes, policing, and so on—have been digitally enabled across one platform, thanks to blockchain and an array of complementary technologies.

Among the hallmarks of the so-called e-Estonia revolution is the blockchain-enabled Estonia ID card, a cryptographically secure digital identity card that unifies access to a mind-boggling array of services. Citizens can order prescriptions, vote, bank online, review school records, apply for state benefits, access medical and emergency services, file their taxes, submit planning applications, upload their will, apply to serve in the armed forces, travel within the European Union without a passport, and fulfill around 3,000 other functions with their Estonia ID. Business owners can use the ID card to apply for licenses, issue shareholder documents, file annual reports, and so on. Government officials can use the ID card to submit information requests to law enforcement agencies, encrypt documents, and review and approve permits, contracts, and applications.[18]

The day-to-day efficiencies for citizens are considerable. Estonia's "once only" data policy dictates that no single piece of information about its citizens should be entered twice. Instead of filling out a detailed loan application, applicants have their data—income, debt, savings—pulled from elsewhere in the system. There are no forms to complete in the physicians' waiting rooms because medical administrators, with permission, can access their patient's medical histories. When a child is born in the hospital, their parents are automatically registered for family benefits. Citizens requiring long-term medication get a digital prescription slip on their medical record, which reduces queues at doctors' offices and hospitals.

Advances such as these have led to exceptional rates of digital public services adoption, making Estonia an e-government leader in the European Union. In 2020, around 97 percent of the adult population in Estonia used the Internet to send filled forms to the public authorities, which is well above the EU average (63 percent).[19] While citizens evidently like the convenience of online services, the savings for government are also significant. Digitizing processes reportedly saves the state 2 percent of its GDP a year in salaries and expenses.[20]

Blockchain-enabled ledgers provide the underlying data management and security technology for much of Estonia's digital public services. The Estonian ID card, for example, records every piece of data with proof of time, identity, and authenticity—providing a verifiable guarantee that records have not been altered. The Estonian government said the keyless signature infrastructure (KSI) that blockchain requires ensures the authenticity of the electronic data stored on its citizens. No one—not hackers, system administrators, or even the government—can manipulate and get away with the data.[21]

Leveraging the blockchain infrastructure means distributing data storage, thus reducing the chance of major breaches of centralized databases. Instead, the government's data platform, X-Road, links individual servers through end-to-end encrypted pathways. The information resides locally: hospitals, educational institutions, banks, and government agencies maintain their own data sets. When a user requests a datum, the system delivers it like a boat through a canal—via locks.[22]

A strict system of permissions and privacy safeguards allows citizens to control who sees or may not see their data. Teachers, for example, can enter student grades but cannot access a student's entire academic history. A file accessible to one medical specialist need not be accessible to other doctors if a patient deems it unnecessary. Few people can say exactly who has looked at their medical records. But Estonians can log into their records and see what medical professionals have viewed and acted on. Citizens could challenge, and justice departments could prosecute any government official who accessed a citizen's data without permission or a legally valid reason.

Estonia's advances are so well regarded that other governments as disparate as Finland and Panama are importing elements of its innovative blockchain-enabled models for government services.[23] Meanwhile, across the Atlantic, examples of blockchain-enabled innovation are popping up in federal agencies and several US states. For example, the US General Services Administration now uses blockchain to automate the most time and labor-intensive aspects of the public procurement process. The agency expects that automation will reduce the amount of human interaction required to review new proposal documents while improving the user experience for offerors and vendors and speeding up the process of awarding contracts and onboarding the companies selected to deliver services.[24] In another recent example, the State of Delaware introduced legislation to allow companies to use distributed ledgers and smart contracts to replace a largely paper-based system for administering stock issuances and transfers. State officials believe the blockchain ledger has enormous advantages both for government and for the companies that are registered in Delaware, including error avoidance, cost savings, and the increased speed and efficiency of administrative functions.[25]

These and other examples suggest that blockchain can be deployed to record, enable, and secure huge numbers and varieties of public-sector transactions, incorporating rules, smart contracts, and digital signatures among many new and emerging technologies. However, there are equally powerful and intriguing examples of blockchain fueling innovation in the broader public and not-for-profit sectors.

Solving Global Challenges

In the humanitarian relief sector, the World Food Program (WFP) is rolling out blockchain technology to provide refugees with improved choices in how they access and spend their cash assistance.[26] The ability to distribute funds has traditionally depended on both relief agencies and refugee populations having access to local financial institutions. In many emergencies, however, the local financial infrastructure is often insufficient or unreliable, and refugees frequently face restrictions in opening bank accounts. To rectify the problem, the WFP built a blockchain solution for authenticating and registering transactions between the WFP and its beneficiaries without requiring a financial intermediary.[27]

After running a successful proof of concept in Pakistan, the WFP made some refinements and is now using its "Building Blocks" platform to deliver more effective food assistance to 106,000 Syrian refugees in Jordan. According to the WFP, more than 100,000 people living in the Jordanian camps are using an iris scanner to purchase groceries at local markets.[28] The Building Blocks app stores the cash value provided to beneficiaries in a beneficiary "account" maintained on the blockchain and compensates retailers with fiat currency using a financial service provider. The WFP says the Building Blocks platform is making cash transfers more secure, efficient, and transparent.

In the global efforts to combat climate change, the Blockchain for Climate Foundation, an international NGO, is putting the Paris Agreement on a blockchain. The organization claims that blockchain technologies are uniquely positioned to enable global collaboration on reducing greenhouse gas emissions.[29] Specifically, the group operates a distributed ledger for national climate accounting that records international transfers in emissions reductions, enables transparency and creates clear accountability on who is doing what for the climate. The global climate ledger, in turn, paves the way for proactive investment into climate projects, technologies, and policies by creating a financial pathway for incentivizing emissions reductions and increased ambition.

The Rise of Web3

Blockchain's most significant and lasting legacy could be a fundamental transformation of the Internet itself. To understand the scope and potential impact of this transformation, it is helpful to break the evolution of the Internet into three eras.

The first Internet era, from 1990 to 2004, is widely referred to as Web 1.0. During this period, websites primarily presented static content and enabled minimal user interaction. Web 1.0 was also commonly known as the read-only web since individuals rarely contributed content.

The advent of social media platforms marked the beginning of the Web 2.0 era in 2004. Unlike its predecessor, Web 2.0 introduced a read-write dynamic. In addition to delivering content, companies like Facebook offered platforms for users to generate and share their own content. As global Internet usage exploded, a small number of dominant companies commanded a disproportionate amount of traffic and value creation on the Internet. Web 2.0 also introduced the advertising-driven revenue model, wherein users could create content but lacked ownership and the ability to monetize it.

Web3 refers to a possible third generation of the Internet, which aims to create a decentralized and user-centric online ecosystem by leveraging blockchain technology. Unlike Web 1.0 (early websites with static content) and Web 2.0 (interactive websites and social media platforms), Web3 is envisioned as a more open, secure, and permissionless Internet built on a decentralized infrastructure. Some describe Web3 as the read-write-own era of the Internet because a key goal is to give users greater ownership and control over their digital assets.

In essence, Web3 is an embodiment of a libertarian-inspired philosophy whose progenitors want to break what they describe as a "corporate stranglehold on the Web" and replace it with an open, decentralized alternative that hands individuals control over their digital identities and data. This philosophy is articulated in the opening pages of a seminal whitepaper authored by the Web3 Foundation:

> *Every day we interact with technologies controlled by a hand-ful of large companies whose interests and incentives often conflict with our own. If we want the benefits of using their proprietary apps, we're forced to agree to terms that most of us will never read, granting these companies complete control over the data we generate through each interaction with their tools. . . .[With] open-source and decentralized technologies like blockchain, we can build systems that prioritize individual sovereignty over centralized control. With these new systems, there's no need to trust any third parties not to be evil.[30]*

The concept of Web3 is best described in Alex Tapscott's new book *WEB3: Charting The Internet's Next Economic and Cultural Frontier* (Harper Collins, September 2023). Web3 (The Read/Write/Own Web) is a decentralized platform where value—including assets like critical information, money, securities, contracts, deeds, intellectual property, and art and music—can be moved, stored, and transacted peer to peer.

By enacting this philosophy, Web3 advocates propose to change the Internet in several significant ways. This will not be easy, the companies that own our data, and their resulting trillion-dollar valuations will not go quietly into the night.

Decentralization

First and foremost, Web3 proponents seek to decentralize power and control by eliminating intermediaries and central authorities. Think financial services without banks or music creation and distribution without record labels. Indeed, Web3 has given rise to a vast ecosystem of decentralized applications, or dApps. These applications are built on open-source protocols, allowing developers to create innovative services without relying on proprietary platforms and ecosystems controlled by Apple, Google, and others.

Unlike traditional apps that operate within walled gardens, dApps can interact with each other and share data, fostering collaboration and interoperability. One of the most prominent families of Web3 applications includes the emerging platforms for decentralized finance (DeFi).

These platforms ideally leverage blockchain and smart contracts to provide financial services such as lending, borrowing, decentralized exchanges, and yield farming without the overhead of traditional financial institutions.

Blockchain technology could play a crucial role in achieving decentralization, as it allows for distributed consensus and the creation of trustless systems. Immutable, auditable, and cryptographically secure transaction records on a blockchain enable users to verify the integrity of data and ensure the transparency of processes, leading to increased trust in online interactions without the need for a centralized authority. To advocates, the resulting disintermediation not only eliminates the middlemen but also streamlines processes, strips out some traditional intermediary fees, and enables direct peer-to-peer interactions.

User Control and Ownership

A second objective of Web3 is to grant users greater control over their data, digital identity, and digital assets. At the core of this transformation lies the innovative concept of self-sovereign identity (a concept I explore fully in Chapter 6). Web3 enables users to have complete control over their digital identities, eliminating the need for intermediaries to verify and authenticate their online presence. By leveraging decentralized identity solutions, the goal is to enable individuals to manage their personal data and selectively share it with third parties, giving them the power to dictate how their information is utilized.

Of course, there are some trade-offs. Retaining full ownership and custody of one's personal information means reducing reliance on popular platforms whose business models are based on collecting and monetizing our data. Traditional social media platforms such as Facebook, Instagram, and TikTok store user data on centralized servers, making it available for aggressive harvesting and misuse. TikTok, in particular, has been criticized for rapacious data collection methods that include the ability to collect user contact lists, access calendars, scan hard drives including external ones, and geolocate devices on an hourly basis.[31]

In the vision for Web3, data is distributed across a network of computers, making it nearly impossible for any single entity to control or manipulate it without consent. This distributed nature of data storage not only enhances security but also ensures that users retain full ownership and control over their information. Alphabet, Amazon, Apple, Facebook, and Microsoft have earned trillions in combined revenues from tracking and monetizing user data. Shifting to a user-centric paradigm where individuals decide how they want to collect and store their data—and if and when they want to sell it—would truly revolutionize the Internet landscape. Whether or not people are willing to pay to protect their privacy from these trillion-dollar corporations is, as yet, an unanswered question.

But are Internet users becoming more discerning about when and how they relinquish control over their personal data? There is some evidence to suggest this is the case. In a recent Pew Research Center survey, more than 80 percent of Americans reported feeling as though they have very little or no control over the data companies collect about them, and 79 percent are very or somewhat concerned about how companies use this data.[32] Meanwhile, a 2023 survey by *Forbes* found that more than 90 percent of respondents are taking increased measures to secure their personal data.[33] Apparently this is more than just talk. When Elon Musk took over Twitter, hundreds of thousands of users fled to Mastodon, a decentralized, open-source social network that prioritizes user privacy and data ownership.[34]

Censorship Resistance

The same decentralized protocols that enhance user control also make Web3 applications resistant to censorship and control by governments. Distributed cloud storage solutions like Filecoin, Storj, and Sia allow users to store their data securely and privately across a decentralized network of computers, thus eliminating reliance on centralized storage providers. For example, Filecoin uses complex algorithms to split up and encrypt digital assets and store them on many different computers around the world. Filecoin keeps a record of how the data fits together and recombines it only when legitimate access to the data is requested.

With decentralized solutions like Filecoin there is no central cloud service provider that can be coerced into disclosing or deleting files or withholding service. For example, human rights organizations may want to host videos documenting abuses, or investigative journalists and whistleblowers may want to store data related to their investigations, such as the data gathered by the International Consortium of Investigative Journalists on the more than 785,000 offshore entities that are part of the Paradise Papers, the Panama Papers, the Offshore Leaks and the Bahamas Leaks investigations.[35]

Concerns that blue-chip cloud providers can be strong-armed into withholding services are genuine. In December 2010, Amazon Web Services discontinued providing its cloud computing services to WikiLeaks, in the aftermath of the organization's publication of hundreds of thousands of classified diplomatic communications leaked from the US government. More recently, Apple yanked anti-censorship tools off its app store in China, and Amazon's cloud computing affiliate told its Chinese customers to cease using any software that would circumvent the country's extensive system of Internet firewalls.[36]

Of course, the ability to evade state censorship, takedown requests, or other coercive measures could make Filecoin an attractive option for less altruistic actors, including distributors of child pornography and other illicit content. The fear that clients could use the network to store illegal content could deter potential users from leasing their excess storage space. Filecoin has taken some measures to address this concern by incentivizing the storage of useful data by clients that have been verified by Filecoin notaries.

A key motivation for Filecoin and the Web3 community more broadly is developing systems that promote less centralized and more anonymized ways to collect, distribute, and trade information and data. However, Filecoin sees distributed data storage as its opening act—the foundation on which to enable decentralized models for exchanging data and information across borders and through time. Filecoin is already building new tools to enable digital marketplaces and provide a vital storage foundation for critically important digital public goods, such as open-access scientific data, creative commons media, and more.

One such example is the Genome Aggregation Database (gnomAD), a growing aggregation of exome and genome sequencing data from a variety of large-scale sequencing projects.[37] Led by a global coalition of scientific investigators, the project is aggregating and harmonizing this data to make it available for the wider scientific community. Filecoin says an agreement is in place to store a copy of what the coalition calls the "v3 short variant data set," which spans 71,702 genomes from unrelated individuals sequenced as part of various disease-specific and population genetic studies. In time, the Filecoin community could unleash a lasting revolution in the way humanity collects, stores, processes, distributes, and protects the data that individuals, organizations, and societies create. Armed with sufficient data, the insights that AI may generate on what and how our genome defines us may be earth-shattering. Dogs live about 12 years, and people about 80. Some species live 200 years or even longer.[38] Can AI with sufficient data find the fountain of youth?

Interoperability

A fourth ambition of Web3 is to promote the use of open protocols and standards that facilitate interoperability between different platforms and applications. This interoperability allows for seamless data exchange and collaboration across the decentralized Web.

To understand the significance of interoperability to the emerging Web3 ecosystem, try to imagine email with SMTP, POP, or IMAP. Now envision the Internet without TCP/IP. It's an impossible ask because the connectivity between email clients, websites, and apps that billions enjoy today is possible only because of these now ubiquitous communication protocols. In other words, absent the communication protocols, each email client, website, app, or database would be an independent island and rendered much less useful by the lack of interconnectivity.

Until recently, this siloed reality was precisely the state of affairs with distributed blockchains. For example, the Ethereum network and Bitcoin network didn't communicate with each other, and neither did the dozens of other prominent crypto blockchain networks in existence today. What exists as value on one network was not visible on—or transferable to—other blockchains, making it difficult to transact without centralized exchanges such as FTX, Binance, Coinbase, and Kraken as intermediaries to transfer funds. Of course, lack of regulation and sloppy engineering in the crypto industry has resulted in staggering losses for some investors and tarnished the reputation of both crypto and their intermediaries, with FTX now bankrupt and Binance,[39] Coinbase,[40] and Kraken[41] in hot water with the SEC for playing fast and loose with the rules.

In these early days of enterprise usage, companies embraced blockchains as a backend ledger through, for example, Hyperledger Fabric. The immutability of this ledger provides significant power, as it eliminates the need for extensive audits and enhances trust, particularly among different institutions. Swift and other financial messaging services have logs and controls that both authorize and authenticate messages. but nothing as powerful as blockchains could provide.

Given the wild swings in crypto prices, few corporations have embraced it as a means of exchange. Further, few companies want to bet on a blockchain solution that won't interoperate with its supply chain partners, its customers, or regulators using crypto for official transactions. The latter concern has led to the creation of networks like Cosmos and Polkadot, both of which are designed to act as connectors that allow blockchain networks to transfer value between crypto tokens.

The Web3 Foundation describes its Polkadot network as a layer zero technology—a fabric or set of protocols that enable data and tokens to pass between independent blockchains. Beyond protocols, Polkadot is also a blockchain development platform that provides the core modules, including shared security and an easy-to-use launchpad, for blockchain developers to build on. Plug-and-play modules like a consensus engine, networking, and security are available to make blockchain development more accessible, allowing developers to focus on their specific area of expertise and save substantial time and effort in the development process. Several teams are already building impactful solutions for Polkadot. The range of projects includes applications for cloud storage, digital identities, finance, gaming, social networking, and supply chain management. These projects are collectively valued at tens of billions of dollars, proving the market demand for interoperable blockchains is real.

New Economic Models

Finally, Web3 aspires to enable novel economic models through the use of cryptocurrencies, tokenization, and decentralized autonomous organizations (DAOs). Each of these developments is important in its own right. But let's take DAOs, for starters.

DAOs are member-owned organizations without a centralized leadership; that is, there is no boss or CEO to make decisions. Instead, DAOs provide a vehicle for dispersed individuals and organizations to collaborate and commit funds to a shared endeavor. Typically, DAOs need rules encoded in the blockchain to govern the organization's operations, a funding source like tokens to reward activities that further the group's interest, and a governance structure, including voting rights, for establishing or amending the organization's ruleset.

In theory, tokenization enables individuals to have a stake and participate in the value created within these networks, fostering a more inclusive and financially equitable Internet. However, voting rights are usually proportional to one's holdings in the native token. Proportional voting might sound democratic and egalitarian, but in practice, it means that raw financial power generally prevails. A June 2022 analysis of the inner workings of 10 major DAO projects by Chainalysis found, on average, less than 1 percent of all holders have 90 percent of the voting power.[42] And, although there may not be a central point of authority or control in theory, in fact there is typically a central point of profitability. Buyers beware.

One of the first known DAOs functioned like a decentralized venture-capital fund, enabling users to invest in new projects using cryptocurrency. Participants could pitch their projects and potentially secure funding upon approval through member voting. The platform gained significant traction, amassing the equivalent of almost $150 million to invest in promising startups. Then things went pear-shaped. Merely two months after its inception, an opportunistic hacker exploited a vulnerability in the platform's code, resulting in the theft of approximately 3.6 million ether, or around $70 million at the time. Blockchains are immutable, and for many, this is an appealing characteristic. It can be a fatal liability as well as a strength. If a hack or inevitable bug writes erroneous data into an immutable ledger, it is there for good. Ironically those blockchains with the most ambitious development plans concurrently face the greatest challenge of not creating an exploitable bug that may be fatal to that ecosystem.

Despite this setback and the inherent risks of a fatal bug, DAOs continue to proliferate, especially in the decentralized finance space. Like the ill-fated VC example, there are countless DAOs that in theory serve as investment vehicles, allowing participants to pool their resources and collectively make investment decisions. One of the biggest and most notable investment organizations is BitDAO, which recently merged with Mantle to create a combined treasury worth $2.5 billion.[43]

There are examples of public-spirited, social-impact DAOs as well. For example, VitaDAO is using a DAO framework to support life-changing healthcare innovation focused on researching, financing, and commercializing longevity therapeutics.[44] In another example, ClimateDAO provides a platform for crowdsourced investor activism. In essence, the DAO is seeking to pool funds from contributors and use the proceeds to purchase shares in publicly traded companies with a view to enacting climate-friendly change through shareholder proposals and proxy voting.[45] In the philanthropic arena, impactMarket has created one of the world's biggest blockchain-driven Unconditional Basic Income (UBI) programs.[46]

NFTs for Christmas

One of the most controversial manifestations of the new economic models unleashed by Web3 was the nonfungible token (NFT). Think of them as a unique digital certificate of ownership, which can be used to establish the authenticity and provenance of a digital asset. This allows creators and collectors to verify the originality and rarity of their digital items, providing a sense of scarcity and uniqueness. As with other scarce assets, frenzied digital marketplaces have emerged to enable users to buy, sell, and trade NFTs for an array of digital assets. On OpenSea, Rarible, and SuperRare, users can auction off NFTs for artwork, collectibles, and virtual real estate—often for mind-boggling sums.

In practice, NFTs are the root of a terrific idea, assigning ownership (and someday income) to things such as music or art. These generally underpaid creators deserve a far greater share of the income than they currently receive. Unfortunately, NFTs are not recognized in law. They are simply a unique pointer to a particular asset; they are *not* the asset. For example, the "owner" of a CryptoKitty does not have exclusive rights to it but is entitled to a "worldwide, nonexclusive, nontransferable, royalty-free license to use, copy, and display" the underlying CryptoKitty art for limited purposes.[47]

But is an exclusive pointer to an image worth anything? In 2021, NFTs were the trendiest of Christmas gifts, supplanting Rolexes and Lambos.[48] Clearly, it's the perfect gift for someone who has everything! Interest in NFTs exploded so much that "NFT" won as Collins Dictionary's "word of the year" in 2021.[49] Twitter founder Jack Dorsey famously turned a digital image of his first tweet into an NFT and sold it for a stunning $2.9 million.[50] Meanwhile, some crypto whales have paid unworldly amounts for these pointers, presumably as marketing expenses. Vignesh Sundaresan parted ways with $69 million for a blockchain pointer to Beeple's digital creation entitled "Everydays: The First 5,000 Days."[51] While anyone can get a full digital copy of Beeple's artwork, Sundaresan describes the purchased pointer as akin to "having an autograph from your favorite artist."[52] Jumping on the bandwagon, the

New York Times created an exclusive pointer to an article entitled "Buy this Column on the Blockchain" and sold it for more than $500,000.[53] Even big corporations are getting in on the NFT market. In August 2021, Visa paid $150,000 for a nonexclusive blockchain pointer to a low-resolution pixelated image of a woman with a mohawk haircut, claiming it wanted to "signal its support" for the burgeoning market.[54]

Not surprisingly a pointer (in bits) from a blockchain (of bits) that few can find that asserts no legal rights has proven to be worthless.[55]

The Future of Blockchains

Setting aside Web3's excesses, the truly decentralized model envisioned by its pioneers holds the potential to create a more inclusive, secure, and equitable Internet where users have more agency, privacy, and control over their digital lives. Naturally, Web3 also has its share of detractors and skeptics. For example, reporters Edward Ongweso Jr. and Jacob Silverman argue that Web3 is nothing more than a giant speculative economy that fuels crypto investment schemes that will further concentrate wealth.[56] Meanwhile, Grady Booch, chief scientist for software engineering at IBM Research, has described blockchain as a software architecture disaster in the making. He cites the inefficiency and incredibly high costs of running "trustless" blockchain systems, which have proven capable of processing only a few transactions per minute—a trivial throughput compared to centralized systems like Amazon Web Services.[57] I examine these and other limitations fully in Chapter 8.

As we look to the future, blockchains will continue to evolve. New frontiers, such as DeFi, NFTs, and DAOs, want to redefine the technical landscape. The most advanced applications are combining blockchain with other emerging technologies like artificial intelligence, the Internet of Things (IoT), and quantum computing (a rapidly emerging technology that harnesses the laws of quantum mechanics to solve problems too complex for classical computers) to open up exciting new possibilities. In this ever-evolving journey, blockchain technologies hold the potential to revolutionize the way we think about trust, security, and transparency. As today's technical limitations are addressed and new use cases emerge, the impact of blockchain may well reshape industries, economies, and society, unlocking unprecedented potential for innovation, collaboration, and decentralized power.

Notes

1. Amit Katwala, "The spiralling environmental cost of our lithium battery addiction," WIRED, 5 September 2018. www.wired.co.uk/article/lithium-batteries-environment-impact

2. Nadia Krieger, "Will Your Electric Car Save the World or Wreck It?" Engineering.com, August 17, 2018. www.engineering.com/ElectronicsDesign/ElectronicsDesignArticles/ArticleID/17435/Will-Your-Electric-Car-Save-the-World-or-Wreck-It.aspx

3. Mitch Jacoby, "It's time to get serious about recycling lithium-ion batteries," Chemical & Engineering News, Volume 97, Issue 28, 14 July 2019. https://cen.acs.org/materials/energy-storage/time-serious-recycling-lithium/97/i28

4. https://pubs.usgs.gov/periodicals/mcs2022/mcs2022-cobalt.pdf

5. "The Human Freedom Index 2020." www.cato.org/human-freedom-index/2022; Transparency International, "Corruption Perception Index 2020" www.transparency.org/cpi2020; UNDP, "Human development index and its components," UNDP Human Development Reports, 2020. http://hdr.undp.org/en/composite/HDI

6. Amnesty International, " 'This is what we die for': Human rights abuses in the Democratic Republic of the Congo power the global trade in cobalt," *Amnesty International Ltd.,* 2016. www.amnesty.org/download/Documents/AFR6231832016ENGLISH.PDF

7. C. Walther, "In DR Congo, UNICEF supports efforts to help child labourers return to school," UNICEF, June 13, 2012. www.unicef.org/childsurvival/drcongo_62627.html

8. E. Airhart, "Alternatives to cobalt, the blood diamonds of batteries," *Wired,* June 7, 2018. www.wired.com/story/alternatives-to-cobalt-the-blood-diamond-of-batteries

9. Z. Yangfan, "Facing challenges, sharing responsibility, joining hands and achieving win-win," *Responsible Cobalt Initiative,* November 14, 2016. www.cccmc.org.cn/docs/2016-11/20161121141502674021.pdf

10. Douglas Johnson-Poensgen, Interviewed via telephone by Anthony Williams, 21 June 2019.

11. Douglas Johnson-Poensgen, Interviewed via telephone by Anthony Williams, 21 June 2019.

12. Anthony Williams, "Blockchain and the Future of Battery Supply Chains," Blockchain Research Institute, December 11, 2019.

13. Drive Sustainability, The Responsible Minerals Initiative and The Dragonfly Initiative, "Material Change: A study of risks and opportunities for collective action in the materials supply chains of the automotive and electronic industries," *The Dragonfly Initiative*, July 2018. https://drivesustainability.org/wp-content/uploads/2018/07/Material-Change_VF.pdf

14. Douglas Johnson-Poensgen, Interviewed via telephone by Anthony Williams, 21 June 2019.

15. Caroline Heider and April Connelly, "Why land registration matters for development," World Bank Group, 28 Jun. 2016. https://ieg.worldbankgroup.org/blog/why-land-administration-matters-development

16. "The Land Registry in the Blockchain," Kairos Future, March 2017. https://chromaway.com/papers/Blockchain_Landregistry_Report_2017.pdf

17. Caroline Heider and April Connelly, "Why land registration matters for development," World Bank Group, 28 Jun. 2016. https://ieg.worldbankgroup.org/blog/why-land-administration-matters-development

18. https://e-estonia.com/solutions/e-identity/id-card

19. https://e-estonia.com/estonia-a-european-and-global-leader-in-the-digitalisation-of-public-services

20. https://apolitical.co/solution-articles/en/e-id-in-america

21. https://e-estonia.com/solutions/cyber-security/ksi-blockchain

22. https://e-estonia.com/solutions/interoperability-services/x-road

23. https://qz.com/1535549/living-on-the-blockchain-is-a-game-changer-for-estonian-citizens

24. Remarks from Jose Arrieta, the director of the General Services Administration's Schedule 70 (IT products and services) operation delivered at the ACT IAC Blockchain Forum, January 31, 2018. www.actiac.org/2018-blockchain-forum-0

25. John Williams, "Stock ledgers revolutionized with Delaware corporate blockchain legislation," *Delaware Business Times*, 28 Jun. 2017. www.delawarebusinesstimes.com/stock-ledgers-revolutionized-delaware-corporate-blockchain-legislation

26. "Building Blocks: Blockhain for Zero Hunger," World Food Programme, November 13, 2019. https://innovation.wfp.org/project/building-blocks

27. "Blockchain 'Crypto' Assistance at WFP," World Food Programme, January 25, 2017. https://innovation.wfp.org/blog/blockchain-crypto-assistance-wfp

28. "Building Blocks: Blockhain for Zero Hunger," World Food Programme, November 13, 2019. https://innovation.wfp.org/project/building-blocks
29. Joseph Pallant and Matt Lockyer, "Putting the Paris Agreement on the Blockchain," Noteworthy—the Journal Blog, July 10, 2018 https://blog.usejournal.com/putting-the-paris-agreement-on-the-blockchain-57eda4c481af
30. https://polkadot.network/Polkadot-lightpaper.pdf
31. www.theguardian.com/technology/2022/jul/19/tiktok-has-been-accused-of-aggressive-data-harvesting-is-your-information-at-risk
32. www.pewresearch.org/internet/2019/11/15/americans-and-privacy-concerned-confused-and-feeling-lack-of-control-over-their-personal-information/pi_2019-11-14_privacy_0-02
33. www.forbes.com/advisor/business/fear-internet-surveillance
34. https://techcrunch.com/2022/11/03/decentralized-social-network-mastodon-grows-to-655k-users-in-wake-of-elon-musks-twitter-takeover
35. International Consortium of Investigative Journalists, "ICIJ Offshore Leaks Database," ICIJ.org. https://offshoreleaks.icij.org
36. Paul Mozur, "Joining Apple, Amazon's China Cloud Service Bows to Censors," *New York Times*, August 1, 2017. www.nytimes.com/2017/08/01/business/amazon-china-internet-censors-apple.html
37. Genome Aggregation Database, https://gnomad.broadinstitute.org
38. www.bloomberg.com/opinion/articles/2023-05-12/how-long-can-humans-live-rockfish-could-help-us-age-healthily
39. www.sec.gov/news/press-release/2023-101
40. www.sec.gov/news/press-release/2023-102
41. www.sec.gov/news/press-release/2023-25
42. https://forkast.news/why-dao-voting-is-problematic
43. https://cryptoslate.com/bildao-mantle-merger-creates-2-5b-dao-led-web3-ecosystem
44. www.vitadao.com
45. https://climatedao.mirror.xyz/crowdfunds/0xAa66700E2425Da3A29E179F50a9bA6B460E28664
46. www.impactmarket.com
47. www.cryptokitties.co/terms-of-use
48. www.bloomberg.com/news/articles/2021-12-08/nfts-are-the-big-holiday-gift-of-2021-and-they-aren-t-just-for-crypto-lovers
49. www.collinsdictionary.com/woty

50. www.cnbc.com/2021/03/22/jack-dorsey-sells-his-first-tweet-ever-as-an-nft-for-over-2point9-million.html

51. www.business-standard.com/article/international/vignesh-sundaresan-paid-69-3-mn-for-an-nft-so-you-can-download-it-for-free-121120100150_1.html

52. https://news.artnet.com/market/updated-most-expensive-nfts-1980942

53. www.nytimes.com/2021/03/25/business/nyt-column-nft.html

54. https://news.bloomberglaw.com/mergers-and-acquisitions/visa-buys-nft-of-digital-avatar-with-mohawk-for-150-000

55. www.unilad.com/technology/news/almost-all-nfts-are-now-literally-worthless-now-806993-20230921

56. https://thedigradio.com/newsletter11

57. www.infoworld.com/article/3689914/the-philosopher-a-conversation-with-grady-booch.html

5 Walking on a Cloud

In a seminal piece of popular science, *The Cosmic Connection*, Carl Sagan postulated that one could measure the progress of any civilization by the scale of information it can access.[1] In other words, a civilization's ability to solve critical challenges, such as reversing environmental degradation or eradicating disease, correlates with its capacity to harness useful knowledge. The capacity to put knowledge to work for the greater good, in turn, depends on the systems and structures that society advances for capturing, distributing, and exploiting the information it creates.

For the last two decades of the Internet age, we have witnessed an epic accumulation of digitized knowledge. For example, websites, online databases, digital libraries, and educational platforms have made an incredible amount of information available to anyone with an Internet connection. From academic research papers and scientific studies to historical archives and cultural artifacts, a wealth of knowledge is now just a few clicks away.

One of the most significant contributors to the accumulation of digitized knowledge is the growth of user-generated content. Platforms such as Wikipedia, online forums, and social media have allowed individuals from all walks of life to contribute their knowledge and experiences. This crowdsourcing of information has expanded the breadth and depth of available knowledge, offering diverse perspectives and insights.

The digitization of books, journals, and other printed materials has also played a crucial role in the accumulation of knowledge. Projects like Google Books and digital libraries have made countless books accessible online, enabling researchers, students, and the general public to access information that was previously limited to physical copies in specific locations.

Of course, there are rival paradigms for managing the world's growing constellation of digitized knowledge. For example, there are open-source advocates who argue that society would be better off placing most of its stock of knowledge in the commons. In this camp, we see Wikipedia, open educational resources, the open-science and open-source software communities, and a legion of other open data projects. On the other hand, there are those who see data and knowledge as proprietary assets that should be closely guarded and exploited for profit. This camp includes the world's large copyright holders and new digital conglomerates like Google and Facebook, which have built global business empires around their proprietary control over data.

Irrespective of which camp you sit in, everyone engaged in the creation and distribution of digital content today fundamentally depends on revolutionary new tools and computing architectures for storing and accessing data and other digitized assets. For example, advances in search engines and data analytics have improved our ability to navigate and extract valuable information from the vast sea of digitized knowledge. Google became ubiquitous because it offers an indispensable tool for discovering information efficiently, allowing users to find relevant content quickly.

In addition to search, one of the most critical developments is what we have come to call the era of *cloud computing*—an era where localized storage of digital assets has been superseded by global data center operators that provide scalable, cost-effective, and flexible solutions for managing the ever-expanding constellation of digital information, on demand.

In the "pre-cloud" era, data was stored in organizational data centers, and the independently maintained infrastructure was a significant cost center. While a dedicated data center gives companies and other organizations full control over not only their data but the hardware itself, doing so entails costly investments in equipment and an in-house IT team to manage it. Independent data centers have finite capacity, and the responsibility and cost for purchasing, installing, and maintaining more equipment to expand the workload of the data center falls on the owner. Planning for adequate redundancy in the event of a system failure, cyber-attack, or natural disaster further inflates the costs of running a network of independently managed data center operations.

In the "cloud-computing" era, the infrastructure for storing and processing data is owned and operated by infrastructure-as-a-service companies like Amazon, Google, Microsoft, IBM, and Oracle. Rather than build and operate their own data centers, organizations with storage and computational needs pay consumption fees for access to computing resources, such as processing power, storage, and massive bandwidth.

Advances in software, processing power, and automation have dramatically increased the capacity to collect, transport, store, and manipulate massive amounts of data in the cloud. Modern cloud computing offers numerous advantages, including lower costs with a pay-per-use model, the elasticity to instantly scale resources to meet demand, and the efficiency benefits of shifting the responsibility for network upgrades, security, and other operational costs to the service provider. In addition to storage, most cloud providers also offer the on-demand computing capacity required for compute-intensive workloads like genomics, crypto mining, risk management, and big data analysis.

Cloud computing has fundamentally changed how enterprises of all sizes manage their IT infrastructure. Large enterprises have leveraged the cloud to streamline their internal IT infrastructures, implement more agile and collaborative work arrangements, and focus more of their resources on the strategic drivers of their business. The biggest beneficiaries of the cloud computing revolution, however, are likely start-ups and small enterprises.

Unlike the previous generations, today's entrepreneurs can rent, off the shelf, practically any function they need to run a company. With storage, computing services, video chat, and other digital utilities on tap, business infrastructures that used to be expensive and complicated are increasingly cheap and easy to use. Users of Amazon's Cloud pay as little as a few cents an hour to harness its nearly unlimited computing and data storage capacity, allowing anyone to leverage the size and reach of the world's greatest e-commerce engine—from the computer geek testing a new algorithm from their dorm room to a Mumbai-based start-up that wants to roll out a new online service.

In this chapter, I argue that cloud computing is not just integral to the Internet; it's part of the fabric of how business is done today, period. The cloud has transformed the way organizations operate, enabling them to streamline processes, enhance productivity, and leverage more advanced technologies for less cost. With cloud-based services, employees can access business applications, data, and resources from anywhere, using any device with an Internet connection. Additionally, cloud storage also offers a scalable and cost-effective solution for storing ever-increasing volumes of information, allowing organizations to leverage analytics, gain insights, and make data-driven decisions.

The cloud is also integral to the Trivergence. Cloud platforms enable organizations to experiment, develop, and deploy new applications and services faster, using cutting-edge capabilities like AI, the IoT, and blockchain. At the same time, one could argue that data- and computationally intensive applications like AI, the IoT, and blockchain would not even exist without access to cloud infrastructures. If you have a trillion IoT devices monitoring vibrations every second, only the cloud is big enough to do so. Before the cloud, it was impossible to find the kind of computer resources necessary to create thinking machines. Even Microsoft in 2020 did not have the computing complex necessary to build Open AI's ChatGPT. Hundreds of millions of dollars of investment later, they now do.

Today, there are only a few companies that possess the massive computer power required to create general AI models. While ownership of the underlying infrastructure for AI may rest with a few, the cloud will lower the barriers to entry to utilizing these advanced capabilities. For example, I will show how eliminating the need for significant upfront investments in infrastructure enables startups, small businesses, and individuals to leverage advanced technologies without substantial financial resources. Democratizing access to AI, blockchain, and the IoT, in turn, will empower a broader range of individuals and organizations to leverage these technologies to foster innovation and drive societal and economic impact.

The Cloud Was Inevitable

Before the cloud, the discipline (based on queuing theory) to determine how much hardware to buy was called *capacity planning*. You needed sufficient capacity to enable a great response time for the peak hour of the peak day of the year. A retailer not being able to meet the demand on Black Friday (in the United States) or on Boxing Day (in the United Kingdom, Canada, Australia, and elsewhere) was clearly unacceptable. The result was that the computer data center was built to handle peak loads, while on an average hour of an average day, most of the capacity sat idle.

In the old arduous paradigm of managing your own data center, CIOs worked with others in their company, typically the CFO and those in profit centers, to estimate the near-term technology-enabled opportunities and resulting transaction volumes. They would then build the business case to pay for the new systems that the capacity plan demanded. In the annual budget process, they would include the costs of purchasing the required software, hardware, and human resources required to build and manage those systems. Once these items were acquired, they would depreciate the costs over a fixed period, hoping that the original business case of expected cost-benefits initially envisioned materialized in the post-implementation review.

Today, those kinds of capacity estimations are nearly impossible. Something as simple as a tweet, or an Instagram post from a social influencer, may increase the demand on your systems by an order of magnitude. If you were clairvoyant and built the capacity in-house for that massive bump, then you have also spent a massive amount of money on hardware capacity that would be vastly underutilized most of the time. Any purchased system that does not run near-peak capacity most of the time to a CFO is wasting capital. But for in-house computing, though, there was simply no other choice.

The introduction of cloud computing has fundamentally changed this equation and subsequently transformed the way organizations operate, enabling them to streamline processes, enhance productivity, and leverage advanced technologies. The benefits for modern businesses are numerous.

- **Scalability and flexibility:** Cloud computing offers businesses the ability to near-instantly scale their resources up or down based on their needs. This scalability ensures that organizations can efficiently accommodate fluctuations in demand, whether it's scaling up during peak periods or scaling down during slower times. The flexibility of cloud services allows businesses to adapt quickly to changing market conditions and operational requirements. For example, an investment bank in the United States typically sees peak demand around 10:30 a.m. and 3:30 p.m. on weekdays, while retailers expect peak demand on Saturdays and in the early evenings.
- **Cost efficiency:** Cloud computing provides cost advantages by eliminating the need for upfront investments in hardware,

infrastructure, and maintenance. Instead, businesses can opt for a pay-as-you-go model, paying only for the resources they consume. This cost-effective approach reduces capital expenditures, enables better budget management, and allows organizations of all sizes to access sophisticated computing capabilities without significant financial barriers.

- **Accessibility and collaboration:** Cloud-based services enable anytime, anywhere access to critical business applications, data, and resources. This promotes remote work, enhances collaboration between teams and individuals in different locations, and facilitates real-time communication and data sharing. Employees can collaborate on documents, projects, and workflows seamlessly, increasing productivity and efficiency.

- **Data security and disaster recovery:** Cloud providers invest heavily in robust security measures to protect data and ensure compliance with industry regulations. Cloud platforms often offer advanced security features, including encryption, access controls, authentication mechanisms, and regular backups. Additionally, cloud-based disaster recovery solutions help businesses safeguard their critical data and applications, ensuring business continuity in the event of unforeseen disruptions. In the old paradigm, having one system engineer part-time who applied patches to your software risked missing a critical one that could result in your company paying millions to a hacker who has encrypted your databases. Cloud vendors deploy hundreds (or perhaps thousands) of engineers to work on security patches, which means the risks of a costly security mishap are much lower.

- **Innovation and agility:** Cloud computing enables organizations to embrace emerging technologies and innovation more rapidly. Cloud platforms provide access to a wide range of services and tools, such as machine learning, artificial intelligence, big data analytics, and IoT capabilities. This empowers businesses to experiment, develop, and deploy new applications and services faster, driving innovation and staying competitive in the market.

- **Scalable storage and data management:** With the exponential growth of digital data, cloud storage offers a scalable and cost-effective solution for businesses to store and manage the growing deluge of critical business information. Cloud storage services provide high reliability, redundancy, and easy accessibility to data, allowing organizations to leverage business intelligence solutions to make data-driven decisions.

- **Integration and interoperability:** Cloud computing offers seamless integration capabilities, allowing businesses to connect different systems, applications, and services. APIs and integration tools enable data synchronization, workflow automation, and interoperability between cloud-based and on-premises systems. This integration facilitates efficient data exchange, enhances operational efficiency, and supports the adoption of hybrid or multicloud environments.

Clearly, there are other benefits as well. Indeed, one of the least recognized benefits of the cloud is the ability to smooth out gross demand profiles and reduce costs in the process. As an example, to save on the tens of millions of dollars necessary to acquire the excess capacity to meet Black Friday credit card processing demand, a major New York bank created a one-day system that authorized every valid credit card request, simply logging the requests in real time into a (much faster) blocked flat file. The transactions that were received were validated and applied to the actual credit card systems at night a day or two later, flattening the peak demand by spreading it across a few days.

Yes, there were credit card losses from authorizing purchases wildly in excess of the card's limits, as well as fake cards. But the bank's statisticians had correctly modeled that the credit losses would be far less than the purchase of the hardware necessary to validate, in real time, this once-a-year demand. They were right: this gamble saved tens of millions of dollars as was anticipated.

But in the age of the ubiquitous Internet, the capacity demands on your retail system, say after a mention on the national news or in a post by a social influencer, are simply impossible to plan or predict, let alone contain. That's where the Borg (now called Kubernetes) can orchestrate this demand across thousands of processors. But there is a catch: to do so, the application needs to be appropriately architected.

To handle possibly explosive peak demand in traditional models, the costs were daunting. If your real-time peak-to-average ratio was, say, 5 to 1, that would mean, on average, your CPU was running at 20 percent or less most of the time. For a real-time system to give a great response time, it, by necessity, had to have short queues on all the resources consistently. Almost every industry has significant economies of scale. But for computer demand, the scales are balanced very differently. For the computer industry, by blending those peaks into a flatter overall demand profile, the economies are much greater than can be achieved in other industries. The cloud is here to stay.

Back in the late 1960s, when the IBM 360 dominated the marketplace, its high-end mainframes were water-cooled. At the time, its management seemed quite content with the current state of the art, the lack of competition, and, of course, the resulting massive profits. Gene Amdahl, the chief architect of the IBM 360, was not comfortable resting on his previous accomplishments. He quit IBM and launched a company to compete with his former employee. He argued and ultimately proved that much faster air-cooled computers could be engineered and built for much less. He recognized that IBM's lack of competition had lulled IBM management into complacency and, as such, became reticent to invest in what he thought was then appropriate for the next generation of technology. One of the then-awesome features of his initial Amdahl V5 and V7 computers was that they could instantly run it much faster, for a per-hour charge, to address those peak loads.

Nearly half a century later, IBM on the z/OS operating system has enabled a similar feature where you can do a nondisruptive upgrade and pay Variable Workload License Charges (VWLC) for IBM (mainframe) z Systems servers running z/OS or z/TPF in z/Architecture (64- bit) mode.[2] This tried-and-true approach can be used to address, say, a weekend sale. But it does have limits. If one company has a peak demand at 10 a.m. and another at 12:30 p.m. and another (in the far east) at 3 a.m. New Jersey time, then before the cloud, each company had to acquire sufficient hardware to service those peaks. But as you can see from Figure 5.1, the peaks of one company's demand will fit into the troughs of another in such a way as to flatten the gross demand profile.

The more companies and industries spanning the most time zones you can get to use a common hardware plant, the lower the gross resulting peaks, the more level the overall demand, the less time the hardware is idle, and the lower the resulting cost.

The cloud, as such, was inevitable. Capacity planners knew 50 years ago that you can supply compute resources far more cost-effectively the larger the base and time zone diversity of companies using them. This is because the larger base results in a flatter demand curve, enabling higher overall utilization and lower overall costs far beyond the simple but significant economies of scale. But back then, network speeds were too slow to make that happen. They no longer are.

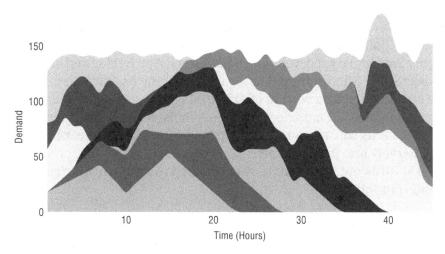

Figure 5.1 The demand peaks of many businesses, when totaled, result in a much flatter and more predictable gross demand profile.

To flatten these demand curves while giving terrific remote response times, the big three plus Facebook are in a competition to lay and buy cable for subsea dominance.[3] There are more than 750,000 miles of submarine cable laid to date.[4,5] It is somewhat ironic that the telecom companies (CenturyLink, Terremark [Verizon], and AT&T) were once the premier providers of cloud services, and a few short years later, the cloud providers are competing with them by laying bandwidth for their own telecom services. The world is quickly changing.

The Cloud's Big Three

The first vendor to build a cloud offering was Linode in 2003. Today, it still offers relatively simple but competitive solutions. There are dozens of vendors in this arena. The first to build a cloud offering at a massive scale was Amazon, which, in 2006, offered disk space and processing power accessible over the Web. Specifically, it offered storage via Simple Storage Service (S3) and cloud CPU processing via Elastic Compute Cloud. These two products were the genesis of Amazon Web Services. Although I am sure that Amazon did the math and fully understood the strategic potential of scale, it chose to downplay it as Amazon simply selling its excess capacity.

As it turns out, the three major players entered the cloud marketplace in three distinct ways. For Amazon, it was originally about renting access to excess infrastructure (hardware). For Google and Microsoft, it was initially about access to their limited but, for certain purposes, highly productive net development platforms (App Engine and ASP.net, respectively). Microsoft soon followed by moving its office products to the cloud with a beta version of Office 365 in the same year it entered the cloud space.[6] In more recent years, Microsoft has been aggressively moving all its software products (such as Office 365, SharePoint, and SQL Server) into its data centers as services.

As it turns out, these are now considered the three main classes of cloud computing:

- **Infrastructure as a service (IaaS):** Think virtualized hardware. The user sees what appears to be real processors, hard disks, and a network. That it is but a sliver of a more massive real infrastructure is not apparent. Think Amazon Web Services.
- **Platform as a service (PaaS):** Think of highly productive development or execution environments such as Microsoft Azure and Google Cloud Platform. These platforms offer an environment for developers to build, deploy, and manage their own applications without having to worry about the underlying infrastructure, such as servers, storage, or networking.
- **Software as a service (SaaS):** Think of end-user apps, be they Office 365, Salesforce, or Dropbox. Today, all three vendors have dozens, if not hundreds, of offerings in all three classes running on their platforms. If you count services, solutions, and components, AWS alone has more than 1,000 elements. Though its pricing models are wildly different (and thus difficult to directly compare), the core offerings have a great deal of overlap.

Microsoft announced Azure as an offering in February 2010. Its first offering was for rendering Active Server Pages on the Internet that could post and gather information by hosting your apps on Microsoft's Internet Information Services (IIS) front end. This would be classified as a PaaS offering. It also included a background "worker" role that, for instance, might process the data gathered as a stand-alone background application.[7] For storage, it offered Blob object storage, a database service branded as SQL Azure (similar to Microsoft SQL Server), and Azure Service Bus, the message middleware product similar to Biztalk that acted as a message broker for business-to-business communication and enabled business process automation within and between firms.[8] If you were comfortable with Microsoft's proprietary and closed software stack and limited volumes, their initial cloud offering was a useful option.

In October of the same year, Microsoft announced Office 365[9] as a key step in its move from a product company to a service company, a massive undertaking. In effect, Microsoft's cloud offering included upgrading and upending its historically purchased products to an on-demand rental software as a service company. Today, a key strategic focus for Microsoft is to convert its massive existing software installation base, be it in your data centers or on your PCs, or Microsoft Office, SharePoint, or Outlook to its Azure cloud. As of 2022, the conversion is nearly complete.[10]

Google's entry to the cloud was comparatively slow. In 2008, the company launched Google App Engine as a full-stack, integrated, scalable web application platform (PaaS). By comparison, Amazon services were much richer, with a multitude of offerings. With Amazon, if you wanted storage, you could just rent storage (IaaS), and if you needed a lot of compute power and little storage, that was fine too. With the original Google App Engine, it was bundled as a highly productive environment that Google built internally to develop and run custom web applications. The apps initially were limited, had to be written in Python, had to use Google's Bigtable non-SQL key database, and had to leverage its proprietary (and extremely powerful for massive amounts of data) Google File System (GFS) data store.

So, Amazon started by offering spare hardware (IaaS), and Google's first offering was a PaaS. In 2010, Microsoft started to offer all three—first PaaS, quickly followed by SaaS (Office) and (to be competitive for large RFPs) IaaS. For initial platform offerings, the choices were between software that was proprietary and limited. In the race for more business, this has quickly and dramatically changed.

When developing your cloud strategy, there will be many drivers. What and how they empower your approach will be discussed later in this book, but for now, let's just say the focus should not be on who has the most check marks on a very long list of cloud capabilities. A more relevant question would be, "Is there a platform or service available on only one cloud provider that may differentiate you from your competitors?" Otherwise, you should plan your future commodity architecture to be as cloud independent as possible. With open systems and open standards, that is becoming ever easier to do.

Cloud Growth Is Explosive

In January 2021, Microsoft stated that its cloud offerings' revenue was up 50 percent to about $15 billion,[11] citing the pandemic as one reason for growth. By 2023, it had grown to over $50 billion.[12] By comparison, AWS in December 2020 announced that it had surpassed $40 billion in annual revenue, adding $10 billion in revenue in the previous 12 months.[13] By 2023, AWS's revenue for a quarter was over $20 billion.[14] Google Cloud revenue reached $8 billion in Q2 2023, up 28% YoY.[15] In a nutshell, in the race for the greatest monetary growth, AWS is in the lead, followed by Azure and then GCP. In the race for percent growth, it is Azure, then GCP, and finally AWS. IBM came in second in cloud revenue, reporting $24.4 billion over the previous 12 months,[16] up 22 percent. What is slightly confusing here is that it appears that IBM (quite rightly) is reporting Red Hat revenue earned from Linux on AWS, Azure, and GCP. Further confusing the issue is that Microsoft counts consulting and hybrid services as cloud offerings.

To keep it in perspective, Facebook—the company that so many love to hate and that seems embroiled in a controversy every week—made nearly $86 billion in revenue in 2020.[17] Each day, 2.6 billion people use either Facebook, Instagram, or WhatsApp. And yes, Facebook does run its own data centers and fiber-optic networks.

The technology in the cloud has matured so much that lower costs are a definite plus. However, the real benefit is that the on-demand offerings from the big cloud providers can decrease your response times while increasing your technical productivity and your security. Better security alone is all the business case some companies need. In addition, the cloud services can unchain your CIO and your CFO from many of your expensive legacy software "maintenance" contracts, as well as from depreciation, hardware failures, and constant security patching. With the cloud's pay-as-you-go pricing, instead of buying, owning, and maintaining physical data centers and servers, you can access technology services—such as high-performance computing software, storage, databases, and even quantum computing— on an as-needed basis. Initially, IT organizations embraced it as a safe place to get the massive compute and storage necessary to test a major release, knowing full well they could release the processing power, storage, and associated costs as soon as the successful results of the test were implemented into their in-house, production environments. If these service offerings failed, there was little risk; it was just a test. But the cloud has gone far above and beyond that initial "testing the waters" use case.

The use cases expanded reasonably quickly as cloud services entered the mainstream. Pay-as-you-go was an obvious place for disaster recovery. This is not to trivialize the complexities of a true disaster recovery plan or to say that in a disaster, you can then take your backups and give Amazon (or Microsoft or Google) a call. However, the geographic diversity of these providers, with up-front planning, coordination, and testing, can radically increase the viability of your plans, expand the range of disasters you have mitigated, and concurrently and dramatically reduce the costs. For example, for some massive organizations (the big five Canadian banks), finding sufficient and timely resources in the case of a loss of a data center was not realistic. As such, their focus was on preventing disasters (through heavily guarded, lights-out data centers in unmarked, hardened bunkers originally in rural areas). But that era has come to an end. All three providers now have sufficient capacity, if properly contracted, planned, and tested, to absorb even the largest of internal corporate IT data center disasters in a timely manner.

But the real business case can be found in the potential new facilities that can be accessed, the productivity software managed and tuned for you in the cloud, and the resulting new applications that can be readily built on the plethora of new services instantly available. Access to high-performance computing—along with the latest in middleware, artificial intelligence, and database software—is all there and on-demand without having to negotiate a multitude of complex contracts.

The final argument for in-house computing was that for the best response time, a local computer could clearly outperform anything off-site that suffered the latency and bandwidth limitations of today's telecommunications networks. That point is now moot since you can put the hardware for the major cloud offerings onsite.[18]

The Cloud, the Future of Computing, and the Trivergence

The cloud has expanded and is now the technological first love for those who want to set up a facility without having to negotiate and purchase software licenses or hardware for those who need a geographically dispersed content delivery network to download their apps and data responsively worldwide. The cloud is also the first port of call for those who want to test their mobile app on the plethora of mobile phones with different display characteristics and for those who believe that their puzzle, beyond the limits of silicon, can be expressed in qubits and solved by a quantum computer. Technology that was once far beyond the reach of many is now available on demand for almost anyone at reasonable prices. The corporate data center is now optional.

The 21st century has brought rapid and radical transformations to many technologies, work processes, and people. Many of the inevitable trends of this decade (such as the gig economy, Zoom, and working from home) have been accelerated by the COVID-19 pandemic. People now widely recognize that commute time spent on driving (or even flying) by knowledge workers to meet in costly vertical silos is a bygone waste. A Zoom call circumventing the unnecessary queues on freeways, in elevators, and in waiting rooms to see your doctor, lawyer, or accountant is far more productive if at first unfamiliar and uncomfortable. Where does Zoom run? On the cloud.[19]

Whether the pandemic has increased your use of Zoom[20] or (worst case through unemployment) your use of Netflix,[21] these cloud services are now central to the digital economy. Some argue that the pandemic will result in the decline of the coastal superstar cities, as commuting to work is recognized as far less important than we recently thought. Will the Fourth Industrial Revolution reverse some of the accomplishments of the Second Industrial Revolution? That does seem possible. Then again, some have predicted the demise of big cities as far back as 1946.[22]

Although it needs to be taken with a large lump of salt, McKinsey says the value derived from the cloud services—that is, the hardware and software components underpinning the cloud, as well as the professional and managed services opportunities around cloud offerings—will surpass $1.0 trillion in 2024.[23] On the other hand, the estimate could be plausible given the cloud provides the essential infra-structure for the three killer apps of Trivergence: artificial intelligence, blockchain, and the Internet of Things.

Here's how cloud computing enables and enhances these technologies:

- For artificial intelligence, cloud computing provides the necessary infrastructure and resources to run computationally intensive applications, including machine learning platforms, natural language processing APIs, and AI model training frameworks. Some AI algorithms require massive computational power and storage capacity to process and analyze large datasets. Cloud plat-forms offer high-performance computing capabilities, distrib-uted processing, and scalable storage, enabling AI developers and researchers to access the resources they need without the need for extensive on-premises infrastructure. In addition to providing specialized services for training ML models, cloud providers will increasingly offer pre-built AI functionalities and APIs that enable organizations to harness advanced AI and ML capabilities on demand, such as automated model training, natural language processing, computer vision, and deep learning frameworks.
- Cloud computing complements and supports blockchain tech-nology in several ways. While blockchain is inherently decentral-ized and distributed, the cloud provides an efficient infrastructure for hosting blockchain networks, especially in scenarios where scalability and performance are critical. Cloud-based platforms can provide secure and reliable environments for blockchain nodes, smart contract execution, and data storage. Cloud com-puting also simplifies the deployment and management of blockchain networks, reducing the complexity and operational overhead associated with running on-premises infrastructure.
- For the Internet of Things, cloud computing is mission-critical for large and expanding IoT ecosystems. The massive amounts of data generated by IoT devices require robust storage, processing, and analytics capabilities. Cloud platforms offer scalable and secure storage for IoT data, enabling real-time and historical data analysis. They provide the computing resources necessary to run IoT applications, manage device connectivity, and support IoT-specific protocols. Cloud-based IoT platforms and services offer

features such as device management, data ingestion, analytics, and integration with other enterprise systems, making it easier for businesses to leverage IoT technologies effectively.

Across all three domains, cloud computing facilitates the integration and analysis of data from AI, blockchain, and IoT applications. Absent the infrastructure, tools, and services the cloud provides, it would be expensive and impractical to aggregate, process, and analyze data at a scale these applications demand. Moreover, the scalability and elasticity of cloud computing are particularly beneficial for managing the fluctuating workloads associated with AI, blockchain, and IoT applications. Computational power, storage capacity, and network resources can be scaled up or down based on workload requirements, providing the flexibility to enable AI models, blockchain networks, and IoT deployments to handle varying data volumes, user demands, and computational complexities.

Over time, cloud computing has the potential to democratize access to advanced technologies like AI, blockchain, and IoT. As already mentioned, there is the benefit of being able to access massive storage and computing power without making substantial financial commitments to building out an in-house infrastructure. This accessibility is a huge benefit for startups, small businesses, and individuals seeking to leverage Trivergence technologies.

Additionally, most cloud providers offer on-demand access to a wide range of AI, blockchain, and IoT services, APIs, and toolkits. These services abstract the complexities of developing and deploying advanced technologies, enabling users to leverage prebuilt components and functionalities. These ready-to-use resources can dramatically simplify the development process and reduce the technical expertise required.

When developers run into problems, they can usually turn to online forums, communities, and documentation provided by cloud service providers, where users share best practices, troubleshoot issues, and learn from experts. These resources level the playing field for utilizing advanced technologies by empowering individuals and organizations to improve their skills and access the collective knowledge of the community.

The scalability of cloud platforms also supports rapid prototyping and experimentation. With easy provisioning and flexible resource management, users can quickly set up development and testing environments for new AI, blockchain, and IoT solutions. This agility supports the ability of organizations to iterate, refine, and scale their ideas and projects, thus reducing their time to market.

By providing affordable resources, prebuilt services, global accessibility, and a collaborative ecosystem, cloud computing helps democratize access to advanced technologies such as AI, blockchain, and IoT. It empowers a broader range of individuals and organizations to leverage these technologies, foster innovation, and drive societal and economic impact.

In the end, the cloud is an inevitable consequence of the digital revolution and a vital infrastructure fueling the ongoing cycle of innovation and creative destruction that defines the modern world. The future of cloud computing will revolve around increased flexibility, deeper integration with Trivergence technologies, enhanced security measures, and the ability to cater to diverse workload requirements. The rise of quantum computing will push the boundaries even further by offering immense computational power and enabling organizations to explore new possibilities and address complex problems that were previously out of reach for classical computing systems. As these powerful on-demand infrastructures mature, cloud computing will continue to be a transformative force, enabling organizations to innovate, scale, and leverage advanced technologies like never before.

Notes

1. Sagan, Carl, The Cosmic Connection: An Extraterrestrial Perspective. Garden City, N.Y.: Anchor Press, 1973.
2. www.ibm.com/downloads/cas/KWXX8XGM
3. https://venturebeat.com/2019/04/06/google-and-other-tech-giants-are-quietly-buying-up-the-most-important-part-of-the-internet
4. https://venturebeat.com/2019/04/24/how-google-is-building-its-huge-subsea-cable-infrastructure
5. https://analyticsindiamag.com/whats-google-doing-under-the-sea
6. Linode is doing well by being the low-cost solution compared to AWS and GCP. They're focused on a particular target: developers with an idea.
7. https://docs.microsoft.com/en-us/azure/cloud-services/cloud-services-choose-me

8. www.forbes.com/sites/janakirammsv/2020/02/03/a-look-back-at-ten-years-of-microsoft-azure/?sh=e2af61149292

9. news.microsoft.com/2010/10/19/microsoft-announces-office-365

10. www.microsoft.com/en-us/licensing/product-licensing/windows-server

11. www.thechronicleherald.ca/business/reuters/microsoft-earnings-rise-as-pandemic-boosts-cloud-computing-xbox-sales-545256

12. https://news.microsoft.com/2023/04/25/microsoft-cloud-strength-drives-third-quarter-results-5

13. www.geekwire.com/2020/reaching-40b-revenue-record-time-amazon-web-services-hints-reinvention

14. www.cnbc.com/2023/08/03/aws-q2-earnings-report-2023.html

15. www.bigtechwire.com/2023/07/26/google-cloud-revenue-reached-8-billion-in-q2-2023-up-28-yoy

16. https://newsroom.ibm.com/2020-10-19-IBM-Reports-2020-Third-Quarter-Results#

17. https://suiting-up.medium.com/the-most-hated-companies-in-the-world-159471b56196

18. www.peerspot.com/products/comparisons/aws-outposts_vs_azure-stack

19. https://explore.zoom.us/en/aws/#:~:text=Zoom's%20cloud%2Dbased%20communication%20and,video%2Dfirst%20communications%20at%20scale

20. www.forbes.com/sites/soorajshah/2020/06/17/zoom-will-mostly-run-on-amazon-cloud-for-foreseeable-future-says-aws-ceo-andy-jassy/?sh=5b1024ed4e2b

21. https://aws.amazon.com/solutions/case-studies/netflix

22. https://archive.macleans.ca/article/1946/12/1/the-big-city-is-obsolete

23. www.idc.com/getdoc.jsp?containerId=US46020420

6

Big Data to Infinite Data

Twenty-five years ago, when I worked at North America's largest nuclear power plant, the operators installed thousands of small (and back then very expensive) sensors throughout the complex to measure temperature, pressure, vibration, and other indicators on the miles of large, brightly color-coded pipes and valves within the facility. (Differing colors indicate the content of the pipe—be it hot or cold, liquid or steam, normal water or heavy water, etc.)

A business case was not needed to install these expensive devices. They were installed in the hope that the mountain of data collected from the thousands of sensors could augment the maintenance, safety, and efficiency of Bruce Power's operations. With restart times for a reactor of at best eight hours and at worst days or even weeks (at Chernobyl, trying to shortcut these processes had devastating results) and revenue of millions of dollars an hour, preventing just one shutdown would more than pay for the expensive monitoring equipment. Nowadays, this equipment would be considered part of the Internet of Things (IoT).

It is interesting to note that the computers that run a nuclear reactor's core systems are vacuum tube based for the simple reason that gamma radiation (from a leak) would play havoc on today's microscopic integrated circuits. And contrary to the plot of some great movies, the critical control systems are not connected to the Internet.

With both Three Mile Island and Fukushima, the lack of transparency to outside experts seriously compounded the problems. If all critical operational information were logged on an external blockchain, it is quite possible that rather than obfuscating the outside world with fragments of information, the whole immutable truth may have been understood by external experts, and both accidents may have been prevented.

My experience at Bruce Power is reminiscent of the early days of computing, where data collection was limited to structured information stored in mainframe databases, primarily used for transactional purposes. However, with the rise of the Internet and the proliferation of Internet-connected devices and sensors, the volume, variety, and velocity of data exploded. Unstructured data, such as text, images, videos, and sensor readings, started to play a significant role, leading to the birth of big data.

The term *big data* itself became popular around the early 2000s. It refers to the massive amounts of data that cannot be easily handled or processed using traditional methods. As technology advanced, organizations started to realize the immense potential of leveraging big data for insights, predictions, and process optimization.

Trivergence accelerates the growth of data, well, infinitely. Today, the cost of sensors has plummeted to near-free. As described in Chapter 3, there is a new generation of connected products with embedded sensors that gather, analyze, and monitor almost everything. Sensors are everywhere, from the smart home to your clothes, from your wristwatch to your sprinkler system, from smart buildings to smart agriculture, and from your fridge to your fish finder. More and more, they are collecting data in real time over the Internet (think Tesla). The 5G protocol and ever faster fiber speeds that can download a movie in a few seconds will be able to transfer this information to feed AI engines.

Blockchain adds to the exponential growth of data as data can now be captured in an immutable record. Add in the ability of AIs to generate limitless new data, and becomes clear that the scale of big data is so mind-boggling that the term *big* no longer suffices.

To coin a term, we are now in a world of *infinite data*. To put this new world of infinite data into perspective, consider some key statistics. According to estimates, around 90 percent of the world's data has been generated in the last two years alone.[1] In fact, the amount of data generated annually has increased by an estimated 60x from just 2 zettabytes in 2010 to 120 zettabytes in 2023.

As a result, the size of datasets has reached astronomical levels. As of 2021, Facebook stores more than 300 petabytes (300 million gigabytes) of user data, consisting of billions of photos, videos, and posts. Similarly, Google's search index contains hundreds of exabytes (1 exabyte = 1 billion gigabytes) of data.

Today's infinite data encompasses increasingly diverse data types, including structured, semi-structured, and unstructured data. It includes text documents, social media posts, sensor readings, geospatial data, audio recordings, videos, and more. Besides traditional enterprise data, organizations now harness data from a rich tapestry of sources ranging from open government databases to scientific repositories for biomedical research.

The speed at which data is generated and processed has also increased. Real-time data streams from sources such as social media, financial markets, and IoT devices require rapid processing to extract valuable insights and take timely actions. For instance, Twitter generates around 500 million tweets per day.

To handle these massive datasets, new technologies and frameworks have emerged. Distributed computing frameworks like Hadoop and Apache Spark enable parallel processing across clusters of computers. NoSQL databases, such as MongoDB and Cassandra, allow flexible storage and retrieval of unstructured data. Additionally, machine learning and artificial intelligence techniques have become integral for extracting insights and making predictions from infinite data. The future of big data is poised for further growth and innovation as the Trivergence accelerates. More and more devices will get connected, while the Internet of Things puts connectivity and intelligence into every inanimate object on Earth. The growing size and complexity of AI models will lead to a surge in data collection, annotation, and management. And, where security and immutability are key, blockchain will offer tamper-proof, decentralized data storage with consensus-driven timestamping and proper audit trails.

The flood of data will unleash enormous economic potential. Retailers like Amazon and Walmart already leverage massive investments in the ability to collect, integrate, and analyze data—including information contained in their suppliers' databases—to predict buying patterns, source popular items automatically, adjust prices in real-time, and optimize logistics and shipping. Layering in increasingly sophisticated AI will put analytical functions like these into overdrive. PWC estimates that AI could contribute up to $15.7 trillion in economic value to the global economy by 2030, more than the current output of China and India combined. Of this, PWC predicts increased productivity will contribute $6.6 trillion, while $9.1 trillion is likely to come from stimulating consumer demand by increasing product variety, personalization, attractiveness, and affordability.[2] Over time, this still largely untapped potential to harness AI to extract insights from big data will become a key dimension of business competitiveness, create entirely new kinds of occupations for data scientists, and generate new consumer services and innovations that we can scarcely imagine today.

In this chapter, I pull together a couple of disparate threads to help illuminate some critical implications of a world with near-infinite access to data. To begin, I look at how combining infinite data with cloud computing will power rapid advances in artificial intelligence, taking several capabilities described in Chapter 2 to a whole new level. Next, we turn to the world of science to examine how infinite data is giving rise to breathtaking advances in scientific discovery and leading to entirely new structures of scientific inquiry. Finally, we examine the dark side of infinite data: the precipitous erosion of personal privacy. Drawing on work by Don and Alex Tapscott, I pose a novel solution to this crisis with a concept we call *self-sovereign identity*.

The Explosion of New Data: The Food for AI

To understand why Google, Microsoft, and Facebook are leading the AI revolution one need look no further than their access to staggeringly deep troves of training data. After all, the first step in any deep learning AI effort is to collect and maintain as much data as you can. Access to infinite data provides the foundation for increasingly sophisticated AI models by supplying the necessary volume, diversity, and quality of data for training, feature extraction, and performance improvement. As big data continues to grow, it will fuel the advancement of AI models, enabling them to make more accurate predictions, adapt to new scenarios, and uncover valuable insights across a wide range of industries and applications.

When gathering and analyzing data, some make the mistake of keeping just the data that they see as relevant. For example, in the early days of credit scoring, bankers felt that income was *the* factor that would correlate most strongly with loan repayments. When Fair Isaac, a credit scoring company, applied statistics to the data available, it turned out that the strongest indicator for repayment was whether the bank had the person's home phone number. Income was a far less significant factor. When I explained this to loan officers, they were stunned. They strongly believed that income was the primary indicator of good credit. They were wrong. In other words, typically, people who can't afford Porches don't apply for loans to purchase them. Statistics and AI can readily spot relationships that are meaningful and powerful but not intuitive to us mortals.

But what is the secret to generating these nonintuitive insights? For starters, big data is often diverse and contains a wide range of features or variables that can be used to train AI models. These features may include structured data such as customer demographics, historical transaction records, or sensor readings, as well as unstructured data such as text, images, and audio. By analyzing these features, AI models can extract meaningful patterns and create sophisticated representations of the input data.

Size matters as well. Adding more data and spanning longer timelines leads to better statistical representations and reduces bias. In other words, the scale of the available data is critical to helping models identify hidden insights, correlations, and trends that may not be evident in smaller datasets.

In dynamic environments where data keeps evolving, a continuous learning loop will ensure that AI models keep improving their performance. By feeding models large volumes of new data, AI systems can refine their predictions, adapt to changing patterns, and offer more precise insights in real-world scenarios. These real-time insights are the key to enabling organizations to make data-driven decisions, optimize processes, identify customer preferences, or develop innovative solutions.

Take the personalized recommendation systems that have driven the success of online retailers like Amazon and streaming media providers such as Netflix and Spotify. By analyzing user behavior, preferences, and historical data from a large user base, AI models can provide tailored recommendations, suggestions, and targeted advertisements. The more data available, the better these systems can understand individual preferences and deliver highly relevant content.

The Internet of Things described in Chapter 3 takes the possibilities for real-time insights from big data even further. Given the plummeting cost of sensors, the scope and business case for retrievable information increases dramatically. If you pause to survey the cookie section in your local grocery store, your social media apps will take note and surreptitiously update your profile. Indeed, with the price of an IoT camera approaching a buck and their size now less than a dime, our historical concept of privacy is gone, or at least requires some rethinking.

Data-collecting sensors have also become an integral component of our cars. There are literally thousands of them in the modern automobile.[3] Let's take Tesla, for example. There is an ongoing debate about whether Tesla is a car manufacturer or a data company.[4] From Tesla's sensors, the data collected can be used for far more than car maintenance. Data can determine where the road may be slippery in certain weather conditions, in what neighborhoods children often play, and what insurance rates one should pay depending on driving patterns. Where people drive will also be of interest to advertisers. And if one is using a company car, the where and when (as well as seatbelt use) is likely available to your boss for their perusal. Will police someday be able to remotely connect to the sensors in one's car and find out every time that person sped in the last year? Ideally not, but in practice, the data for such an analysis is already available.

Building the Infrastructure for Infinite Data

Gathering and making sense of these mountains of data is one thing. Feeding these AI engines also requires high transmission speeds, massive storage, and massive computational power suitable for repetitive bursts of data processing over longer periods of time.

Transmission speeds are broadly improving. Advances in fiber and 5G speeds into the gigabits per second have made the real-time movement of IoT data to fully centralized hubs possible. The challenge in 2025 will be how companies will store and analyze the estimated 7 zettabytes (30 zeros) of information generated by more than 75 billion connected IoT devices.[5] The answer is two words: the cloud.

When Microsoft invested $1 billion in OpenAI in 2019, it realized that even its Azure cloud service was not up to the task of providing the horsepower required for OpenAI to build and train its massive neural networks. In fact, it asserted that it was not even sure it could build the supercomputer required to build and train such a massive neural network. Scott Guthrie, the executive vice president of Microsoft, said the investment here was "probably larger" than several hundred million dollars to acquire, configure, and power the tens of thousands of NVIDIA's A100 graphics chips that built and trained ChatGPT.

Nevertheless, having succeeded in such a massive task, it has significantly increased the credibility of Microsoft as a cloud player. Having proven the hardware to build super large neural networks, Microsoft plans to build many more—including a new AI-based version of its search engine Bing. It is now available for Microsoft Edge.[6] Whether Bing can capture more than a sliver of the marketplace has yet to be seen. In 2021, the number-one search term on Bing was to find "Google."[7]

One can build these facilities in-house, but the erratic demand profile of these apps makes renting on the cloud highly cost-effective. IDC, a global market intelligence firm, predicts that by 2025, nearly 50 percent of all accelerated infrastructure for performance-intensive computing (e.g., AI, high-performance computing, and big data analytics) will be on the cloud. I suspect that number will be higher.

Until recently, advances in computational power generally followed Moore's law, which hypothesizes that the number of transistors in an integrated circuit (IC) doubles about every two years. In the early 1950s, one transistor was about the size of a thumbnail. Notable progress was made from the four transistors in the somewhat bulky and heavy portable radio of the 1960s. Over the last 60 years, the advances in chip density have been nothing short of breathtaking.

TSMC (in Taiwan) is now manufacturing 3 nanometer (nm) chips with a density of about 300 million transistors per square millimeter, or roughly 200 billion per square inch. IBM, Intel, and TSMC are now planning for even denser 2 nm chips in 2024. For comparative purposes, a human hair is about 90 nm thick, and a copper atom is about 0.15 nm in diameter.

While rumors of the death of Moore's law have been greatly exaggerated, the years of dramatic increases in speed for two-dimensional flat chips may finally be numbered. To give a second life to Moore's law, three-dimensional chips and the new massively parallel chip designs may be the answer. As far as neural networks are concerned, massive parallelism of processing on simple reduced instruction computer (RISC) chips has made data access, not compute speed, today's bottleneck. Now that storage no longer rotates but is solid state, expect continuous improvements in speed. Data access speed is still the rate-determining step.

Some of the credit for the advances in AI can go to Satoshi Nakamoto and blockchain—not for what blockchain software or cryptocurrency do, but for funding (in the tens if not hundreds of billions of dollars) the design and development of this new massively parallel processing architecture. These graphical processing units were first leveraged for high-end graphics for gaming and not much else. That architecture (with thousands of simple GPUs as opposed to a few complex CPUs) turned out to be ideal for crypto mining, and as a result, with massive demand, it was heavily funded. In another twist of fate, these new very simple processors eventually morphed into the massively parallel processing required to train AI systems today. When Ethereum 2.0 was launched in 2022, the demand for (and the price of) these reduced instruction set-based processors dropped dramatically. Moving from proof-of-work to proof-of-stake (which is much less computationally intensive) has freed up much of the demand for GPUs that can now be redeployed for AI systems.

Where can one find these massive GPU complexes to produce a timely result? The answer is, yet again, in the cloud. Ironically, when the demand for GPUs for blockchain mania fueled the demand for NVIDIA graphics cards, their management forgot to tell their shareholders, resulting in a $5.5 million fine.

"Using GPUs to accelerate AI is dramatically faster and more efficient than CPUs—typically 20x more energy efficient for certain AI workloads, and up to 300x more efficient for the large language models that are essential for generative AI," NVIDIA said in a statement.

To get perspective, let's compare processing throughput. An Intel i9 will crypto mine at about 10 kilohashes per second (10^4), while the application-specific integrated RISC circuit (ASIC) Bitminer Antminer can mine at about 110 terahashes per second (10^{14}). For 10x the price of an i9, we get an increase in throughput of about $10^{14}/10^4 = 10^{10}$, or an increase of about 10 billion. Wow! Forget Moore's law (whose math compounded predicts a thousand-fold [3 zeros] increase every two decades) and think of a multiplication factor with 10 zeros in less than a decade. So, the increases in processing speed expected "in a decade or two" (or more like four or five) have suddenly arrived, thanks first to gaming and then crypto mining. NVIDIA's core business was once graphics (then mining) and has now transformed into powering the AI data centers of the future. Both AMD and Intel have announced plans to focus here to reduce NVIDIA's lead.

High transmission speeds, massive storage, and massive computational power are all essential ingredients for a new era of generative AI. But above all, the world of infinite data will be the engine that feeds rapid advances in general artificial intelligence. As the available data grows, large language models will continue to improve their understanding of human language, including nuances, context, and cultural references. They will become more adept at grasping complex queries, generating coherent responses, and providing accurate information across a wide range of domains such as medicine, law, finance, and scientific research.

Future AI models will also harness infinite data to provide better contextual adaptation. For example, AI models trained on increasingly diverse datasets will be able to understand and generate language that is specific to particular domains, industries, or user preferences. This adaptability will enable more personalized and tailored interactions, making the models more useful and relevant to diverse individual users. Integrating other modalities to understand and generate content that combines images, videos, audio, and sensor readings could also lead to richer and more immersive user experiences. And, when large language models begin to work alongside developments such as computer vision and robotics, we will witness the emergence of the most comprehensive and powerful AI systems yet.

Science's Infinite Data Revolution

The big data revolution arguably hit science before it hit other institutions. Powerful scientific instruments and pervasive computing have driven quantum leaps in the amount of data available to scientists, raising new challenges for researchers who have had to develop new methods, tools, and institutions for managing and exploring massive datasets. Thankfully, their efforts are surfacing valuable lessons for data innovators in other fields, such as public administration, journalism, and healthcare.

The ability to distribute billions and eventually trillions of connected sensors around the planet is having a profound effect on the scientific endeavor. Sparsely distributed and intermittently connected devices gave us an imperfect and often dated picture of reality. Now this old analog understanding of the world is being replaced by something new: a real-time, always-on live stream of our natural and man-made environments.

With the right tools and the right training, scientists can harness this vast cloud of data to derive increasingly granular insights into an array of natural phenomena, from long-term evolutionary trends like climate change to previously inaccessible environments like the depths of the oceans and the far reaches of outer space. At the same time, access to infinite data will revolutionize the practice of science and even alter the basic skill set required to enter the field.

Data granularity is already ushering in some big changes, including a growing reliance on cloud computing. It is also stirring up new controversies as societies wrestle with the social implications of a world with ubiquitous connectivity, where every minute movement or trivial utterance could be detected and recorded for subsequent analysis.

The real challenge for scientists is not collecting the data but analyzing and making sense of it. And not just each individual data stream in isolation but the larger emergent patterns arising out of the cacophony of information we are constantly assembling. "We already have orders of magnitude more data than before," says Euan Adie, who works in the online division of Nature Publishing Group. "It's not like one person can collect the data, analyze it, and then exhaust all the possibilities with it."

Mapping the Universe

The new data-rich reality has already started driving some fundamental changes in scientific practices and even the structure of scientific communities. Take astronomy, where increasingly powerful space telescopes and the data they generate have fundamentally changed the discipline. A couple of decades ago, astronomy was still largely about small and mostly isolated groups of researchers keeping observational data proprietary and publishing individual results. Now, it is organized around large datasets, with data being shared, coded, and made accessible to the whole community. In the process, astronomers went from having dozens and hundreds and thousands of galaxies to handling hundreds of thousands and now millions.

The Sloan Digital Sky Survey (SDSS), for instance, has collected terabytes of astronomical data, helping astronomers map millions of celestial objects and identify transient events like supernovae. Collaborative projects like the Square Kilometre Array (SKA), a radio telescope array, will be the most sensitive telescope in the world once completed.[8] In just one year of activity, it will generate more data than the entire Internet and revolutionize our understanding of the universe. Some have suggested SKA could be capable of detecting airport radar stations of alien civilizations up to 50 light-years away.[9]

These ambitious projects will push the boundaries of computational power and test scientists' ability to sift through and analyze mountains of imagery. The challenges in analyzing large datasets have already prompted scientists to pursue some intriguing experiments. In one instance, a team at Oxford and Yale launched Galaxy Zoo, a clever online citizen science project where anyone interested can peer at the wonders of outer space while simultaneously helping scientists classify the millions of galactic images they have stored in their databases. At first, researcher Kevin Schawinski assumed "that there may be a couple of dozen hardcore amateur astronomers who might possibly be interested in this." Three years later, the Galaxy Zoo community was thriving, with more than 275,000 users who have made nearly 75 million classifications of one million different images—far beyond the project's original goal of classifying 50,000 galaxies. If the scientists behind the project were still laboring on their own, it would have taken them 124 years to classify that many images!

Astronomy is hardly alone in wrestling with the challenges of handling near-infinite data. In the world of theoretical physics, large-scale particle physics experiments generate massive amounts of data. The Large Hadron Collider (LHC) at CERN, for example, produces petabytes of data every second from particle collisions. Big data technologies enable the storage, distribution, and analysis of this data to unravel the fundamental properties of matter, search for new particles, and test theoretical models. The worldwide computing grid used for processing LHC data, known as the Worldwide LHC Computing Grid (WLCG), combines about 1.4 million computer cores and 1.5 exabytes of storage from more than 170 sites in 42 countries. According to CERN, this massively distributed computing infrastructure provides more than 12,000 physicists around the world with near real-time access to LHC data and the power to process it.[10]

The Rise of Big Genomics

Some of the most data-savvy scientists are arguably in the biomedical sciences, where researchers have become accustomed to readily accessible "big genomics" databases and networks at a cost no higher than that of connecting to the Internet. Big data analytics is crucial for processing, analyzing, and interpreting genomic data to understand the complexities of genetic variation, disease mechanisms, and personalized medicine. The 1000 Genomes Project, which aimed to build a comprehensive map of human genetic variation, generated more than 2.5 petabytes (2.5 million gigabytes) of genomic data, requiring sophisticated big data infrastructure and analysis techniques.[11]

Data-intensive science is truly revolutionizing many fields. However, does more data automatically lead to better outcomes and faster rates of scientific discovery? Not always. For example, following the sequencing of the human genome, many believed that a pharmaceutical renaissance was just around the corner. And yet, as Gigi Hirsch, executive director of the Center for Biomedical System Design at Tufts Medical Center has argued, "It is perhaps the most frustrating fact of the industry that despite an enormous increase in R&D investment, and historical advances in technology through genomics, automation and computation, the number of new drugs produced each year remains at the same level that existed over 40 years ago (about 20 per year)."[12]

You can point the finger at the industry's extremely long product development times and the high cost of R&D. Both have arguably led to a very competitive industry culture, with little interest in cooperative ventures and a bias toward fiercely protecting its intellectual property. For decades, these inefficient practices have become deeply ingrained by a highly risk-averse and legalistic corporate culture, often at the expense of opportunities to co-develop early-stage technology tools, establish data standards, share disease target information, or pursue other forms of collaboration that could lift the productivity of the entire industry.

Thankfully, this is beginning to change with an infusion of new thinking about intellectual property throughout the life sciences industry. Scientists Stephen Friend and Eric Schadt at Sage Bionetworks in Seattle have argued that human disease biology is so complex, interconnected, and expensive to research that the existing dominant business strategies of building and patenting unique models need to be replaced by an open source alternative.

"Human disease biology has no common languages, no accessible communal repositories and no government, corporate or foundation investment in generating an inclusive resource," they argue. "Disease biology is characterized by many intelligent academic and commercial researchers in fragmented public and proprietary efforts. As a result, data are often stored as specialized and insulated collections, and even when accessible, there are barriers to integrating it into complex disease models required to guide research or trials in a meaningful way."[13]

Sage Bionetworks' answer is to build a digital commons for biomedical data and predictive disease modeling. At the inception of Sage Bionetworks, Friend and Schadt suggested that the best way to evolve necessarily crude initial models of human disease is to have them nurtured by an open contributor network. Over the years, their network has evolved into a truly collaborative global engine of human disease model building—one that bridges public and private research institutions around the world. Pooling data and talent from across the life sciences community, in turn, has enabled researchers and drug manufacturers to launch a more coordinated and comprehensive attack on the intractable diseases that have so far stymied the industry. For example, in 2020, Sage Bionetworks and the Michael J. Fox Foundation launched a global challenge to develop new methods for converting sensor-based data—including data from smartphones, watches, and fitness trackers—into digital biomarkers that will help medical practitioners predict the progression of Parkinson's disease in individuals.[14]

Preparing for Infinite Data

So, what are some of the lessons for data innovators in other fields? I'd like to highlight four insights that stand out for me.

- The first is to prepare for exponential change. More powerful instruments and sensor networks have led to exponential increases in the amount of data available to scientists. This is not only true of data-intensive disciplines such as biomedicine and astrophysics but also of other fields such as oceanography, where sensor networks are providing researchers with an astonishing wealth of undersea data once accessible only through costly marine expeditions. For example, Ocean Networks Canada (OCN) operates the world's first regional-scale cabled observatory network to provide real-time ocean intelligence to more than 32,000 scientists around the world. Located off the west coast of Vancouver Island, British Columbia, the network extends across the Juan de Fuca plate, gathering live data from a rich constellation of instruments deployed in a broad spectrum of undersea environments. Data is transmitted via mobile and high-speed fiber-optic communications from the seafloor to an innovative data archival system at the University of Victoria. This system provides access to an immense wealth of both live and archived data through the OCN's fully open-source Oceans 3.0 data portal.[15]

- A second insight concerns the growing imperative to invest in data literacy. Basic data literacy is assumed among scientists, but the general population has nowhere near the level of data literacy that will be required in most professions in the near future. Even in science, recent developments have upped the ante. To do path-breaking science, scientists need to be fluent in large-scale data analytics, or need to partner with someone who is. Skills in managing, presenting, and extracting insight from data will be increasingly valuable in other professions, too, including marketing, public policymaking, and journalism, to name a few.

- Intellectual property is another pillar of industrial-era economic policy that we should revisit. Data is a valuable asset. It can be costly to gather and manage. For marketers, politicians, and other professionals, possession of high-quality data can yield lucrative insights and strategic advantages. It's not surprising that many organizations—and indeed many scientists—prefer to keep their data proprietary. And yet, the advantages of pooling data through shared repositories and open standards are compelling as well. Less redundancy. Lower costs. Increasingly comprehensive datasets. And a more diverse and capable network for generating new insights. Even traditionally secretive governments are sensibly concluding the public data created with public dollars should be treated as public assets that anyone can access and use. But data ownership and control issues will certainly become a fault line over which many institutions battle.

- Perhaps the biggest benefit of the big data revolution in science is that the research community increasingly recognizes that no one scientist, team, or organization has the scale to create and curate the deluge of data on its own. Research organizations have little choice but to pool the financial and human resources necessary to undertake these large-scale projects. In the process, social media has become an increasingly important tool for breaking down institutional barriers. Researchers using OCN's Oceans 3.0 platform, for example, can tag everything from images to data feeds to video streams from undersea cameras, identifying sightings of little-known organisms or examples of rare phenomena. There are shared collaboration spaces for group learning and discussion, while a Facebook-like social networking application helps connect researchers working on similar problems.

The same kind of cross-institutional collaborations will be key to making effective use of open data in other fields too. Public servants and citizens will need to collaborate across agency walls and jurisdictional boundaries. Journalists will need to join forces to interpret and report on breaking stories that contain a significant data component, like the recent Wikileaks disclosures. Healthcare providers will use medical data to collaborate around patient health needs, and so on.

A data-rich world will generate many new opportunities. In astronomy, physics, biomedical research, and other domains, we are seeing a new kind of analysis, a new kind of science, and a whole new kind of organization come into being. Of course, there will also be some difficult adjustments and issues such as privacy, intellectual property, and national security to confront along the way. "We're going from a data-poor to a data-rich world," said Larry Smarr, a distinguished physicist at the University of California and a global leader in scientific supercomputing. "And there's a lag whenever an exponential change like this transforms the impossible into the routine." People aren't necessarily good at thinking about exponential changes, he argues, and as a result, he suggests scientists will need to massively ramp up their investments in tools and infrastructure required for the era of infinite data.

Infinite Data and the Era of Self-Sovereign Identities

While a new age of scientific discovery highlights the upside and opportunity associated with a world of infinite data, the precipitous erosion of personal privacy provides a cautionary tale of its dark side. In this era of Trivergence, Internet users are collectively creating, storing, and communicating information at nearly exponential rates of growth. Most of this data is personally identifiable, and much of it is controlled by third parties. Practical obscurity—the basis for privacy norms throughout history—is fast disappearing. More and more aspects of our lives are becoming observable, linkable, and identifiable to others. Thanks to networked computing technologies, this personal data will be archived online forever and be instantly searchable.

Online or off, our digital footprints and shadows are being gathered together, bit by bit, megabyte by megabyte, terabyte by terabyte, into personas and profiles and avatars—virtual representations of us in a hundred thousand simultaneous locations. These are used to provide us with extraordinary new services, new conveniences, new efficiencies, and benefits undreamt of by our parents and grandparents. At the same time, novel risks and threats are emerging from this digital cornucopia. Identity fraud and theft are the diseases of the Trivergence, along with new forms of discrimination and social engineering made possible by the surfeit of data.

Personal information, be it biographical, biological, genealogical, historical, transactional, locational, relational, computational, vocational, or reputational, is the stuff that makes up our modern identity. It must be managed responsibly. When it is not, accountability is undermined, our personal security is threatened, and confidence in our society is eroded.

All this data constitutes a "virtual representation" of every Internet user. The digital crumbs people leave in daily life create a mirror image that knows more about individual Internet users than they do. Most people probably can't remember dozens of their personal identifiers: their driver's license details, credit card numbers, and government information. But they definitely don't know their exact location a year ago; what they bought or what amount of money they transacted; what they said online; what medication they took, or diagnosis they received. However, when data aggregators link all these different data points, they can create a detailed and intimate picture of an individual's life, interests, and even vulnerabilities.

And that's just the beginning. In the future, private companies will amass detailed medical information and myriad other real-time measures of what people do, how they function, where they are, and even how they feel. AI systems could foreseeably analyze this data to make accurate predictions about individuals' choices, preferences, and future actions.

What irks many Internet users is the lack of personal control or agency over how their personal data is used. In many cases, individuals have limited control over their personal data once it is collected by organizations. Terms and conditions, privacy policies, and consent mechanisms are often complex, lengthy, and difficult to understand, making it challenging for individuals to make informed decisions about their data.

To compound matters, big data ecosystems often involve the sharing of data between multiple entities, including companies, advertisers, and data brokers. Personal data collected by one organization can be shared or sold to others without individuals' knowledge or control. This unregulated data sharing introduces privacy risks, as data can end up in the hands of unknown parties or be used for purposes beyond individuals' expectations or intentions.

Stop-gap measures have emerged to help individuals reassert some autonomy and control. For example, anonymization and de-identification techniques are often used to protect privacy in big data analysis. However, research has shown that it is increasingly difficult to completely anonymize data due to the availability of auxiliary information and the potential for re-identification. As a result, even supposedly anonymized data can be linked back to individuals, posing privacy risks.

Breaking Free of Our Digital Landlords

The tension between big data analytics and personal privacy remains an ongoing challenge that requires ongoing efforts to strike a balance between innovation and privacy protection. To address these privacy concerns, regulatory frameworks such as the European Union's General Data Protection Regulation (GDPR) and the California Consumer Privacy Act (CCPA) have been introduced to provide individuals with more rights and control over their data.

The ultimate solution, however, must exist independent of any corporation, government, or other third party and should not be subject to the agency risk of executives or political parties. As Don and Alex Tapscott argued in *Blockchain Revolution*, the solution to personal privacy in the world of infinite data resides in the notion of self-sovereign identity.[16]

Here's how it works.

To bootstrap identity, we first need a model that is distributed among and maintained by the people whose identities it protects. This means that everyone's incentives align in an identity commons, with clear rights for users to steward their own identity, protect their privacy, access (and allow others to access) and monetize their own data, and participate in rule-making around the preservation and usage of the commons.

Each identity is in a black box on a blockchain. It sweeps up the exhaust of everyone's daily transactional and information data—from purchases to biological data—protecting it and enabling every citizen to use it in any way they want. Several identity projects in the block-chain space are working to provide such structure and capabilities. They include companies such as Civic, which offers an ID verification solution called Civic Pass through an Ethereum-based platform.[17] Users collect verifiable claims of attributes from validators—such as banks, governments, and universities—but when a third party wants to learn something about a user, the user can decide whether and how much to reveal. The third-party must then pay the validator of the relevant attribute, which is an incentive for validators to participate.

Services like Civic Pass represent a starting point for digital identity and privacy solutions. To function effectively, the self-sovereign identity must interoperate with a vast range of private and public institutions, even as it outlasts them. In fact, it must be built to *outlive* its users and enforce their right to be forgotten.[18] This would mean separating data rights from the actual data so that the rights holder could delete it. To be inclusive, it must be user-friendly with a low-tech mobile interface and low-cost dispute resolution.

This transition will take time. I challenge corporations to take at least three actions to rebuild the trust of those whose data they hold.

The first involves governance. Many large corporations and government agencies have strong governance mechanisms for their hard assets but really poor governance of information assets.[19] Companies must define decision rights around their data and develop an accountability framework that disciplines how employees use data.

The second involves the discontinuation of practices that collect and store customer data. This could involve either destroying these massive customer databases altogether (after returning files and records to customers) or migrating this data to distributed storage systems, such as the IPFS, and then transferring control to customers.[20]

The third involves the cultivation of a new core competence: the ability to work with huge, anonymized datasets rented from large numbers of people, all handled in a distributed and trust-minimized manner. It will remove data as a toxic asset from the corporate balance sheet and make it a fundamental human asset from birth. It would flip the data-analytics business model on its head and reward corporations for serving as data brokers on behalf of individuals. This will see the end of the large, centralized data frackers that scrape, hoard, and rent but don't protect this data.

These new approaches to privacy and ID management give citizens ownership of their identities, the facts of their existence, and the data they create as they live their lives. The self-sovereign identity is one of the pillars of a new social contract for the digital economy and will be critical to the transformation to a more open, inclusive, and private economy.[21]

Notes

1. https://explodingtopics.com/blog/data-generated-per-day
2. www.pwc.com/gx/en/issues/data-and-analytics/publications/artificial-intelligence-study.html
3. www.nytimes.com/2021/04/23/business/auto-semiconductors-general-motors-mercedes.html
4. www.aidataanalytics.network/data-monetization/articles/tesla-automaker-or-data-company
5. www.statista.com/statistics/471264/iot-number-of-connected-devices-worldwide
6. Your AI-Powered Browser | Microsoft Edge
7. www.lifewire.com/top-bing-searches-4120761
8. www.skao.int
9. www.smithsonianmag.com/science-nature/next-big-discovery-astronomy-scientists-probably-found-it-years-ago-they-dont-know-it-yet-180969073
10. https://home.cern/science/computing/grid#:~:text=WLCG%20combines%20about%201.4%20million,the%20power%20to%20process%20it

11. www.internationalgenome.org/about
12. www.evidera.com/advancing-healthcare-through-innovation-and-collaboration
13. https://pimm.wordpress.com/2009/10/08/sage-bionetworks-update-building-an-oa-standard-for-human-disease-biology
14. www.michaeljfox.org/news/mjff-and-sage-bionetworks-launch-data-challenge
15. www.oceannetworks.ca
16. www.amazon.com/Blockchain-Revolution-Technology-Cryptocurrencies-Changing/dp/1101980141/ref=sr_1_1?keywords=blockchain+revolution&qid=1566845965&s=books&sr=1-1
17. https://civic.com
18. www.theguardian.com/technology/right-to-be-forgotten
19. http://mitiq.mit.edu/IQIS/Documents/CDOIQS_200777/Papers/01_08_1C.pdf
20. https://ipfs.io
21. www.blockchainresearchinstitute.org/socialcontract

7

The Trivergence in Action

At this point in our journey, I have provided a detailed account of the three essential components of the Trivergence. Individually, AI, blockchain, and the IoT have already made significant waves in their respective domains.

Deep learning AI, the late bloomer, emerged from the depths of academics into a household word in 2023. Modeled on the human brain, it possesses the ability to learn, reason, and make decisions like its human creators. With its insatiable hunger for data and its uncanny knack for pattern recognition, AI has ushered in a new era of intelligent automation, transforming industries one algorithm at a time.

On a parallel path, blockchain has demonstrated the ability to be an incorruptible guardian of trust and transparency. However, as blockchains enter their second decade, we have seen some fascinating implementations of this novel technology, as well as the collapse of some proprietary, permissioned, or poorly engineered solutions. Properly implemented blockchain ledger technology can ensure that every transaction and record is securely stored, immutably recorded, and accessible to all participants in a network. It holds the promise of revolutionizing finance, supply chains, and even governance itself.

Meanwhile, the IoT is weaving its web of interconnectedness. Everyday objects are transforming into intelligent entities connected to a vast digital network. From smart homes to smart cities, sensors and devices are generating a deluge of real-time data, creating a fabric of information that can be harnessed to improve efficiency, enhance decision-making, and bring unprecedented convenience to our lives.

Each of these foundational technologies is uniquely and individually powerful. However, their convergence promises something extraordinary. This is a classic case of the whole being greater than the sum of its parts.

The IoT will create an era of pervasive computing where billions of people, trillions of devices, and countless decentralized autonomous organizations are connected to the Internet. With the addition of blockchain, connected people, devices, and organizations can do much more than communicate; they can perform transactions, create markets, and trust each other. Add in AI, and we can also analyze and make sense of the massive datasets this connectivity generates. Subject to benign governance, we can use this power to make better decisions and take actions that sustain the planet—all in a secure, encrypted, and entity-to-entity manner.

In short, the marriage of AI, blockchain, and the IoT holds the potential to unlock a realm of possibilities across industries and sectors, where seamless automation, verifiable transactions, and intelligent insights could reshape the very fabric of society. To better understand this potential, let's examine how the Trivergence is underpinning profound transformations in three critical sectors of our economy: agriculture, transportation, and healthcare. As a starting point, let's look at healthcare—a sector rife with both deep-rooted challenges and abundant opportunities for life-changing innovations.

Trivergence and the Future of Healthcare

Despite the miracles of modern medicine, the fundamental model of healthcare has remained largely unchanged for decades. Doctors diagnose patient conditions based mainly on the signs and symptoms presented by the patients and prescribe treatment according to the experience, knowledge, and intuition of the physician.

Today, advances in genomics are combining with the Trivergence to drive a shift from one-size-fits-all medical care to a new model of personalized medicine tailored to your exact genome. AI algorithms are already enabling doctors and hospitals to better analyze data and customize their healthcare to the lifestyle, environment, and genetic makeup of each patient. From diagnosing cancerous tumors to deciding which course of treatment will work best for an individual, AI can enhance both the speed and efficacy of care. For example, medical imaging, such as X-rays, MRIs, and CT scans, plays a crucial role in diagnosing and monitoring diseases. However, the interpretation of these images can be time-consuming and prone to human error. AI has the potential to revolutionize this process and improve patient outcomes.

Consider the case of diagnosing diabetic retinopathy, a leading cause of blindness. Traditionally, ophthalmologists analyze retinal images to identify signs of the disease, a task that requires expertise and can be subjective. With AI, algorithms can be trained on vast amounts of retinal images, enabling them to detect subtle abnormalities and accurately classify different stages of diabetic retinopathy.

In 2016, Google developed an AI system called GoogleNet and collaborated with doctors to test its efficacy in diagnosing diabetic retinopathy. The AI system was trained on a large dataset of retinal images and achieved remarkable accuracy in identifying the disease's severity. When compared to human experts, GoogleNet demonstrated a higher accuracy rate in detecting diabetic retinopathy, leading to the potential for early intervention and treatment.

AI algorithms have also shown promise in detecting lung cancer, breast cancer, and other conditions using medical imaging. In these instances, AI-enabled diagnoses are not based on the career experience of a single doctor but on an analysis of an enormous reservoir of medical data. By trolling through health records and images, population data, insurance claims data, and clinical trial data, AI technologies can uncover patterns and insights that humans could not find on their own, leading to better patient outcomes and potentially saving lives. Additionally, AI-based diagnostic tools have the potential to bring improved healthcare access to underserved areas where specialists may be limited.

While AI provides powerful new analytic tools, IoT and blockchain are combining to create a revolutionary new model for health informatics. For several decades, the proliferation of simple health monitoring devices have been empowering patients and doctors to share data and collaborate in new ways. A growing array of connected devices—digital heart monitors, Bluetooth-enabled scales, glucose monitors, skin patches, and maternity care trackers, to name a few—can provide insights into both general health conditions, such as weight loss and allergies, and very specific disorders, such as infertility and diabetes. Several pilot studies aimed at reducing the cost of chronic care confirm that such self-monitoring technology reduces errors, improves communication with doctors, and helps patients better manage their illnesses. Physicians increasingly encourage the use of smart web-based applications and self-monitoring tools for patients so they can spend less time on routine check-ups and queries and more time delivering care to patients with acute needs. These advances, in turn, decrease emergency department trips, unnecessary doctor's office appointments, and costly home nurse visits.

The promise of IoT-enabled healthcare is that it will generate vast amounts of anonymous data that becomes part of the knowledge base for science, health, and medicine. From the data, AI will deduce correlations and insights beyond the imagination of us mortals. However, add in blockchain—with its capacity to enable secure, permissioned access to data—and it's possible to envision the rise of a community-driven Internet of health data, gathering researchers and patient communities, social networks, and Internet of Things data flows into a seamless environment for wellness promotion and medical research.[1] Adults would own and control their own data, but healthcare professionals (and perhaps family members) could access it as required with appropriate levels of privacy and security.

Medical researchers are also enthusiastic about deploying the Trivergence in their research. For example, blockchain-enabled clinical data repositories could help enable large-scale medical and pharmaceutical research efforts to co-develop early-stage technology tools, establish data standards, share disease target information, or pursue other forms of collaboration that could lift the productivity of the entire industry.

Aled Edwards has seen the benefits of such collaborations firsthand in his role as CEO of the Structural Genomics Consortium, a global biomedical research collaboration involving scientists in hundreds of universities around the world and in nine global pharmaceutical companies. Edwards cites a range of industry problems where more collaboration between big pharma, biotech firms, and university researchers would yield better results: anti-bacterial research, developing more intelligent approaches assessing drug toxicology, reducing the industry's reliance on animal testing, and even tackling grand medical challenges like cancer, diabetes, and Alzheimer's. "These are areas in which a purely market-driven approach is sub-optimal and where the sharing of information makes a great deal of sense," he said.[2]

Blockchain could also enable better digital rights management in medical research, such as enforcing rules about who owns and can see DNA data. For example, IBM is working with the US Food and Drug Administration (FDA) on a blockchain-based method to manage large file transmissions related to clinical trials, where the data must be divided and carefully protected. Blockchain provides the cipher and permissioning system to maintain the integrity of the reassembled files.[3]

As healthcare systems around the world grappled with the crippling impact of COVID-19, the Trivergence was instrumental in arming healthcare practitioners and public health officials with new tools to fight the pandemic. In late February 2020, for example, AbCellera Biologics, a Canadian biotech firm that develops antibody therapies using artificial intelligence, found itself on the front lines of the global pandemic.

The Vancouver-based company, which employs about 300 people, received a blood sample from a patient who recovered from COVID-19. AbCellera screened more than 5 million immune cells and used its AI-power drug discovery engine to identify those that produce the antibodies that helped that person neutralize the virus and recover from the disease.[4] As Carl Hansen, AbCellera's CEO, explains, "Our system identifies those antibodies, using AI to generate hundreds of millions of images per month. Machine learning then deconvolutes their genetic codes to find the patterns that best match the best properties for a drug. Humans can never detect all the patterns there, but an AI algorithm can. If you give it enough data, you can start to get insights that apply to multiple problems."[5]

According to Hansen, the process identified more than 500 promising antibodies for therapeutic use and eventually led to emergency FDA approval of Bamlanivimab, a successful antibody therapy marketed by AbCellera's pharmaceutical partner, Eli Lilly. Incredibly, the initial discovery process took less than a week. The FDA would eventually revoke the EUA for Bamlanivimab in 2021 as the virus' mutation rendered the treatment less effective. Nevertheless, the speed of drug discovery enabled by AI has forever changed the way healthcare professionals and pharmaceutical companies will confront pandemics in the future.

The development of COVID-19 vaccines and antibody therapies highlights how AI-enabled breakthroughs in drug discovery are compressing years-long processes down to weeks and months. However, distributing these vaccines and therapies to every living person around the globe represented yet another truly unprecedented public health challenge. In this global endeavor, the Trivergence also played an essential role.

In March 2021, Moderna and IBM announced that they were running a pilot program to trace the distribution of COVID-19 vaccines so that healthcare providers can see the status of specific vaccine batches as they travelled from the manufacturer to the clinic.[6] Moderna's vaccine needed to be warehoused and shipped at a temperature of minus 20 degrees Celsius, but hospitals and clinics could store it for up to one month in a regular refrigerator (2-8 Celsius). Storing vaccines properly is critical to maintaining their efficacy and could literally mean the difference between life and death. With vaccine hesitancy presenting a thorny and unwelcome factor in prolonging the pandemic, trust in the safety and efficacy of the supply chain was paramount.

IBM and Moderna tackled this problem with an IoT and blockchain-enabled solution that enabled governments and healthcare providers to quickly and securely share data about individual vaccine batches at each step in their journey through the complex COVID-19 supply chain. Sensors embedded in shipping containers provided real-time status updates on the location and storage conditions of individual vaccine batches. Capturing the status updates on a blockchain, in turn, offered an immutable, tamper-proof record to ensure all parties that vaccine supplies were being stored and handled properly, removing any logistical concerns about whether the vaccines were safe and effective.

The same traceability system for vaccines can deliver other benefits. For example, pharmaceutical companies and governments can track whether the agreed quantities of vaccines are delivered to their destinations on time. Distributors can analyze the shipping data to identify potential efficiencies in the distribution system. Clinics and hospitals can anticipate supply conditions and better manage their inventories. The COVID pandemic may be over, but future pandemics are sure to arise. When they do, one hopes that the learnings from IBM and Moderna's efforts can help streamline the distribution of vaccines around the world.

In the meantime, there is much work to do to leverage the Trivergence to make modern healthcare more accessible, efficient, and fiscally sustainable. While technological advancements have undoubtedly brought numerous benefits to healthcare, they have also contributed to increasing costs. Sophisticated medical equipment, advanced therapies, and innovative medications often come with high price tags, making healthcare more expensive.

The global population is also aging, and chronic diseases are on the rise. The treatment and management of chronic conditions require ongoing care, medication, and monitoring, leading to increased healthcare costs. The aging population also puts a strain on healthcare systems, as older individuals typically require more healthcare services and long-term care.

Additionally, there are systemic challenges related to healthcare administration. The administrative complexity of most modern healthcare systems adds to the overall cost burden. In the United States, billing, insurance claims processing, and compliance with regulatory requirements involve significant administrative costs. The complex reimbursement systems and bureaucracy can lead to inefficiencies and higher healthcare expenses. Fragmented care, where patients receive healthcare services from multiple providers without efficient coordination, can also result in duplication of tests, inefficient care delivery, and increased costs. In many cases, lack of care coordination and information sharing leads to preventable medical errors and unnecessary hospital readmissions.

The Trivergence is no silver bullet for addressing the crisis of healthcare affordability, but it does offer solutions. For example, AI and IoT will enable the collection of individualized health data, genetic information, and lifestyle choices, allowing healthcare providers to create tailored treatment plans, preventive strategies, and wellness programs. Patients will be actively involved in their own care decisions, leading to better health outcomes and increased patient satisfaction.

A focus on preventive care rather than reactive treatment could help address the growing burden of chronic diseases. AI algorithms could analyze patient data to identify early signs of diseases, predict risk factors, and provide personalized preventive measures. IoT devices could monitor health parameters and send alerts to healthcare providers and patients in case of abnormalities. Proactive approaches such as these could lead to early interventions, reduced hospitalizations, and improved population health outcomes.

In the administrative realm, AI automation could streamline administrative processes, reduce paperwork, optimize resource allocation, and improve operational efficiency. Tasks such as appointment scheduling, billing, and claims processing could be further streamlined, allowing healthcare providers to allocate more time and resources to direct patient care. This efficiency would result in cost savings, shorter waiting times, and enhanced overall healthcare delivery.

Then again, not all implementations of AI are necessarily benevolent. Cigna has employed an AI engine to assist their doctors in reviewing claims.

By law, to reject a claim for medical reasons, a doctor must review them and conclude they are medically unnecessary. With the help of an AI engine, doctors at Cigna are rejecting claims at a staggering 1.2 times a second.[7] Only 0.2 percent of the time, customers appeal these decisions.[8] For a typical doctor's office in the United States, managing claims is a tedious and time-consuming administrative task. The power of AI is a double-edged sword.

The integration of blockchain technology could also revolutionize data sharing and interoperability in healthcare. For example, sharing medical records, research data, and treatment outcomes across different healthcare providers could improve the continuity of care and reduce the duplication of tests and procedures.

Overall, the rising costs of healthcare services and treatments have become a significant concern for individuals, governments, and healthcare organizations worldwide. However, a focus on data-driven decision-making, proactive preventive care, streamlined administrative processes and improved interoperability would go a long way to putting modern healthcare on a sustainable foundation.

Trivergence and the Future of Agriculture

Humans have engaged in agricultural practices since around 10,000 BCE, a period that marks the transition from a hunter-gatherer lifestyle to settled farming communities. Human civilization evolved in tandem with modern agriculture, as increasingly sophisticated farming practices allowed for the production of surplus food, which led to population growth, the emergence of complex societies, and the specialization of labor.

Of course, food production today is radically different from the past. Modern agriculture is highly industrialized and commercialized, with a focus on meeting market demands and maximizing profitability. Large-scale farms, agribusiness corporations, and contract farming are prominent features. So too is the globalization of agricultural supply chains, with deep interconnections to global trade allowing for a wide variety of food choices and access to seasonal produce year-round.

Above all, modern agriculture is increasingly technology-intensive, with mechanization, genetic modification, and data-driven approaches driving superior yields and efficiency. In Chapter 3, I briefly explained how Trivergence can optimize farming practices with sensors, drones, and satellite imagery providing real-time data on weather conditions, soil moisture, and crop health. The convergence of AI, blockchain, and IoT is also revolutionizing agricultural supply chains. Indeed, some of the most advanced efforts involve global food retailers using an array of Trivergence technologies to track meat or other agricultural products from the farmer's field to the supermarket shelf.

Trivergent Food: From the Field to the Supermarket Shelf

The focus on using AI, blockchain, and IoT to establish the authenticity and provenance of food comes with considerable justification. The World Health Organization estimates that contaminated food makes one in ten people ill every year, with 420,000 dying as a result.[9] One reason is that the global food supply has grown so complex that food producers and retailers find it nearly impossible to guarantee the provenance of their products. Regulatory investigations seeking to trace contaminated foods back to their origins often take months rather than hours, days, or even weeks.[10] In the wake of numerous food scandals, food retailers are under pressure to instill greater trust and safety into their supply chains.

Until now, supply chain transparency and traceability in agriculture and food production have been hampered by the Byzantine nature of the global food system. The Food Safety Modernization Act (FSMA) in the United States, for example, requires food producers only to provide "one back, one up" traceability.[11] "One back" refers to where the food came from, and "one up" refers to who bought it. In short, tracing the origins of food poisoning incidents requires a lengthy, one step at a time, process. The problem is compounded by the fact that each company in the supply chain has its own system for recordkeeping, and each processes its transactions in separate databases using different data standards. Many participants must dig through paper records to assist in efforts to determine the ultimate source of the contamination. Erroneous or incomplete data can further delay investigations. With multi-ingredient foods, including materials from a variety of food chains and countries, importers might end up relying on the arcane traceability systems (if any) of other countries up to the point of import.[12]

Now, some of the world's biggest companies, including Walmart and Nestle, are working with vendors such as IBM to remake how the industry tracks food worldwide. Leveraging blockchain and IoT technologies, the proposed solution will make the complete history and current location of any food item along with its accompanying information (i.e., certifications, test data, temperature data) readily available in seconds.[13]

For Walmart, the technology will be used to tell stakeholders that a particular head of lettuce came from a particular harvest on a particular farm, so if a consumer gets sick, government investigators will have a head start on the investigation. Rather than chasing a paper trail for days, they can get to the source of a tainted head of lettuce within seconds, and that should mean less wasted produce, fewer sick people, and more confidence in the food system.

For meat products like pork, the tracking process begins in the pens—where every pig is smart-tagged with bar codes—and reaches all the way to the supermarket shelf, where packaged pork can be traced back to its origins. A combination of RFID, cameras, and various sensors help document the journey at each step in the supply chain—from cameras installed in slaughterhouses to capture the entire production process to shipping trucks equipped with temperature and humidity sensors to ensure the meat arrives at the supermarket under safe conditions.[14] With global positioning systems, retailers like Walmart can trace the whereabouts of trucks and monitor conditions in each refrigerated container. If conditions exceed established thresholds, the system will send alerts to prompt corrective action.[15]

All of this data is captured in an immutable and tamper-proof ledger, arming everyone from importers and retail procurement managers to consumers and regulators with a veritable smorgasbord of information. Blockchain network participants can fetch data about farm origination, batch numbers, food processing methods, expiration dates, storage temperatures, shipping details, and, for some food products, soil quality and fertilizers. All this can be uploaded on an e-certificate and linked to the product package via a QR code.[16]

Getting an entire supply chain on board with the traceability effort required a complex and coordinated approach. The first step was identifying a clear value proposition and business case for investment in Trivergence technologies. As Walmart's vice president of food safety, Frank Yiannas put it, Walmart's solution needed to be "business-driven and technology-enabled."[17] For Yiannis, that value proposition was clear. Walmart's need for traceability arose from its focus on food safety and its need to safeguard its corporate reputation and brand. Both require Walmart to be able to prevent or respond quickly to contamination, fruit and animal disease, harmful drug or pesticide residues, or attempted bioterrorism incidents. A Trivergence-enabled solution also promised to help the retail giant identify new efficiencies in the supply chain, lower its costs, and increase its margins by reducing food spoilage and costly mass recalls.[18]

The second step was to ensure that there was also a compelling value proposition for all participants in the supply chain. The success of Walmart's food traceability initiative depended on the willing participation of a disparate group of players ranging from breeders and farmers, food processing plants, cold storage facilities, wholesale distribution centers and transport operators, and more. Granting access to the blockchain records ensured that every participant at each step in the food chain could derive clear business benefits from greater supply chain transparency and traceability.

For example, farmers will gain better visibility into international market prices for their goods and enhance their bargaining power accordingly. Food processors will be able to analyze data on the impact of harvest maturity, method of harvesting, food packaging, and modes of transportation on the quality of produce coming into their processing facilities. Transport operators will have access to real-time information about food import quantities to optimize their distribution networks. "This is not about competition; this is about collaboration," said Yiannas. "[It's about] creating solutions that offer shared value for stakeholders."[19]

The third step was ensuring that the solution was easy for its partners to adopt. For example, Walmart worked with IBM to identify a technology platform that could integrate well with its existing supply chain operations. Brigid McDermott, IBM's vice president of blockchain business development, said Walmart chose IBM's solution because it was "not re-creating supply chain, but leveraging existing technologies [such as sensors and global positioning] to enhance supply chain traceability using Hyperledger."[20] Traceability systems that are integrated with existing company business practices are more likely to be maintained, according to McDermott, and more likely to be accurate than stand-alone traceability systems.

Walmart and IBM also deployed an incremental approach to testing and refining new solutions for increasing food safety. In 2016, for example, Walmart launched a few blockchain pilot projects focused on discrete food items like mangos and pork.[21] The pilots not only provided a testbed for new technologies and processes but also helped Walmart build confidence in the potential for shared value across the supply chain. As its food traceability effort matures, Walmart will continue to experiment, scale, and learn from its pilots as it builds coalitions within the supply chain ecosystem where members are seeking to implement the applications more broadly.

Finally, Walmart built a broad knowledge network around global food safety. The knowledge network gives its partners and collaborators a voice in setting industry standards and conducting research that will support the effective implementation of industry-wide solutions for food safety. To date, the network has brought American and Chinese academics together with Chinese poultry producers to study safety in poultry supply chains.[22] Walmart has also pooled talent from top academic institutions working on IoT and supply chain analytics solutions—including Massachusetts Institute of Technology, Zhejiang University, and Tsinghua University—to improve the capacity of supply chain participants to predict and detect areas of greatest vulnerability for food adulteration in global food supply chains.[23] Walmart said this knowledge network is just getting started and could eventually include other research and development centers, primary production facilities, aggregation and mobilization providers, farm input supplies, trading and grading participants, wholesalers, retailers, and even customers.[24]

Walmart also recognized that early cooperation with governmental regulators would be crucial to its success. The good news was that regulators were enthusiastic about blockchain technology and its potential. A transparent ledger to enhance food traceability aligned with their need for better tools to investigate contamination incidents and monitor the safety of the food supply.[25] With collaborators in place and a green light from regulators, Walmart was ready to roll out its food traceability platform across the supply chain. One early result is promising: the time taken to track contaminated food to its origin has dropped from approximately seven days to only 2.2 seconds, which minimizes the chance of tainted food ever reaching consumers.[26]

Rise of the Digital Farm: Accelerating Innovation in the Global Food System

While the initial focus is supply chain traceability and food safety, the solutions pursued by giants like Walmart and IBM could easily grow into something much bigger. Layering in artificial intelligence will yield ever more powerful possibilities to enhance food safety, productivity, and innovation. Data gleaned from traceability systems, for example, could help supply chain participants streamline distribution, better manage inventory, reduce food waste, and identify other efficiencies. In other words, everyone from retailers to producers to farmers could use the Trivergence as a platform for accelerating innovation in the global food system.

Such innovation is already taking root in other domains of the agricultural sector. Take Milk Moovement, an AgTech company that provides supply chain management solutions for the dairy industry. Co-founded in 2018 by Robert Forsythe and Jon King, the company's AI and IoT-powered software tracks raw milk shipments from dairy farmers to processing plants, delivering real-time quality and quantity information to producers, processors, transporters, and cooperatives.

Like the broader agricultural sector, the dairy industry has been lagging on digitization. Milk producers, transporters, and processors typically rely on siloed, paper-based systems to record vital information, resulting in errors and inefficiencies. Milk Moovement replaces these disparate systems with a streamlined, cloud-enabled solution that makes the entire supply chain more efficient, sustainable, and profitable. "Our software democratizes the dairy supply chain by connecting key stakeholders and ensuring everybody is working off of a single dataset," said Forsythe, Milk Moovement's CEO.

According to Forsythe, streamlining the dairy supply chain requires two steps. The first step is digitization. Milk Moovement installs digital sensors across the supply chain, including dairy farms, milk processors, and transportation vehicles. The data gleaned from real-time monitoring of these operations feeds the second step: supply chain optimization. Here, Milk Moovement uses analytics to generate insights into on-farm milk pricing and help optimize pickup and delivery routes.

Globally, dairy producers are facing financial strains as costs for essential inputs such as feed, fertilizer, and fuel continue to rise.

Similarly, dairy processors are experiencing challenges as rising raw milk prices and energy costs put pressure on profit margins. In an industry where margins are a recurring concern, Milk Moovement's solution enables dairy farmers and producers to enhance the efficiency and profitability of their businesses.

As of 2022, Milk Moovement is working with more than 2,500 farms and 11 dairy cooperatives across the United States and managing more than 30 billion pounds of dairy.[27] According to Forsythe, the whole US dairy sector produces about 230 billion pounds annually, which means Milk Moovement is tracking about 13 percent of all US dairy.

On the immediate horizon, Forsythe sees opportunities to deepen the company's relationship with the dairy industry. "We started by tracking milk. Now we are tracking feed, and we see opportunities to go closer to end-consumers," said Forsythe. "We also sit in a place where we could be facilitating industry payments, including how dairy processors pay producers. There is a large fintech play in our future. That's where we see the potential to become a billion-dollar company."

Global aquaculture production has increased rapidly since the 2000s. According to Food and Agriculture Organization of the United Nations data, aquaculture eclipsed traditional capture fisheries as the leading source of fish production for human consumption in 2016.[28] More recently, operators have been bringing fish farming on land to circumnavigate regulation and overcome some of the problems that have plagued ocean-based fish farms. For example, so-called land-based aquaculture operations can control everything from the temperature, salinity, and pH of the water to its oxygen levels, artificial currents, lighting cycles, and carbon dioxide and waste removal. Land-based operators can also locate their fish farms closer to processing sites and end consumers, thus significantly reducing transportation costs.

Halifax-based ReelData provides an artificial intelligence solution to bring the world's most sustainable aquaculture practices to the main-stream. With reliable, real-time monitoring and analysis, ReelData works with each farm to increase operational efficiency, reduce costs, grow fish faster, and eliminate risks related to contamination and parasites. "We are the digital operating system behind land-based aquaculture," said co-founder and CEO Matt Zimola.

Zimola and his cofounder, Houssein Salimian, are computer scientists. Neither cofounder has a background in aquaculture or fisheries, but both shared a desire to impact the world positively.

Being in Halifax, they also saw aquaculture as a space where they could marry their tech skills with a mission to boost global sustainability. Zimola explains that using aquaculture to produce protein for human consumption is 10 times more carbon efficient than producing beef. "But when we looked at the aquaculture industry, we realized that operators had problems monitoring the growth and health of their fish stocks," said Zimola. "With our background in machine vision and AI, we felt that was a problem we could help solve."

Poultry and cattle farmers can visually inspect their herds. But that's much harder to do in a fish farm aquarium the size of a hockey rink. "We saw the potential for automation," said Zimola. "With our machine vision tools, we can quickly assess how much the fish weighs, whether they are hungry, and how healthy they are."

While land-based aquaculture is relatively new, the industry is poised to grow 50-fold in the next 8 years, providing a sizable addressable market for ReelData's solution. "The land-based operators are also digitally under-served," said Zimola, "because most vendors optimize their tech solutions for ocean-based fish farms." Today, ReelData has customers in Denmark, the Netherlands, Canada, Norway, and the United States. However, plans are in the works to open a satellite office in Europe, where land-based aquaculture operations are more advanced than those in North America.

Across the board, the agriculture sector highlights the increasingly vital role of Trivergence technologies. Artificial intelligence, blockchain, and the IoT are giving rise to incredibly powerful information systems that will become indispensable tools for driving innovation, productivity, and profitability. While global giants like Walmart are using these tools to boost supply chain transparency and efficiency, everyone from dairy farmers to aquaculture operators are leveraging similar information systems to track assets, analyze performance, and gather insights to design and lead innovative initiatives.

Trivergence and the Future of Transportation

The evolution of autonomous transportation has been a remarkable journey, reshaping the way we envision mobility and transforming the possibilities of transportation. It all began with a vision to develop vehicles that could navigate and operate without human intervention, relying on advanced sensor technologies and artificial intelligence. In other words, autonomous vehicles are yet another perfect illustration of the Trivergence in action.

The early stages of autonomous transportation can be traced back to the 1920s when radio-controlled vehicles were experimented with for remote control. However, significant progress in this field was not achieved until the latter part of the 20th century.

In the 1980s, research institutions and automotive companies began exploring the concept of autonomous vehicles more seriously. The focus was primarily on developing advanced sensors, computer vision systems, and control algorithms to enable vehicles to perceive and understand their surroundings. Experimental autonomous vehicles made their debut on closed tracks and controlled environments, showcasing the potential of this technology.

The 2000s marked a turning point as advancements in computing power, sensor technology, and machine learning algorithms propelled autonomous transportation to new heights. The Defense Advanced Research Projects Agency (DARPA) played a pivotal role by organizing the DARPA Grand Challenges, which spurred competition among researchers to develop fully autonomous vehicles capable of completing challenging off-road courses.

Major automotive companies also entered the race, investing heavily in autonomous vehicle research and development. They focused on refining sensor technologies such as light detection and ranging (LiDAR), radar, and cameras, as well as developing sophisticated AI algorithms to process and interpret sensor data in real time.

By the 2010s, autonomous vehicles started hitting public roads, albeit in limited testing environments and under strict supervision. Companies like Google's Waymo, Uber, and Tesla gained significant attention for their efforts in advancing autonomous driving technology. The industry witnessed a rapid expansion of testing programs in various cities worldwide, accumulating valuable data and insights for further refinement.

In addition to significant advancements, this work also highlights several limitations that need to be overcome before widespread adoption of fully autonomous vehicles can occur. For example, while autonomous systems are designed to operate safely, unpredictable scenarios and edge cases can pose risks. Adapting to rapidly changing road conditions, unpredictable human behavior, and extreme weather conditions remains a complex task for autonomous vehicles. So far, Google and others have spent more than $100 billion trying to solve this conundrum, yet they are still years off. Navigating through dense urban environments with intricate traffic patterns, pedestrians, cyclists, and various road users is particularly challenging. Creating and maintaining detailed maps of road networks, including lane markings, traffic signs, and temporary construction zones, is another ongoing challenge.

Above all, autonomous vehicles pose ethical dilemmas that remain unresolved. For example, autonomous vehicles may confront situations where harm to humans is possible, such as choosing between two potential collision scenarios. Deciding how autonomous vehicles should prioritize human life, follow traffic laws, or respond to unexpected events presents complex ethical challenges that need careful consideration and consensus. Without resolution of these concerns, industry leaders could fail to win the widespread public acceptance and trust required to successfully integrate autonomous vehicles into society.

Given these limitations, the focus has shifted toward developing autonomous technology for specific use cases, such as ride-sharing services, delivery vehicles, and public transportation. Companies like Waymo, Cruise, and various start-ups have launched pilot programs and commercial services, bringing autonomous transportation closer to everyday life.

At the same time, Trivergence is also enabling a new kind of transportation economy. A great case in point is the Mobility Open Blockchain Initiative (MOBI), a nonprofit alliance of public and private organizations working to make transportation more efficient, affordable, greener, safer, and less congested. Backed by many of the world's largest vehicle manufacturers, infrastructure providers, and tech companies, the consortium's focus is simple blockchain-based standards to streamline mobility transactions by promoting secure protocols for vehicle-to-vehicle (V2V) and vehicle-to-infrastructure (V2I) communications and payments. According to MOBI, these standards will permit any smart device—vehicles, road sensors, toll bridges, or other pieces of mobility infrastructure—to have an identity, to communicate, and to participate autonomously in economic transactions as an independent agent.[29]

Some of the earliest blockchain-based vehicle value transfer systems emerged to tackle issues associated with parking fees, toll road billing, and other roadside services. In 2019, MOBI convened five major auto manufacturers, including Renault, BMW, General Motors, Honda, and Ford Motor, to begin field tests for a blockchain-based vehicle identification system that will enable drivers to pay highway tolls and parking fees automatically.[30]

The proposed system will assign digital IDs to individual vehicles and record details such as ownership information and service history on a blockchain. Data covering the lifetime of the vehicle will then be used to identify cars on the road, enabling the owner to purchase goods and services automatically with no need for the specialized tags or transponders required in existing electronic tollbooth systems.

MOBI and its partners are optimizing the blockchain-based system for connected EVs. This way, transactions for tolls, car maintenance, and even rest stop snacks can be recorded on the fly and then paid all at once when the vehicle is plugged in to a charging station. In a recent analysis, Juergen Reers, Stephen Zoegall, and Pierre-Olivier Desmurs of Accenture predict that transactions like these will become a multitrillion-dollar global ecosystem that enables new pay-as-you-go mobility services, with blockchain providing the infrastructure for data sharing and security across manufacturers, suppliers, and other relevant parties.[31]

Of course, autonomous vehicles and mobile transactions are just the tip of the iceberg. AI and IoT technologies will also combine to optimize traffic and enable predictive maintenance on transportation infrastructure. For example, NoTraffic, an Israeli start-up, uses machine vision, IoT connectivity, and radar to analyze traffic data and adjust traffic signals in real time. Pilots of the AI-powered system in several cities in California, Arizona, and Texas have proven it can reduce congestion and promote the efficient movement of people and vehicles. Using IoT sensors installed at eye level, NoTraffic's platform automatically identifies different classes of road users—including pedestrians, bicycles, cars, heavy trucks, transit, and emergency vehicles—and makes intelligent routing decisions. In Redlands, California, the system reduced traffic congestion in one highly trafficked intersection by 50 percent, saving 2,700 hours of delays and cutting 33 tons in carbon dioxide emissions during a one-year period.[32]

Pilots in Redlands and other areas demonstrate that progress toward increasingly intelligent transportation continues to accelerate, driven by ongoing advancements in AI, sensor technology, blockchain, and smart infrastructure. The pursuit of fully autonomous vehicles capable of navigating complex urban environments and interacting with pedestrians and other road users is still some distance away. However, once we get there, a future with fully autonomous transportation holds the promise of safer roads, reduced congestion, increased accessibility, and enhanced efficiency.

Get Ready for Trivergence-Driven Disruption

We have seen how the convergence of AI, blockchain, and the IoT is powering disruptive innovation and enabling new business models in agriculture, healthcare, and transportation. Over time, the Trivergence will usher in a next-generation Internet where nearly every animate and inanimate object on Earth generates data, a distributed ledger records and secures the data, and AI analyzes the data, communicates with the objects, alerts their owners, and continuously adjusts and improves the efficiency of the economy and the sustainability of its effects on the environment. Inevitably, new business models enabled by this Trivergence will disrupt most industries and provide a platform for innovation in the economy for decades ahead.

In financial services, AI, blockchain, and IoT integration will transform payments, fraud detection, and identity verification, reducing costs and enhancing trust in financial systems. In manufacturing and supply chain management, AI algorithms can analyze real-time data to predict equipment failures, optimize production schedules, and improve overall efficiency. In the energy sector, blockchain can be deployed to create energy trading platforms, while IoT and AI can combine to optimize energy distribution, predict demand, and automate energy-saving actions. And the list of transformative opportunities goes on.

To be sure, the Trivergence also has weighty implications for every business, government, and individual. Concerns about privacy, autonomy, and jobs, among other things, cannot be dismissed lightly. Interdisciplinary partnerships between technologists, industry professionals, and policymakers are needed to explore the societal implications of innovative use cases. Support for academic institutions, start-ups, and research organizations can drive advancements and discover novel ways to integrate these technologies for maximum socio-economic impact. Further research and multistakeholder discussions will be required to develop ethical guidelines and frameworks for the development and deployment of AI, blockchain, and IoT applications. These guidelines should encourage transparency, fairness, accountability, and responsible use of these technologies, considering potential biases, unintended consequences, and social impacts.

In some cases, regulatory frameworks will be necessary to create an environment that promotes innovation while safeguarding privacy, security, and the broader public interest. Across most industries, there will also be an imperative for greater investment in education and training programs to equip the workforce with the necessary skills to understand and leverage these technologies effectively. By following these recommendations, we can overcome the dark side and leverage the Trivergence to improve global health outcomes, instill trust and transparency into our agricultural supply chains, modernize transportation, and help solve a host of other intractable problems.

Notes

1. Aaron Stanley, "Big Pharma Seeks DLT Solution for Drug Costs," CoinDesk, Digital Currency Group, 9 Jan. 2018. www.coindesk.com/blockchain-day-big-pharma-seeks-dlt-solution-drug-costs
2. Aled Edwards, interviewed via telephone by Anthony Williams, 13 Feb. 2019.
3. Jerry Cuomo, interviewed via telephone by Robert Morison, 3 April 2018.
4. "AbCellera and Lilly to Co-develop Antibody Therapies for the Treatment of COVID-19," AbCellera.com, March 12, 2020. www.abcellera.com/news/2020-03-abcellera-and-lilly-codevelopment, accessed 22 October 2021.
5. Gail Dutton, "AbCellera and Lilly Slash Antibody Selection Time for COVID-19 With AI/Machine Learning," Biospace.com, April 28, 2020. www.biospace.com/article/abcellera-and-lilly-slash-antibody-selection-time-for-covid-19-with-ai-machine-learning
6. N.F. Mendoza, "Moderna and IBM partner on COVID-19 vaccine supply chain, distribution data sharing," Tech Republic, March 17, 2021. www.techrepublic.com/article/moderna-and-ibm-partner-on-covid-19-vaccine-supply-chain-distribution-data-sharing

7. www.propublica.org/article/cigna-pxdx-medical-health-insurance-rejection-claims

8. www.pbs.org/newshour/show/how-algorithms-are-being-used-to-deny-health-insurance-claims-in-bulk

9. "Food Safety," World Health Organization, 31 Oct. 2017. www.who.int/news-room/fact-sheets/detail/food-safety, accessed 9 Nov 2018.

10. See, for example, the recent incident with E.coli contaminated romaine lettuce in North America. www.cnn.com/2018/06/29/health/e-coli-romaine-lettuce-outbreak-cause/index.html and www.canada.ca/en/public-health/services/public-health-notices/2018/public-health-notice-outbreak-e-coli-infections-linked-romaine-lettuce.html

11. "FDA Food Safety Modernization Act," US Food and Drug Administration, US Department of Health and Human Services, last updated 15 Nov. 2018. www.fda.gov/food/guidanceregulation/fsma, accessed 4 March 2019.

12. Bruce Welt and J. Ralph Blanchfield, "Food Traceability," IUFoST Scientific Information Bulletin, International Union of Food Science and Technology, March 2012. www.iufost.org/iufostftp/IUF.SIB.Food%20Traceability.pdf, accessed 4 March 2019.

13. Ian Allison, "IBM Enlists Walmart, Nestlé, Unilever, Dole for Food Safety Blockchain," International Business Times, 24 Aug. 2017. www.ibtimes.com/ibm-enlists-walmart-nestle-unilever-dole-food-safety-blockchain-2582490, accessed 28 Aug. 2017.

14. "IFA Accuses Pig Processors of Undermining Pigmeat Market," ThePigSite News Desk, 7 Aug. 2017 www.thepigsite.com/swinenews/43938/ifa-accuses-pig-processors-of-undermining-pigmeat-market; Jeff Clark, "Pig Premise ID Registrations Top 13 Thousand & Growing," ThePigSite News Desk, n.d. www.thepigsite.com/swinenews/43919/pig-premise-id-registrations-top-13-thousand-growing, accessed 7 Aug. 2017.

15. Fred Gale, "China's Pork Imports Rise Along with Production Costs," Economic Research Services, US Department of Agriculture, Jan. 2017. www.ers.usda.gov/webdocs/publications/81948/ldpm-271-01.pdf?v=42745, accessed 30 June 2017.

16. Dan Murphy, "Meat of the Matter: When Solutions are Seen as Problems," Farm Journal's Pork, 29 Nov. 2016. www.porknetwork.com/community/contributors/meat-matter-when-solutions-are-seen-problems, accessed 29 June 2017.

17. Frank Yiannas, interviewed via telephone by Reshma Kamath, 28 June 2017.

18. Frank Yiannas, interviewed via telephone by Reshma Kamath, 28 June 2017.

19. Frank Yiannas, interviewed via telephone by Reshma Kamath, 28 June 2017.

20. Brigid McDermott, interviewed via telephone by Reshma Kamath, 23 June 2017.

21. Michael del Castillo, "Walmart Blockchain Pilot China Pork Market," CoinDesk, Digital Currency Group, 19 Oct. 2016. www.coindesk.com/walmart-blockchain-pilot-china-pork-market, accessed 7 Aug. 2017.

22. Laurie Burkitt, "Walmart to triple spending on food safety in China," *The Wall Street Journal*, 17 June 2014. www.wsj.com/articles/wal-mart-to-triple-spending-on-food-safety-in-china-1402991720, accessed 29 June 2017.

23. Laurie Burkitt, "Walmart to triple spending on food safety in China," *The Wall Street Journal*, 17 June 2014. www.wsj.com/articles/wal-mart-to-triple-spending-on-food-safety-in-china-1402991720, accessed 29 June 2017.

24. Laurie Burkitt, "Walmart to triple spending on food safety in China," *The Wall Street Journal*, 17 June 2014. www.wsj.com/articles/wal-mart-to-triple-spending-on-food-safety-in-china-1402991720, accessed 29 June 2017.

25. Kim S. Nash, "Walmart Readies Blockchain Pilot for Tracking US Produce, China Pork," *The Wall Street Journal* CIO Journal, 16 Dec. 2016. blogs.wsj.com/cio/2016/12/16/wal-mart-readies-blockchain-pilot-for-tracking-u-s-produce-china-pork, accessed 15 Aug. 2017.

26. Ron Miller, "This Is How Blockchain Can Keep Your Food Safe," WEForum.org, World Economic Forum, 23 Jan. 2019. www.weforum.org/agenda/2019/01/walmart-is-betting-on-the-blockchain-to-improve-food-safety, accessed 15 Feb. 2019.

27. www.newswire.ca/news-releases/milk-moovement-raises-20-million-usd-to-transform-the-dairy-industry-s-supply-chain-893569906.html

28. https://link.springer.com/article/10.1007/s12571-021-01246-9

29. https://dlt.mobi

30. Keiichi Furukawa, "Blockchain turns cars into payment vehicle for drivers," Nikkei Asia, October 14, 2019. https://asia.nikkei.com/Business/Automobiles/Blockchain-turns-cars-into-payment-vehicle-for-drivers

31. Juergen Reers, Stephen Zoegall and Pierre-Olivier Desmurs, "V2X is close. Here's what still needs to happen," Automotive World, May 31,

2021. www.automotiveworld.com/articles/v2x-is-close-heres-what-still-needs-to-happen

32. www.thestar.com/autos/2022/07/30/like-a-huge-chess-game-start-up-is-revolutionizing-traffic-light-timing-with-ai-and-the-internet-of-things.html

8

Challenges of the Era of Trivergence

The era of Trivergence has ushered in a new frontier of possibilities, promising to reshape business models and unlock unprecedented opportunities for growth and innovation. The convergence of AI, IoT, and blockchain allows organizations to harness the strengths of each technology, while synergistically overcoming their individual limitations. This convergence creates a new paradigm where the whole is greater than the sum of its parts. It empowers organizations to navigate the era of Trivergence with reduced risks and increased potential for innovation and growth. However, embracing these transformative technologies goes beyond simply adopting them. It requires careful consideration of the challenges and implications that lie ahead. While a few pioneering applications have successfully integrated AI, IoT, and blockchain, they are still the exception rather than the norm. Before the era of Trivergence becomes a widespread reality, we must identify and address the challenges it presents.

Trivergence technologies present two types of challenges: technological challenges and social challenges. Technological challenges involve understanding the complexities and limitations of the technologies themselves, and the trade-offs that need to be made for them to function effectively. On the other hand, social challenges force us to consider the complex dynamics that come into play as society adopts these technologies. Technology doesn't exist in a vacuum—it's not just about the gadgets and systems. It's about how people use them and the impact they have on the world. For these three emerging technologies, the social challenges and associated labor disruptions will be far more difficult to overcome than the technical ones. Expect significant societal disruption.

As we navigate the era of Trivergence, we need to tackle these challenges head-on. By gaining a deeper understanding of the technology and addressing the complexities of human interaction, we can pave the way for successful adoption and make the most of what the era of Trivergence has to offer.

Technological Challenges

Data Integrity

In the era of Trivergence, data plays a central role, fueled by the proliferation of IoT devices generating vast amounts of data, extended further by the people and programs constantly adding more. All this data is used to glean further insights through the correlations of artificial intelligence. However, ensuring data integrity poses a significant challenge due to trust issues arising at the physical-digital interface. For example, IoT devices today are typically small, easily accessible, and lack physical security measures, making them vulnerable to tampering or unauthorized access. Some do not offer remote password management, which significantly increases the likelihood that they will be hacked. This raises concerns about the reliability and authenticity of the data they generate. Additionally, the sheer volume of data produced in varying formats adds complexity to the task of verifying its accuracy, completeness, and reliability. With such a massive influx of data, distilling meaningful insights becomes increasingly challenging.

The impact of data alteration can have far-reaching consequences. Let's consider a few examples to understand the potential risks involved. Imagine a scenario where vital signs recorded by an IoT-enabled medical device, such as a pacemaker, insulin pump, or glucose monitor, are hacked. This could lead to incorrect medical treatment, even death. Similarly, in smart grid systems that rely on IoT devices to monitor and control electricity distribution, data integrity issues can wreak havoc. When the data used to calculate power supply and demand is compromised, it can lead to equipment failures and even widespread long-lasting blackouts, that when they effect the sick, can kill. IoT-enabled vehicles that rely on accurate data for navigation, safety, and autonomous driving functions could, if compromised, crash. Likewise, in industrial settings, compromised IoT devices can lead to data manipulation that affects critical processes, leading to faulty product quality, equipment damage, or even safety hazards.

Compromised data becomes a significant concern when it comes to training AI systems. These systems learn from input data, and any biases or inaccuracies present in the training data will persist in the algorithm's predictions or decisions. This means that if the training data is biased or contains inaccuracies, the AI models will perpetuate these biases or produce erroneous outcomes. In the context of automated decision-making, such biases can result in everything from crashing aircraft to discrimination or financial loss.

The issue of data integrity in the context of AI is a double-edged sword. On the one hand, AI exhibits the capability to intelligently identify and reject suspicious data and software, safeguarding the quality of the information it processes. Conversely, AI can generate misleading or false data, exemplified by the emergence of deepfakes—AI-generated content that convincingly mimics reality. Given that many people prefer their news pre-filtered to reinforce their pre-existing biases the impact on democracy could be devastating. As AI systems traverse the vast expanse of the internet, they amass a wealth of valuable information, but they will also ingest a considerable volume of spurious or misleading content. AI lacks "common sense" filters. Consequently, AI today cannot readily distinguish fact from fiction, or the morally right from the wrong—a task that remains beyond its current capabilities. Further by the time you are reading this book, an AI routine will likely have already scanned and learned from its contents without attribution.[1]

What sets blockchain logged data apart from other data is its immutability. For example, when anomalies arise in your transaction processing system having an immutable back-end log of all transactions is an incredibly powerful tool in determining what went wrong. Having, in my younger career, spent many a sleepless night trying to understand why a financial system hickuped and crashed at say 1:30 AM, it is a tool I wish I had had. For backend blockchains, once data is recorded, it cannot be altered or deleted. For distributed ledgers it takes longer to be sure validated transactions stay in the ledger. For bitcoin, experts say to wait somewhere between ten minutes and an hour then check it is still there, with Ethereum, you need to confirm only after about 15 seconds. Critical data from IoT on things along the supply chain, transaction logs, financial records, or security footage stored immutably on a private backend blockchain dramatically increases the trust of those that review it. On the front end with distributed blockchains there are still challenges, resulting from the immaturity of the ledgers, and the speculation on the tokens.

Let's explore the power of a distributed blockchain ledger to disintermediate. Today we have a challenging situation where climate change has made it too risky for insurance companies to provide flood insurance in certain areas of Florida, or fire insurance in the woods of California, British Columbia, Spain, or the islands of Hawaii or Greece. As the world warms, we can expect these uninsurable areas to dramatically expand. If you own a home in any of these regions, how do you hedge the risk of a catastrophic event?

Through a distributed ledger homeowners in those regions could contribute a monthly payment to a smart contract. Then software could monitor reputable IoT udometers, combined with satellite imagery, to determine which areas have been burned or which areas have been flooded. The smart contract would then automatically distribute a percentage of the funds to those homeowners who have been affected. This process eliminates the need for insurance companies with their expensive overhead. No actuaries, no brokers, no sales agents, no adjustors, no lawyers, no inspectors, no claims processors, no subjectivity, no management overhead, no head office to rent—and for the customer no fear of their claim being challenged. With the creation of a distributed smart contract, with no central point of control, the insurance process becomes more transparent and far more efficient, as real-time data from external sources can be securely integrated into blockchain smart contracts.

For IoT, data integrity is not just about protecting the physical devices themselves, but also about making sure the data they produce is captured intact. The usual security methods, like cryptography, don't always fit well with these devices. Today, these devices have limitations in terms of energy and memory, which makes it hard to implement complex security measures. To tackle this issue, experts are now exploring lightweight security algorithms that rely on simpler techniques. For example, they analyze factors such as arrival times, angles, signal strength, history, input from other nearby devices, and other characteristics to verify the authenticity of the data.

With sufficient compute time, almost any form of encryption can be hacked. The rule of thumb of how complex your encryption scheme need be to crack is as follows. If it takes $100,000 in computer time to steal your $10,000, then you are reasonably safe. At least until the cost of compute time to crack your system drops to $9,000.

Integrating AI into IoT networks and infrastructures presents another effective method for enhancing data integrity. With the help of AI, IoT systems can better detect and mitigate various risks that threaten the security of data, such as malware, phishing attacks, and other malicious activities targeting IoT devices. Traditional anti-virus software looks for code that it knows to be malicious. Today AI is smart enough to look for code that is similar. By harnessing the power of AI, IoT networks can continuously monitor device behavior, identify any unusual patterns or signs of potential threats, and respond swiftly to maintain the security of devices and data. This combination of AI and IoT not only reinforces data protection but also establishes a dynamic and adaptable security framework. AI algorithms will learn from the observed behavior in IoT networks, enabling them to detect emerging threats and develop effective defense mechanisms. As technology progresses, the integration of AI and IoT security will continue to evolve, providing robust safeguards to uphold data integrity in the face of ever-evolving risks.

The Trivergence Trilemma

We have discussed the potential of modern distributed networks, with blockchain being a key example. In 2021, Vitalik Buterin, the founder of Ethereum, articulated the weaknesses of distributed ledgers when he wrote about what he called the "blockchain trilemma."[2] He then argued that public blockchains, which aim to be secure, decentralized, and scalable, need to make trade-offs among these three factors. Bottom line: be careful in deploying or depending on these technologies.

For example, the Bitcoin blockchain offers decentralization, and when valid transactions do make it to the ledger, it can only manage about six transactions a second. In my experience, that is about what 150 clerical staff generate, a far cry from the needs of say international banking. On the other hand, enterprise blockchains like Hyperledger's Fabric can handle much higher transactional throughput but typically are deployed for private ledgers. Buterin argues that decentralized blockchains that prioritize speed must do so at the expense of security opening them to long-term vulnerabilities. In simpler words, if your system in the future may need to scale to any significant volume, don't put it on a distributed ledger, you should never compromise security.

As a former bank CIO, hearing that this class of software needs to make tradeoffs between security and throughput was disconcerting. The CEOs and CFOs I have worked with have demanded that the systems I have designed are both secure and capable of very high transaction volumes. As a rule of thumb in capacity planning, if a class of software cannot scale to meet ten times your anticipated requirements, then it is clearly best to use other technologies. But with blockchains, that is not conservative enough. With public blockchains, you need to remember that you may be one of a hundred applications running on the same Ethereum shard. The implementation of any technology has risks. No doubt there are cases where the implementation of a public distributed ledger can disintermediate a bloated and entrenched legacy player and in doing so be highly profitable, and as such is well worth the risk. The risks Buterin highlights are the reasons why deployment of (high speed) private blockchains are far more common than decentralized ones. Nevertheless, Buterin's framework is an interesting one to discuss not just distributed blockchains but the overall trivergence.

Decentralization

In the history of computers, technology typically converges toward monopolies. WordPerfect was arguably better than Word, and Lotus 1-2-3 was arguably better than Excel, but the business world converged on one office software product (Microsoft Office), on one search engine (Google), and on one online store (Amazon). While alternatives like Google Docs and Wayfair do exist, it's a common pattern in the technology market to see a single player, or a very limited few, gaining dominance. (Does anyone you know use Bing?). This consolidation occurs often as a desire for standardized solutions in a department, then within a company, then an industry, and eventually the world. Consequently, each instance of such technological consolidation results in a company assuming a near-monopoly position, posing a challenge for government regulators tasked with reintroducing healthy competition. That this history is likely to repeat itself in artificial general intelligence is most disconcerting. More specifically, the smartest system will likely get the most business, resulting in more customers and, as a result, their data. That added data will make them even smarter, resulting in even more customers with ever more data . . . and so on.

The concept of decentralization, the first component of Buterin's trivergence trilemma, in theory could offer a solution to this monopolistic trend. Decentralization, when faithfully implemented, entails shifting control and decision-making power from a single authority to a network of many participants, reducing the reliance on trust in a central entity and preventing excessive control. Decentralization and democratization were and still are core aspirations of blockchain, ideally removing the need for intermediaries across different sectors. Depending on the implementation, it could allow all network participants to collaborate toward achieving consensus on the state of the network.

If tokens are widely distributed, then no one person or organization can control or manipulate the data that is recorded and shared, nor the price of the associated crypto assets. It is true that crypto has the potential of being widely distributed, and a force for liberation and democratization.

Unfortunately, this aspiration has yet to materialize. So far, most, if not all, founders of these crypto networks have pre-allocated millions, if not billions, of tokens to themselves before launch. They were falsely marketed as a force for democratization[3], but today's implementations simply are not. For example, just 0.01% of bitcoin holders controls 27% of the currency in circulation.[4] For bitcoin the top 2.8 percent of wallet addresses control 95 percent of the supply.[5] With Ethereum, just 10 wallets control 31 percent[6]. What is clear from the wild swings in crypto prices is that their current prices are based on speculation not utility. For the founders of these crypto currencies, there are untold riches. For those that bought the hype in 2022, they suffered 2 trillion dollars in losses.[7] Buyer beware.

Today, it is difficult to determine to what degree the wild swings in crypto pricing are the result of radical and rapid change in people's perception of their value (speculators), or if they are being manipulated by the token rich founders, often referred to as "whales." If and when the intrinsic value of supporting smart contracts is known, we can hope for some price stabilization. Until then, it is risky to depend on a system of smart contracts whose future price (of tokens) to run, is a big unknown. That is not to say that distributed ledgers with widely distributed ownership can't exist, though I suspect regulation to that effect may be a prerequisite to less speculative use. The democratic aspirations of this original movement are still possible,

In this era of Trivergence, the principle of decentralization extends to IoT. With billions of connected devices producing enormous amounts of data, the success of the IoT ecosystem relies on providing services that are scalable, reliable, and high performing, while being available everywhere. Currently, most IoT software systems depend on middleware to coalesce the information before storing it on the cloud. For IoT, centralized remote systems can face challenges in terms of propagation delays, connectivity issues, and limited (or expensive) bandwidth, which may not be able to meet the diverse and time-sensitive needs of various IoT applications.

To overcome these limitations, new computing models are emerging, such as Mobile Edge Computing, Cloudlet, Fog Computing, and Transparent Computing. These distributed approaches bring computing power closer to the devices at the edge of the network, bridging the gap between the cloud and IoT devices. They can summarize the data that reflects the "normal" state and highlight the anomalies worthy of attention. This shift allows for faster and more efficient processing of data, and less network demand in meeting the specific requirements of different IoT applications. It also means that relevant information is reduced to the point where it can readily be stored on the cloud.

Decentralization is a construct under discussion in the realm of AI. Deep learning, a key aspect of AI, relies on vast amounts of data for training models and improving decision-making capabilities. Currently, only a few large technology companies, such as Facebook, Apple, Amazon, Microsoft, and Google "own" our data and have access to the computing power necessary to create generalized natural language processing systems such as ChatGPT. Advocates of Web3 argue, that a new paradigm should emerge where users own their own data so that we, as individuals might have more control over our part in these massive datasets that AI ingests enabling a less biased and democratic understanding of the world. To prevent that from happening, expect the trillion-dollar internet empire (known as FAAMG) to fight back. To regain control of our personal data, it will take a social movement. Time will tell. In the meantime, Consumer Reports now offers simple, free software that will request (and in some jurisdictions require) the tech companies to delete what they know about you. It can be found here.[8]

Security

Security is the second component of the trivergence trilemma, and it plays a crucial role in maintaining the integrity of any system. Blockchains, when properly implemented, can increase security and reliability. Buterin argues that there is a trade-off between network throughput (the speed at which transactions are processed) and decentralization. Having thousands, or even millions of redundant nodes doing the same thing is arguably more secure, though it is clearly far more expensive, and painfully slow. As someone who has designed many a system, redundancy and resulting fault tolerance is important, but to me thousands or even millions of levels of redundancy seem like overkill. The electricity bill for bitcoin alone is that of a small country. The argument for decentralization is that if it can disintermediate an expensive legacy player then it will be worth it.

Blockchains are a double-edged sword. When good data is logged into a blockchain, immutability is a great asset. When corrupt or hacked data is logged into a blockchain, its immutability is a liability. For some business models, it has proved to be a fatal one.

When smart contracts first emerged, they were highly limited in what could be coded in radically subsetted computer languages. Over the last decade, the various distributed ledger systems have become "Turing Complete" meaning that they now fully support powerful programming languages giving you the flexibility to build any system that you can imagine. That is unfortunately a double-edged sword. The more powerful and innovative the smart contract system is, the more code is written to execute it, the more likely the code has bugs, or worse, can be hacked. When your bug or the hacker's virus writes bad data into your immutable ledger, it may be the end of your business. Assuming that you can write bug-free code is certainly bold, but you need a hedge when that assumption is disproven. One crypto marketed how well they vetted their code, to then be hacked through open-source software they had used to build their system.

Achieving the right balance between scalability and security is a difficult task, if you plan on integrating blockchain into IoT environments that are exploding in number, though have limited computational resources. The existing security protocols for IoT—like Datagram Transport Layer Security (DTLS) and Transport Layer Security (TLS)—bring complexity and computational demands to IoT devices. Additionally, these protocols often require centralized management and governance, typically done through Public Key Infrastructure (PKI). The current challenges with PKI, including its resource demands and operational complexities, have prompted the exploration of decentralized and more efficient approaches for managing device identity and authentication in IoT networks.

Integrating AI into the system may further strengthen security. AI algorithms can analyze the vast amounts of data generated by IoT devices to identify patterns or behaviors that may indicate cyber threats such as malware, phishing attacks, or unauthorized access attempts. Through supervised and unsupervised learning algorithms, the AI component can continuously adapt and improve its ability to detect and mitigate potential security threats over time.

Scalability

In the context of the era of Trivergence, scalability refers to the ability of the entire system—comprising blockchain, IoT devices, and AI—to effectively handle the increasing volume, velocity, variety, and veracity of data generated by these interconnected components. It extends beyond traditional notions of scalability focused solely on transactional throughput. To achieve scalability in the era of Trivergence, it is necessary to address not only the performance demands and limitations of these networks, but also the interoperability, reliability, and efficiency of IoT devices and the massive computing power necessary to train and run AI algorithms.

To address the challenge of scalability in IoT systems, you can employ two key strategies: edge computing (EC) and fog computing (FC). Edge computing means placing computing resources, such as storage and processing power, close to where data is generated or used. This reduces delays and enables faster device responses, akin to having a nimble local computer rather than relying on distant data centers. Fog computing, on the other hand, acts as a mediator between the edge and the cloud within the IoT network. It expands upon edge computing by dispersing computing resources and services across various network points known as fog nodes or gateways. These nodes serve as local hubs for efficient data processing and analysis, working collaboratively with the edge devices. Once the data is summarized and the exceptions are noted, then you can connect to the cloud as necessary. This distributed approach overcomes the limitations of relying solely on a centralized cloud-based system, enhancing the speed and efficiency of data processing closer to the devices' location.

By employing AI, IoT systems can further optimize the resources, networks, and systems involved in edge computing. One important way AI helps improve IoT scalability is through a process called *task offloading*. This means transferring computational tasks from less powerful devices to more capable ones, typically from resource-constrained devices to intermediaries with more computing power. Another AI-driven technique is *selective sensing*—a method that carefully selects and focuses on the most relevant data in noisy environments with limited resources. By leveraging filtering logic, including AI algorithms in the sensing layer, we can extract the most important insights from the data while reducing network demand. The aim is to summarize and extract valuable data close to the source, minimizing data transmission and associated delays and costs. For example, when monitoring a person's heartbeat over the course of an hour, AI can condense the 59 minutes of regular heartbeats into a concise summary, while giving special attention to the noteworthy one-minute irregularity.

Interoperability

Interoperability is all about different systems, devices, or technologies being able to work together smoothly and exchange information effectively. In the era of Trivergence, technologies like AI, IoT, and blockchain each face their own set of challenges when it comes to interoperability. Modern coding standards, such as Amazon's API Mandate,[9] have greatly simplified efforts for interoperability, though there are still some daunting challenges. For instance, AI systems often have their own specific data formats, models, and interfaces that might not easily match with other technologies. This lack of plug and play compatibility can make it time consuming to integrate AI with other systems.

To address these issues, there are efforts like the Open Neural Network Exchange (ONNX).[10] It's an open-source ecosystem that brings together technology companies and research organizations. Their main goal is to establish interoperability between different deep learning frameworks such as TensorFlow, PyTorch, and Microsoft Cognitive Toolkit. With ONNX, models can be trained in one framework and then easily deployed in another. This promotes flexibility and interoperability in AI development, making it easier for different systems to work together.

In the world of IoT, there are many different types of devices that use various communication protocols, different data formats, and interfaces. Making all these devices work together smoothly and exchange data seamlessly is quite complicated because of these differences. Moreover, IoT systems generate huge amounts of data, and making sure this data can easily be shared and integrated with other technologies presents a significant challenge. To tackle these issues, there are organizations like the Open Connectivity Foundation and OneM2M that are dedicated to solving the problem of interoperability in IoT.[11] They focus on developing open standards and specifications that define how IoT devices can work together. These standards provide guidelines for discovering devices, establishing connections, and exchanging data across different IoT ecosystems. By establishing these open standards, these organizations are making it easier for IoT devices and platforms from different manufacturers to communicate with each other. This promotes compatibility and simplifies the integration of IoT systems with other technologies. Ultimately, their efforts aim to create a more connected and interoperable IoT environment where devices can work together seamlessly, regardless of their differences. When contemplating IoT implementations having them all conform to the same standard can make the benefits more easily accessible. This issue may require some serious upfront analysis.

To address interoperability challenges, collaboration is key. Your CIO needs to ensure that stakeholders from AI, blockchain, and IoT domains work together to develop common standards, protocols, and interoperability frameworks that bridge the gaps between these technologies. These frameworks should enable seamless integration, data exchange, and communication while accommodating the specific needs of each technology. Establishing technical standards is crucial to ensure compatibility and collaboration. This involves defining common data formats, communication protocols, and interfaces that facilitate the smooth integration of AI models, IoT devices, traditional databases and blockchain networks. These decisions may drive your choice of vendors. Furthermore, establishing semantic standards is equally important. Through these standards, stakeholders can define common data models, ontologies, and schemas that enable the consistent interpretation and exchange of information. This ensures that data from AI models, IoT devices, traditional databases, and blockchain networks can be effectively understood and utilized across the trivergence ecosystem.

By actively addressing interoperability challenges and promoting collaboration among stakeholders, we can achieve seamless interoperability between AI, blockchain, IoT, and other data sources. This opens opportunities for the development of robust and interconnected systems that fully harness the potential of data, intelligence, and trust. Ultimately, this fosters innovation and drives transformative outcomes in the era of Trivergence.

Software Limitations and Risks

Artificial Intelligence

AI's potential in the coming decade is truly staggering, offering the prospect of groundbreaking advances in almost everything, reshaping all aspects of our work and daily lives. However, alongside these remarkable possibilities, there are critical considerations for businesses and society. AI, if not handled cautiously, presents significant risks. One of the most pressing concerns in the realm of AI development revolves around the potential for misuse. Eminent figures in the AI community have even called for temporary pauses in its development due to the potential for catastrophic outcomes.[12] One of many concerns is that AI has the capacity to learn, adapt, and potentially operate autonomously. These characteristics present formidable challenges in terms of control and oversight, making responsible AI governance a paramount priority.

Recent advancements in neural networks enabled by smarter software and massive parallel processing, have led to deep learning's reemergence, from a 70-year history of try and fail, and try again. Neural networks, at the core of deep learning, can process an incomprehensible volume of data to draw conclusions, a feat far beyond we mortals.

One of the critical risks associated with AI is bias. If the training data contains biases or inaccuracies, AI models may well amplify them, potentially leading to discrimination and when caught, inevitable legal disputes. Neural networks have far too many nodes to give (to us) predictable outcomes, but unlike humans they can be asked to perform say a hundred thousand applicant screenings overnight. Humans are far better at hiding our biases. And once you have done the exhaustive training to minimize your systems bias, the introduction of the latest data has the risk of opening Pandora's box.

Despite these limitations and risks, AI continues to advance at an astonishing pace. The recent 40 percent improvement in accuracy from Chat-GPT 3.5 to ChatGPT 4 in less than four months underscores AI's recent explosive progress.[13] Expect it to continue. As businesses navigate this rapidly evolving landscape, they must remain vigilant, ensuring responsible AI development and addressing the ethical, legal, and operational challenges it presents.

Blockchain

Blockchain's immutability is a core feature that when properly implemented offers undeniable historical records that strengthen data integrity. As a back-end system, setting up a blockchain as an immutable ledger of activity is straightforward and widely accepted. It provides a transparent and powerful audit trail, bolstering trust within ecosystems and aiding auditing, debugging, and analysis. It has been called "the trust protocol." However, at the front end, this very immutability can be a double-edged sword. Once data is recorded on a blockchain, it becomes nearly impossible to alter or delete. In traditional databases, administrators can correct inaccuracies, but on a blockchain, errors will remain indefinitely. Businesses must implement rigorous testing and quality control measures to minimize the chances of erroneous data being added to the blockchain. When the near-inevitable bug or hack corrupts your data, you need to have built, pre-implementation, a plan to mitigate the damage.

Forgive my EUOA over the next few paragraphs. Oops, by that I mean my *excessive use of acronyms*. Originally, computer databases had no concept of what a business transaction was. If there was a transaction with one debit for $100 and three debits totaling $100 and the system crashed after posting, say only the $100 debit, your system would be out of balance. When this occurred, you had to be both a data scientist and a sleuth to find the problem. Eventually, a software solution was found in a database management system called SQL (or sequel) that understood what a transaction was. It would "commit" all the transactional data together or roll it back altogether. That way, you could ensure the debits equaled the credits. Today, these database management systems are atomic, consistent, isolated, and durable (ACID) databases.[14]

Historically, the best data management practices for synchronizing multiple databases were to have one central hub database that was updated and other spoke databases that synchronized to it. An example might be rates for a bank, where the central database was in the head office, and the replicated databases were in the branches. If you applied multiple-way replication, what happens if two branches do an update to a rate at about the same time? Which is right? Chaos. In pre-blockchain think, two-way replication was a recipe for disaster.[15] Personally, I would never have let such a construct survive a system design review.

To rise above this conundrum, Natashi Sakomoto had a simple, elegant, and heretical solution. When conflicts occur keep one transaction and throw out the rest. Then the system applies one transaction across all the databases, the direction of replication changing on a transaction-by-transaction basis. In blockchain speak when conflicts arise, the system keeps the transactions "on the longest chain." If there are small volumes of transactions, these will be a very rare event. If the blockchain is pushed near its full capacity, it will occur more often.

In distributed blockchains, Brewer's CAP theorem applies. It states that it's impossible to simultaneously achieve *consistency*, *availability*, and *partition tolerance* in a distributed system. Consistency refers to all nodes in the network having the same data at the same time, availability ensures that every request receives a response without guaranteeing it's the most recent data, and partition tolerance allows the system to continue functioning despite network splits.

So today, as distributed ledgers enter the world of finance, there needs to be a small adjustment to ensure that no deposits or withdrawals are discarded. Yes, the lower the activity on a distributed public blockchain the less likely this is to happen. But if your application is very low volume, on a public blockchain you still must worry. You need to remember that it is about all the applications on that public blockchain (or shard), not just your own. Although a challenge, this is far from a fatal limitation.

In distributed ledgers, integrity in transactions can be achieved through what is called an ordering service. Here one of the nodes is arbitrarily assigned to validate and order the transactions for the current block and another arbitrary node is assigned to do the same for the next. To blockchain purists, any hint of even temporary centralization may be unacceptable. But to enter the world of banking and go beyond the prototyping stage, a financial system cannot drop transactions, even rarely. The two reasons why the aspirations of the last decade for wide and deep penetration of distributed ledger technology into various industries have not materialized, are one the possibility of lost transactions and two, the need to acquire highly speculative crypto to power them. I suspect that this could soon change. Today, Hyperledger Fabric has an ordering service[16] and Hashgraph[17] and FlureeDB[18], are also ACID compliant.

The implications of quantum computing on blockchain could be profound. If quantum computers advance to the point where they can efficiently crack cryptographic keys, the security of existing blockchains (and many other things) may be compromised. Transactions could become vulnerable to unauthorized access and alteration, potentially undermining trust in blockchain-based systems. To mitigate this threat, ongoing research is focused on developing post-quantum cryptographic algorithms that are resistant to quantum attacks. Transitioning to these quantum-resistant algorithms in a timely manner will be crucial to ensuring the long-term security and integrity of existing distributed blockchain networks in the trivergent age. The million traditional computers competing to win the next crypto will soon find that they can't compete. When quantum computing can win every PoW or PoS challenge, then those who are the first to be quantum enabled would be wise to win say every 20th crypto lottery, and not win them all, protecting the value of the cryptocurrency, and making a fortune in the process!

Internet of Things

One of the significant challenges in the IoT landscape is ensuring that devices remain secure and functional over time. This requires regular firmware and software updates to patch vulnerabilities, introduce new features, or enhance device performance. However, managing updates in IoT ecosystems can be a daunting task. Many IoT devices are designed for low-power or resource-constrained environments, making them less capable of handling frequent software updates.

Manual intervention is often required to initiate updates, and users may not be aware of the need for these updates or find the process cumbersome. As a result, many IoT devices remain unpatched, leaving them susceptible to known security vulnerabilities. Manufacturers must prioritize building mechanisms for automated and secure updates into IoT device designs to ensure that these devices can receive critical patches in a timely manner. This requires a shift in mindset, with a focus on long-term support and maintenance.

A second IoT software challenge is related to the power constraints of IoT devices. A significant portion of IoT devices operate on battery power or have limited access to continuous power sources. Optimizing software to operate efficiently under these power constraints is vital. Power-efficient programming involves minimizing energy consumption during both active and idle states. For example, devices can be programmed to enter low-power sleep modes when not actively collecting or transmitting data, thus extending battery life.

However, power optimization can be complex, as it often involves trade-offs between performance and energy efficiency. Striking the right balance is critical, especially for IoT applications where battery replacement or recharging is impractical, such as remote environmental sensors or wearable health devices. Advanced techniques like dynamic voltage scaling and asynchronous processing can be employed to manage power consumption effectively, but these optimizations require specialized knowledge and careful software design.

Finally, a third IoT software challenge is related to latency and real-time processing. In many IoT applications, real-time or low-latency processing is essential. For instance, autonomous vehicles must make split-second decisions, and industrial automation systems require precise timing for coordinated operations. Achieving low-latency processing in IoT environments can be challenging due to the inherent complexities of data transmission and processing.

IoT data typically flows through multiple layers of the network before reaching its destination, which can introduce latency. To address this, software developers must prioritize optimizing data routing and processing. As discussed previously, edge and fog computing—where data processing occurs closer to the data source—can help reduce latency by minimizing the distance data needs to travel. Additionally, real-time operating systems (RTOS) and specialized hardware accelerators can be used to ensure rapid response times.

Furthermore, IoT developers often rely on messaging protocols like MQTT or CoAP, which are designed for efficient and low-latency communication. Implementing Quality of Service (QoS) mechanisms within these protocols can prioritize critical messages, ensuring they are processed with minimal delay. In essence, optimizing for low-latency and real-time processing in IoT software involves careful architecture design and a focus on reducing data transit times, which are crucial for applications where timing is of the essence.

Social Challenges

Speculation and Hype

As with any emerging technology, one of the major social challenges we face in the era of Trivergence is the excessive hype and speculation surrounding AI, IoT, and especially blockchain technologies. Many decades ago, Gartner described this phenomenon as new technologies at first reaching the "peak of inflated expectations," which is followed by the subsequent "trough of disillusionment" then as reality slowly sets in a rising slope of enlightenment as the technology proves useful.[19] Gartner argued that eventually, expectations and reality align into a "plateau of productivity."

Today, AI is climbing the rising slope while blockchain is deep in its trough. Media sensationalism, hype-driven public relations, questionable marketing practices, and the spread of misinformation creates an environment where expectations are often blown out of proportion, and irrational investment behavior is common. This issue is further amplified by the influence of social media and behavioral economics, leading to a phenomenon known as the fear of missing out (FOMO) and the resulting impulsive decision-making.

The bubble for crypto currency defied all logic, burning smaller investors for trillions. The regulators were surprisingly late to the table and did not protect naïve investors. Historically, those that print private currency are soon shutdown by the regulators.[20] With crypto for reasons that are difficult to understand, this did not happen.

The launch of cryptocurrencies fascinated many including anarchists and libertarians, fiscal conservatives, the young, everyone in countries with unstable currencies, and many others disenchanted by the tsunami of government spending accelerated by the pandemic. The value of Bitcoin and other digital assets originally exploded, making the founders instant billionaires. Smaller investors who entered the market later were burnt with $2 trillion in losses. We need to approach these technologies with a discerning mindset, questioning exaggerated claims and seeking reliable sources of information. Ironically, these external factors may contribute to the wild swings in the price of crypto assets, thus interfering with the adoption of smart contracts that need stable crypto pricing to gain credibility.

Ideally, collaboration among industry, academia, and regulatory bodies is essential in promoting ethical practices, ensuring accurate reporting, and fostering responsible investment. By fostering responsible engagement, education, critical thinking, and transparent communication, we may be able to reduce the inevitable speculation and hype in the era of Trivergence and approach these transformative technologies in a more balanced and informed way. Hopefully, generations X, Y, and Z may develop skills here that much of the boomer generation seems to have forgotten. The bottom line on crypto is that today its mostly speculation about the value of bits. The sudden rise and then collapse of so-called non-fungible tokens being a case in point. Buyer beware.

Effective regulation in the era of Trivergence is not just a necessity but a cornerstone for fostering responsible innovation. Regulations provide a framework for ethical behavior, accountability, and risk management. In this sense, businesses are not only dealing with rapid technological advancements but also facing a complex global regulatory landscape. The era of Trivergence transcends borders, making the global regulatory landscape elusive. For businesses operating on a global scale, this poses challenges and for the unscrupulous it also offers opportunities. Navigating a patchwork of regulations should require a comprehensive strategy that ensures compliance across jurisdictions. Beware of cryptos that hide in remote jurisdictions or claim to operate in no jurisdiction at all.

The challenges posed by this intricate web of regulations are particularly evident in the context of each trivergence technology. On the AI front, different countries have varying approaches to regulation. For example, the EU has proposed the Artificial Intelligence Act, which aims to create a comprehensive framework for AI regulation. This proposed regulation explicitly addresses high-risk AI systems, mandating that they meet rigorous ethical and safety standards. It imposes fines for non-compliance, reinforcing the importance of adhering to ethical guidelines. In contrast, the United States has a more decentralized approach, with regulatory oversight dispersed among different agencies, such as the Federal Trade Commission (FTC) and the National Institute of Standards and Technology (NIST). OpenAI's CEO, Sam Altman, emphasizes the essential role of regulation and expresses eagerness to collaborate in shaping policies. The challenge lies in avoiding a scenario where those deeply embedded in the AI industry will have the lobbying power to influence the regulatory framework to their advantage. I and others[21] are somewhat pessimistic here.

The Internet of Things presents similar challenges, as connected devices transcend national boundaries. IoT regulations often revolve around data privacy, security, and interoperability. For instance, the European Union's GDPR has strict requirements for data protection and user consent, impacting IoT devices that collect personal data. The United States has seen state-wide initiatives like the California Consumer Privacy Act (CCPA) with implications for IoT device manufacturers and service providers. Other countries, such as Japan, have introduced cybersecurity guidelines for IoT manufacturers to ensure the security of connected devices.

Blockchain technology, known for its borderless and decentralized nature, faces regulatory challenges related to financial transactions, digital assets, and smart contracts. Some countries, like Switzerland and Singapore, have embraced blockchain and cryptocurrency innovation, creating regulatory sandboxes to encourage experimentation. Others, like China, have imposed strict regulations on cryptocurrency trading and initial coin offerings (ICOs). The United States has a patchwork of regulations at both federal and state levels, with agencies like the Securities and Exchange Commission (SEC), the Commodity Futures Trading Commission (CFTC), the Federal Trade Commission (FTC), and the Department of the Treasury providing (potentially conflicting) guidance on digital assets.

In the cryptocurrency domain, regulatory oversight has historically been lax, exposing the industry to vulnerabilities and tarnishing its reputation. Recent SEC lawsuits against major players like Binance, Coinbase, and Ripple indicate a belated yet necessary intervention, particularly in the aftermath of the 2022 collapse of FTX and other crypto scandals. However, it's important to understand that the collapse of companies like FTX is not inherent to the technology itself but is instead attributed to the hubris or incompetence of those wielding it. FTX's downfall exemplifies the risks associated with a "too big to fail" organization, echoing the concerns initially voiced by Bitcoin's creator, Satoshi Nakamoto, who sought to circumvent such centralized vulnerabilities. As regulatory bodies step in to address these issues, it becomes essential to distinguish between the inherent potential of the technology and the consequences of the absence of governance.

Regulations are constantly evolving. Businesses should implement systems for ongoing monitoring and compliance updates to ensure that they remain aligned with the changing regulatory landscape. Regulation is not solely about compliance; it also shapes organizational culture. In the era of Trivergence, a culture of ethical innovation is not born out of fear of regulatory penalties but from a genuine commitment to responsible practices. Business leaders must champion ethical innovation, embedding it into their company's DNA. This involves proactive engagement with regulatory bodies to provide input on regulations that impact their industry. Collaboration between industry leaders and regulators can result in regulations that foster innovation rather than impede it.

Privacy

The era of Trivergence has brought about a profound transformation in the landscape of personal data ownership, challenging the dominance of tech giants and reshaping the discourse on privacy in our interconnected world. Prior to the era of Trivergence, concerns about data security and privacy were heightened as companies like Google, Apple, and Amazon wielded unparalleled control over individuals' personal information. The widespread deployment of surveillance technologies, geo-locators, online trackers, and wearables intensified these concerns, sparking debates on the boundaries of personal privacy.

In the healthcare sector, for example, there is a significant challenge related to the rapid growth of IoT data, which includes information from Electronic Health Records (EHR) systems, wearable devices, pacemakers, labs, and other sources. This abundance of data holds immense potential for new business models and medical research. However, healthcare practitioners understandably have reservations about sharing sensitive patient information due to privacy concerns.

To address this challenge, different regions have implemented regulations to protect personal health data. In the United States, the Health Insurance Portability and Accountability Act (HIPAA) sets standards for safeguarding health data. In Europe, the General Data Protection Regulation (GDPR) emphasizes clear communication with users about their data and provides protection. Similarly, regulations like the California Consumer Privacy Act (CCPA) and China's Internet Security Law also prioritize data security.

While these regulations are essential for protecting privacy, they create challenges for researchers and data analysts who need to comply with multiple regulations when working with data from different sources. This complexity can slow down progress in medical research. Furthermore, medical data generated by IoT devices, such as wearables or remote monitoring devices, is constantly evolving. It may include real-time measurements and updates, requiring researchers to merge and analyze the data repeatedly to both protect privacy and obtain meaningful insights. This iterative process of data merging adds an additional layer of complexity to the research, compared to accessing the data just once. Researchers must ensure the accuracy and integrity of the merged data while complying with the relevant regulations, further complicating their work.

The introduction of AI in medical IoT systems presents additional challenges related to data privacy and related regulations. Consequently, important and valuable data often goes unused, which restricts the potentially revolutionary insights that AI can bring. To address this, new techniques have been developed in the field of Collaborative and Privacy-Preserving Machine Learning (PPML).[22] One popular technique is called *Federated Learning*, which allows machine learning models to be trained using distributed data without the need to exchange sensitive information. Another technique, called *Homomorphic Encryption*, allows computations to be performed on encrypted data, ensuring that privacy is maintained throughout the analysis process. *Secure Multi-Party Computation* is a method that allows participants to jointly perform computations together while keeping their inputs private. This technique ensures that sensitive information remains protected during collective analysis. Additionally, *Differential Privacy* introduces controlled noise to sensitive data, striking a balance between privacy protection and meaningful analysis.

In the era of Trivergence, blockchain technology has emerged as a game-changer, enabling decentralized and tamper-resistant storage of personal data. This shift from centralized databases to blockchain may empower individuals to own and control their personal information through cryptographic keys, reducing reliance on centralized authorities. Smart contracts introduce programmable and automated agreements for managing data consent. Users can define granular privacy controls, specifying how their data is accessed or shared. This dynamic and automated approach ensures that data usage aligns with predefined conditions, offering users responsive mechanisms for controlling their information.

Overall, the era of Trivergence marks a paradigm shift where individuals could regain control over their personal data, challenging the traditional dominance of tech giants. Blockchain, smart contracts, and innovative techniques in AI and privacy preservation are pivotal in this transformation. As we navigate this era, it is crucial to strike a balance between leveraging the potential of data for revolutionary insights and safeguarding privacy rights. The empowerment of individuals in data ownership aligns with the principles of autonomy and user-centricity, promising a future where privacy is not compromised in the pursuit of technological advancements.

Governance

Governance refers to how decisions are made and implemented in organizations, communities, or societies. When it comes to technologies like AI, blockchain, and IoT, governance is about the principles, policies, and practices that guide their development and use. It includes creating rules and mechanisms to ensure responsible and ethical use, as well as addressing concerns like data privacy, security, and accountability. Governance also involves setting standards and regulations to promote transparency, trust, and compliance. It includes involving stakeholders, making decisions, and managing risks to handle the social, legal, and ethical impacts of these technologies. Effective governance frameworks help maximize the benefits of these technologies while minimizing risks and aligning with what society expects and values.

While the rapid advancements in AI, IoT, and blockchain are reshaping industries and societies, they also present challenges for traditional governance models. In traditional hierarchical organizations, managers and reporting lines are ultimately responsible to a board of directors and majority shareholders. In the era of Trivergence, technologies create complexities in addressing vital concerns like data privacy, security, and ethics. To address these challenges, we must develop new approaches and frameworks to ensure the responsible and ethical use of these technologies.

For example, decentralized autonomous organizations (DAOs) have re-emerged as one possible solution to governance challenges in the era of Trivergence. DAOs are like software programs that run on blockchains and are, in theory, not controlled by any central authority. They operate through a set of rules encoded in smart contracts, which encourage transparency, security, and accountability. In this approach, decision-making is reflected through code rather than by a select few individuals. In a regulated environment, DAOs could introduce governance tokens, empowering holders to actively participate in decision-making—a potentially impactful concept. These tokens could be used for voting on proposals or staking on specific initiatives.

Consider a hypothetical example of a DAO dedicated to advancing trivergence technologies in smart cities. This DAO's specific mission is to back projects promoting sustainable urban development, enhancing citizen well-being, and improving resource management. Citizens participating in this DAO would possess the right to vote and influence fund allocation. Project teams can submit proposals seeking financial support for their trivergence-based initiatives. For instance, a team of researchers might present a proposal for an AI-powered system optimizing energy usage in smart buildings, explaining how it aligns with the DAO's objectives—like reducing energy consumption and enhancing environmental sustainability. DAO token holders review the proposal, assess its potential impact, and vote on funding. If the project proves profitable in the long run, returns could fund other DAO initiatives. Upon receiving sufficient votes, the DAO allocates funds to support the project. This approach, maintaining widespread ownership, enables the DAO to foster innovation in trivergence technologies by providing financial support to initiatives aligned with its objectives.

In the absence of regulation, caution is necessary. Some founders or other entities may exploit the concept of decentralization to make deceptive claims, masking a centralized control structure. This deceptive practice often involves the pre-allocation of tokens, where founders retain a disproportionate number, contradicting the essence of decentralization. To address this issue, projects should provide detailed information about the allocation of tokens among founders, developmental teams, and the public, ensuring that investors and participants are aware of the distribution structure. If ownership of governance tokens remains widely distributed, DAOs could stimulate innovation in trivergence technologies by offering financial resources to initiatives that match its objectives.

Another framework to consider is the Decentralized Resource Governance (DRG) model, developed by the Blockchain Research Institute in collaboration with Input Output and Boston Consulting Group.[23] The DRG framework combines the transparency, democratization, and decentralization offered by blockchain solutions with well-established principles of management and oversight. The DRG framework provides a way to govern initiatives, allowing for efficient allocation of resources, shaping of events, and meaningful engagement of many stakeholders in co-creating a decentralized future. By integrating both bottom-up and top-down approaches, DRG may ensure sustained productivity, competitiveness, and integrity within the ecosystem, setting the stage for effective decentralized governance.

Access and Inclusivity

Ensuring equitable access to trivergence technologies is crucial for harnessing their transformative potential, yet addressing this challenge remains elusive. By 2030, AI alone is projected to boost world GDP by 21 percent, potentially lifting billions out of poverty. However, the critical question is, who stands to gain from these advancements? In the pursuit of efficiency and profit, we may inadvertently face potential displacement by the very tools designed to assist us.

The challenge of access to trivergence technologies is multifaceted. True access goes beyond mere connectivity, requiring the provision of resources, infrastructure, and supportive environments that empower individuals across diverse backgrounds to utilize and benefit from AI, blockchain, and IoT. It demands breaking down barriers and offering equal opportunities, regardless of geographic location, socioeconomic status, or physical ability. Despite this vision, trivergence technologies, in the short term, may widen the digital divide.

One example of a barrier to accessing trivergence technologies is the lack of reliable high-speed internet in certain rural or remote areas. Because trivergence technologies heavily rely on internet connectivity, people living in these regions may face challenges in accessing and using these transformative technologies. The full deployment of Elon Musk's Starlink combined with wider distribution of 5G will help. Another barrier may be the cost associated with trivergence technologies. Limited financial resources hinder access to the compute power, internet services, IoT devices, and necessary tools to leverage this new paradigm. Additionally, a lack of digital literacy skills poses another barrier to access. Individuals who lack the necessary skills to navigate and leverage these technologies may find themselves excluded from the opportunities they present.

On the other hand, "inclusivity" refers to the principle of embracing diversity and accommodating the needs, perspectives, and experiences of all within the era of Trivergence. It involves designing and implementing technologies, policies, and practices that do not exclude or marginalize any group or individual. This approach considers the diverse needs, preferences, and abilities of individuals, with the aim of fostering a welcoming, accessible, and supportive environment for all users. Inclusivity prioritizes equity, fairness, and the elimination of barriers to participation, ensuring that everyone has an equal opportunity to engage with, contribute to, and benefit from trivergence technologies.

One key aspect of addressing this challenge is through inclusive design and user experience. This involves engaging diverse user groups and incorporating their perspectives throughout the design process. Conducting user research, usability testing, and gathering feedback from individuals with diverse abilities, backgrounds, and experiences can help identify barriers and inform design decisions. For example, consider a smart home automation system that relies heavily on voice commands as the primary mode of interaction. Users are required to verbally control various devices and perform tasks such as adjusting lighting, temperature, and security settings. However, this design overlooks individuals with speech disabilities, those hard of hearing, or those who may not be comfortable using voice commands due to privacy concerns.

Feedback from users with diverse abilities and experiences can shed light on the importance of finding different ways to interact with technology. For instance, people with speech impediments might suggest incorporating visual interfaces or gesture-based controls instead of relying solely on voice commands. Those with hearing impairments might request visual or tactile cues to ensure they can effectively engage with the system. To make the design more inclusive, developers would incorporate these suggestions into subsequent iterations. They could add visual cues, written prompts, and haptic feedback to enhance accessibility for people with hearing or visual impairments. They could also allow users to personalize settings, adjusting how the system responds to their unique needs.

In the era of Trivergence, prioritizing inclusive design and user experience is not only a matter of ethical responsibility but also a strategic imperative. By ensuring that trivergence technologies are accessible and inclusive, we can unlock the full potential of these transformative technologies, foster equal opportunities, and create a future where innovation and progress benefit everyone.

Notes

1. www.theatlantic.com/technology/archive/2023/09/books3-database-generative-ai-training-copyright-infringement/675363
2. Buterin, Vitalik. "Why Sharding Is Great: Demystifying the Technical Properties," April 7, 2021. https://vitalik.ca/general/2021/04/07/sharding.html.
3. https://medium.com/@VitalikButerin/liberation-through-radical-decentralization-22fc4bedc2ac
4. www.wsj.com/articles/bitcoins-one-percent-controls-lions-share-of-the-cryptocurrencys-wealth-11639996204
5. https://finance.yahoo.com/news/five-reasons-why-bitcoin-wealth-155752613.html
6. https://news.bitcoin.com/exploring-crypto-whale-concentration-unveiling-the-rich-lists-of-the-top-10-cryptocurrencies
7. www.cnbc.com/2022/11/11/crypto-peaked-in-nov-2021-investors-lost-more-than-2-trillion-since.html
8. https://permissionslipcr.com
9. Biehl, Matthias. "The API Mandate — Install API Thinking at Your Company." API-University (blog), March 27, 2020. https://medium.com/api-university/the-api-mandate-install-api-thinking-at-your-company-4335433b7d0b.
10. Open Neural Network Exchange. https://onnx.ai, accessed 14 June, 2023.
11. Open Connectivity Foundation. https://openconnectivity.org, accessed 19 June 2023; OneM2M. www.onem2m.org, accessed 19 June 2023.
12. Roose, Kevin. "A.I. Poses 'Risk of Extinction,' Industry Leaders Warn." *The New York Times*, May 30, 2023, sec. Technology. www.nytimes.com/2023/05/30/technology/ai-threat-warning.html.
13. OpenAI. "GPT-4 Technical Report." arXiv, March 27, 2023. https://doi.org/10.48550/arXiv.2303.08774.
14. www.datasciencecentral.com/understand-the-acid-and-base-in-modern-data-engineering

15. https://medium.com/brainendeavor/2-way-data-synchroniza
    tion-is-often-a-lazy-and-naive-strategy-9c7d0c08b572
16. https://developer.ibm.com/articles/blockchain-hyperledger-
    fabric-ordering-decentralization
17. https://docs.hedera.com/hedera/core-concepts/hashgraph-
    consensus-algorithms
18. www.infoq.com/presentations/flureedb
19. Linden, A, and J. Fenn. "Understanding Gartner's Hype Cycles,"
    May 30, 2003. http://ask-force.org/web/Discourse/Linden-
    HypeCycle-2003.pdf.
20. www.clevelandfed.org/publications/economic-commentary/2007/
    ec-20070101-private-money-in-our-past-present-and-future
21. www.newyorker.com/news/daily-comment/congress-really-
    wants-to-regulate-ai-but-no-one-seems-to-know-how
22. Firouzi, Farshad, Shiyi Jiang, Krishnendu Chakrabarty, Bahar Farahani,
    Mahmoud Daneshmand, Jaeseung Song, and Kunal Mankodiya. "Fusion
    of IoT, AI, Edge-Fog-Cloud, and Blockchain: Challenges, Solutions,
    and a Case Study in Healthcare and Medicine." *IEEE Internet of Things
    Journal* 10, no. 5 (March 1, 2023): 3686–3705. https://doi.og/10.1109/
    JIOT.2022.3191881.
23. Input Output, Boston Consulting Group, and Blockchain Research
    Institute. "Decentralized Resource Governance: A New Model of
    Engagement, Execution, and Trust." Research Brief. Blockchain
    Research Institute, June 2022. www.blockchainresearchinstitute
    .org/project/decentralized-resource-governance.

9

The Executive Guide to the Era of Trivergence

The era of Trivergence is a defining moment in both business and technology history. We are amid a significant shift in the ways that businesses are organized, innovate, and create value. More specifically, it will redefine the relationships between shareholders, suppliers, producers, and consumers, resulting in more automated, less human-intensive processes than those that exist today. Traditional corporate structures, with their multilevel, inward-focused, hierarchical command-and-control systems, are no longer effective. Yet many businesses struggle to adapt to new ways of operating because they are constrained by traditional mindsets, legacy technology systems, and entrenched organizational cultures. Worse, because they lack vision of what their future architecture should be, and a plan to attain it, firms often perpetuate these legacy perspectives with each new investment.

This situation has created a "demand pull" for a new paradigm in enterprise architecture as we enter the era of Trivergence. Simultaneously, there is a "technology push" from these emerging technologies themselves. AI, empowered by a new generation of massively parallel reduced instruction set computers (RISC), can analyze vast amounts of data, discover new patterns and even insights, and make intelligent predictions. Additionally, AI can now recognize individuals by their facial geometry and walking patterns; generate coherent paragraphs, essays, and even books; compose music; write software and make decisions. When implemented correctly, blockchains enhance trust and transparency, keeping all involved parties informed about historical and current conditions. Furthermore, the IoT connects physical objects and devices, providing real-time proactive insights for critical aspects of businesses.

There is now an emerging consensus on how these three technologies can transform many if not most businesses. This has far-reaching implications for your business strategy. So-called "strategic plans" for information technology of the past are being bypassed as Trivergence technologies become part of the business strategy itself. Today, every business strategy will have a technological component just as it might have a component dealing with marketing, financial, and human resources. It's not merely about implementing the latest buzzwords; it's about understanding how these technologies can create value and drive business objectives. It requires organizations to evaluate their readiness, assess the unique challenges and opportunities in their industry, and chart a clear path for integration. Gone are the days of "big bang" implementations. Instead, a gradual migration toward a cloud-based target architecture, taken in well-managed incremental steps, can help reduce costs, enhance flexibility, and position the company to harness the potential of the Trivergence era.

In this chapter, we will delve into practical recommendations and key considerations for business leaders to evaluate their organizational readiness, vision, and strategy for the era of Trivergence. By engaging with these recommendations and considerations, business leaders can position themselves and their organizations to thrive, capitalizing on the immense potential of AI, the blockchain, and the IoT to drive growth, innovation, and sustainable competitive advantage.

Evaluating Organizational Readiness

Incorporating Trivergence into your business strategy requires a thorough evaluation of your organization's readiness to embrace these transformative technologies. It involves assessing various factors to determine whether your organization has the necessary foundation, resources, and capabilities to leverage AI, blockchain, and the IoT effectively. By conducting a comprehensive evaluation, you can identify strengths, weaknesses, and areas of improvement to guide your Trivergence journey.

Identify Business Objectives and Opportunities

Aligning Trivergence technologies with your business objectives is essential for successful integration. Evaluate your organization's strategic goals, both short-term and long-term. Identify the areas where AI, blockchain, and the IoT can have the greatest impact on achieving these objectives. Consider how these technologies can improve operational efficiency, enhance customer experiences, drive innovation, and open new business opportunities.

While these considerations are essential, they may not be enough on their own. Some lateral thinking is necessary. Involving recent graduates who bring fresh knowledge and creativity to the table is vital. Create a thought experiment of what a new company harnessing these technologies could do to disrupt your business. Shift your focus from merely competing to challenging your existing operational paradigms and, where possible, murder your competitors in the process.

It's important to recognize that the current AI revolution is fundamentally driven by data. Therefore, a robust data strategy is now critically important. Establish a data strategy that captures and retains a wide range of relevant information, ensuring it can be effectively utilized by AI engines. Data is the new oil. A collaborative data access strategy with stakeholders in your ecosystem can help maximize the potential of Trivergence technologies. The more credible data you can gather, the greater the intelligence of your AI engines. Initiate a corporate commitment to acquiring data with the understanding that as your software capabilities improve, you'll translate these insights into action.

Opportunities may also arise from data that spans your entire ecosystem, including customers, suppliers, and their suppliers. For instance, if your support service archives all past customer queries and interactions, that is useful. Additionally, if you have obtained customer feedback after each interaction, that is powerful. By strategically utilizing data and leveraging Trivergence technologies, businesses can unlock a wide array of possibilities and create significant value for their organization.

Review Existing Infrastructure

The next step in the integration process is to double-check that you have a solid understanding of your existing technological infrastructure. Know your organization's hardware, software, networks, and systems to understand their capabilities, limitations, and compatibility with Trivergence technologies. Pay particular attention to data integrity and security as these are critical considerations when incorporating AI, blockchain, and the IoT.

With AI now being used by foreign governments and large criminal organizations, evaluate the security of your data management practices, including storage, transmission, and access control, to identify potential vulnerabilities. Ensure your organization has plans in place to safeguard data privacy, confidentiality, and protection against cyber threats when integrating Trivergence technologies into your cloud environment. Following best practices for cloud security is essential, especially for IoT devices, which are often remote and difficult to access, making them prime targets for cybercriminals. To secure IoT devices effectively, consider investing in high-quality, secure devices to protect your entire network. Segment your networks to prevent breaches in one area from compromising others and maintain a detailed map and inventory of IoT devices, including hardware, firmware/software, and passwords. Regularly update device software when available, and avoid using default passwords, opting for strong, randomized ones instead. If you can't update your IoT network's passwords and software, develop a plan to replace those older devices with more secure ones.

Furthermore, it's important to realize that even with your best security practices in place, your systems may still get compromised. To prepare for such situations, ensure you have the essential resources and tools on hand, if possible offline, to get your systems back up and running after a significant cyberattack. For real-time databases, ensure you have logs of the updates to, post hack, and re-create correctly what may have been compromised. If time and resources permit, conduct tests to ensure your recovery plan works as intended. In some industries, that is regulated. Additionally, when possible, create immutable logs of system activities that cannot be tampered with to help speed up the process of restoring your systems.

If you are a newly appointed CIO, reviewing historical technology adoption patterns within your organization may provide valuable insights. Identify technologies that have been successfully implemented in the past and learn from previous experiences and challenges. By understanding your organization's strengths and weaknesses in technology adoption, you can develop strategies for a smoother integration of Trivergence technologies. This comprehensive review of your existing infrastructure and technology adoption history will help ensure a successful and more secure integration of AI, blockchain, and the IoT into your organization's operations.

Assess the Digital Skills and Attitudes of Your Workforce

In the Trivergence era, effectively integrating AI, the blockchain, and the IoT technologies into your business strategy requires a thorough understanding of your workforce's digital skills and attitudes. Identify skill gaps and opportunities for growth to stay ahead in the rapidly evolving technological landscape. Determine which areas will require upskilling, training, or recruitment of specialized talent.

This is not a one-off. As Trivergence technologies continue to advance, it is crucial to maintain a culture of continuous learning, as the demand for AI expertise, for instance, is projected to far outpace supply in the coming decade. Encourage employees to embrace new technologies and seek opportunities to apply them creatively to solve business challenges. An organization that cultivates a growth mindset and openness to change will be better positioned to leverage the full potential of Trivergence technologies.

Recognize the transformative impact of AI on various white-collar jobs. Emphasize the importance of AI upskilling your existing workforce rather than viewing it as a replacement for human roles. For example, AI can streamline tasks such as generating initial drafts of analysis, reports, and blogs freeing up employees to focus on higher-value analysis and decision-making.

Providing basic programming skills to a broader group of staff, enabling them to access tools such as ChatGPT's open API, will distinguish your organization, showcasing a powerful combination of human intelligence and AI capabilities. Should they encounter any coding challenges, they can simply seek assistance from ChatGPT. By embracing these emerging technologies, you can position yourself as an indispensable asset to your organization, and the rewards will reflect this commitment.

By engaging key stakeholders throughout the assessment process, such as employees, managers, and technology users, you create a sense of ownership and collaboration in the integration journey. Avoid platitudes where possible, and act in good faith. Gather feedback, conduct surveys, interviews, or focus groups to understand their experiences, challenges, and suggestions.

Ultimately, the successful integration of AI, the blockchain, and the IoT technologies relies on a skilled and adaptable workforce. A workforce that embraces the Trivergence era with enthusiasm and continues to acquire new digital skills will be better prepared to drive innovation, efficiency, and success in this transformative technological landscape.

Deliberating Key Considerations

Integrating Trivergence technologies into your business strategy requires some analysis of the potential risks, costs, and benefits involved. By weighing these considerations, you can make informed decisions and develop mitigation strategies to ensure successful integration. Given the low cost of these cloud-based services, some experimentation is appropriate. The following are the key steps to consider.

Identify Risks and Trade-Offs

Incorporating Trivergence technologies into your business strategy involves inherent risks that need to be carefully managed to ensure success. Failures, particularly when they come at a low cost, can provide valuable learning experiences. Some of the executives I have had the pleasure of working with strongly believe that no decision is a far better choice than the risk of a wrong one. The cloud has upended that paradigm. Encourage low-cost experimentation.

An essential aspect to evaluate are the trade-offs associated with the Trivergence trilemma, particularly regarding security. Balancing the need for secure, scalable, and where appropriate decentralized systems requires a careful examination of potential vulnerabilities. Deep learning systems, while offering improved intelligence, also carry the risk of biased or erroneous results. It is important to consider the legal implications, such as anti-discrimination laws, when deploying AI solutions. Testing and monitoring for bias in algorithms can help mitigate this risk and ward off potential litigation.

When incorporating distributed blockchain solutions, it is critical to mitigate the risk of bugs or hackers inserting incorrect records into the immutable blockchain. The reliability of knowing that validated transactions are securely recorded in the ledger is a powerful advantage. However, any immutable error resulting from a hack or a bug can be detrimental, even fatal, to a business relying on a distributed blockchain. It is essential to bear in mind that in distributed ledgers, there is no central authority to call to resolve such errors, making prevention and robust security measures of utmost importance.

Compliance with relevant regulations and laws is also crucial. Identify the specific legal and regulatory requirements pertaining to your industry. For example, in the field of AI, it may be wise to consider compliance with the EU's regulatory framework, such as the AI Act, as it could provide valuable insight into potential future regulations in North America.[1] Additionally, consider EU and Californian privacy policies to prevent the inclusion of data that "has the right to be forgotten" into an immutable ledger. By proactively addressing compliance considerations, implementing data protection measures, and thoroughly testing and vetting algorithmic decision-making, you can mitigate compliance risks and demonstrate a commitment to ethical practices. This not only helps you avoid legal penalties and reputational damage but also builds trust among your customers and stakeholders. As the general population learns how disruptive the Trivergence will be, expect the unexpected in regulations.

Assess Costs and Resource Requirements

Optimizing your cloud spend is the new paradigm for capacity planning. Designing your systems to reliably span multiple data centers is a science. Doing so at an optimal spend is an art. Having professionally trained cloud staff can lead to significant cost savings, especially when designing systems to reliably span multiple data centers. Leveraging off-peak hours for training AI models can also result in substantial discounts.

While the CFO may request up-front cost and benefit estimates, the dynamic nature of Trivergence technologies calls for a more iterative approach. Rather than providing fixed estimates, it's best to fine-tune your approach as you gain a deeper understanding of the potential benefits. Adopting an iterative Agile or Lean methodology with a DevOps implementation strategy is ideal for these technologies. Many major corporations are likely already following this path to efficiently manage resources and costs throughout the integration process.

Evaluate Potential Benefits

Organizations that effectively integrate Trivergence technologies can expect to achieve improved operational efficiency and enhanced customer experiences. By leveraging the capabilities of AI, blockchain, and IoT, businesses not only can streamline and automate existing processes but also eliminate outdated ones. AI algorithms enable real-time analysis of vast amounts of data, leading to quicker and more accurate decision-making. Blockchains can ensure transparency, trust, and security in transactions, while IoT devices enable data collection and monitoring for proactive maintenance and optimizations. Evaluating how these technologies can improve customer interactions, deliver personalized experiences, and build trust will revolutionize the overall customer experience.

However, it's important to note that these technologies are advancing rapidly. Relying solely on what they can currently do and forming a strategy accordingly may lead to obsolescence. To stay ahead, consider setting aside 10 percent of the savings generated by each technology implementation for further research and experimentation. Organizations that focus on what these technologies can achieve in the future are more likely to remain competitive. In this context, the architectural aspect is of critical importance.

Embracing Trivergence technologies and enabling your employees to harness their potential will position your organization as a forward-thinking and adaptable industry leader. By promoting these technologies to enhance efficiency, innovation, and customer experiences, you can garner strong support from your workforce. On the other hand, adopting a narrow focus solely on cost-cutting measures, such as the massive layoffs in the 2020s, could lead to disruptions and hinder your ability to fully leverage the benefits of Trivergence. As we progress into the 2030s, assumptions about workforce dynamics may shift, with potential implications for staffing and workweek structures. By embracing these technologies thoughtfully, you can create a sustainable and successful integration that propels your organization to thrive in the era of Trivergence.

Cut out unnecessary middlemen. While complex derivative products on Wall Street may require experts to translate from business needs, to math, to code, this is not the norm for most businesses. You can do away with system analysts in many cases. Instead, encourage your technical team to spend some time directly working in the business. If you are a bank CIO, spend some time in the branches as a teller. Throughout IT's history, we've seen many project failures *lost in mistranslation.*

When businesspeople who aren't tech-savvy request solutions, they often ask for what they think is possible, rather than what's truly feasible and beneficial. Blindly following these requests, especially with traditional methods, can be harmful when using emerging technologies, potentially putting your company at risk. In my experience, it's usually easier for a programmer to learn about the business than the other way around. So, focus on getting your technical team to understand the business well enough to bridge the communication gap effectively. Once I had a business manager ask for a report to better understand the existing six-week inventory management process. When I finally understood it end to end, I was able to reduce it to less than an hour.

Weigh the Risks Against the Benefits

Hedging the risks while embracing the benefits is a crucial step in implementation. Let's consider an insurance company that uses IoT devices to collect data on insured properties. AI algorithms can analyze the data and make far smarter predictions proactively for underwriting and reactively settling claims far faster than is done today. Blockchain technology can offer an indisputable record of what happened and when.

The integration of the IoT, AI, and blockchain technologies will bring several benefits to the insurance company. Tangible benefits may include improved risk assessment and underwriting accuracy, streamlined claims processing, reduced manual paperwork, and dramatic operational cost savings. Intangible but measurable benefits include enhanced customer experiences, increased customer satisfaction, and improved brand reputation. To estimate the impact of these benefits, the insurance company may focus on measuring increases in policy sales, customer retention rates, customer lifetime value, or all three. They can also evaluate the impact on operational efficiency, such as reduced administrative workload or improved claims settlement accuracy. An old truism in IT is "nothing measured, nothing gained."

Piloting Trivergence technologies is relatively cost-effective thanks to the accessibility of cloud computing resources. Cloud platforms offer scalable and flexible infrastructure, making it easier and more affordable to experiment and test new technologies. For example, by leveraging cloud-based AI services and APIs, businesses can easily integrate AI capabilities into their existing applications, reducing the up-front costs associated with building AI solutions from scratch.

The cloud's flexibility enables organizations to easily scale their resources up or down based on project needs, optimizing costs and avoiding unnecessary expenses. In this way, the cloud's accessibility has opened exciting opportunities for businesses of all sizes to explore and harness the power of Trivergence technologies without breaking the bank.

Open-source platforms also present a cost-effective solution for piloting Trivergence technologies. For example, Hyperledger offers ready-to-use frameworks and tools that simplify the development of blockchain solutions, reducing the initial investment required for experimentation. This makes it ideal for testing and exploring the potential benefits of blockchain technology. Moreover, blockchains often have features that allow the creation of smart contracts using Turing-complete programming languages. This feature allows developers to create sophisticated and flexible smart contracts that can perform a wide range of functions on the blockchain, making it relatively straightforward to create a pilot for a solid use case.

Recognize that there may be others who are thinking of ways to employ these technologies to disintermediate your business. Given you know your business better than they do, a thought experiment of how it might be done is necessary. The result may be modifications to products or the launch of low-cost products that will mitigate that risk.

In the context of IoT integration, there are also risks and benefits to consider. The benefits are evident, as they empower organizations to gather valuable and actionable digital intelligence. However, business leaders must carefully assess the risks associated with IoT implementation, including concerns about data security and privacy, challenges in seamless integration with existing IT infrastructure, and potential technical malfunctions impacting decision-making and resource allocation. IoT devices with simple passwords will be hacked. You need to plan on what you will do when they are hacked.

To weigh the risks against the benefits, business leaders must ask themselves several critical questions. For example, what measures are in place to safeguard the data collected by IoT sensors, and how can the organization proactively address potential security breaches? What are the costs involved in implementing and maintaining the IoT infrastructure, and how can the expected benefits justify these expenses? Recognize that IoT devices are constantly dropping in price while increasing in capabilities. The real question may be when, as opposed to how. Does the organization have the necessary expertise and support to handle the technical complexities of IoT integration, and if not, how can they bridge this gap? What redundancies and fail-safes can be implemented to ensure the reliability and accuracy of the IoT system?

By weighing the risks against the benefits, companies can tune their organization's integration of AI, the blockchain, and the IoT. They can ensure that the potential benefits materialize as streamlined processes, enhanced data insights, and improved customer experiences. This approach helps them allocate resources effectively, mitigate risks through proper safeguards, and align their integration strategy with their organizational goals and risk appetite.

Crafting a Trivergence-Focused Business Strategy

After evaluating organizational readiness and identifying the key considerations for the integration of Trivergence technologies, the next step is to develop a roadmap that enables phased implementation and continuous improvement of your Trivergence initiatives.

Step 1: Define Phases and Milestones

Defining phases and milestones is a critical first step. It involves breaking down the integration process into manageable stages, each with its specific objectives and deliverables. When defining phases, consider the complexity and interdependencies of your Trivergence initiatives. Start by identifying the longer-term goals you aim to achieve through the integration. These goals may include enhancing operational efficiency, improving customer experiences, streamlining processes, launching new products or services, and where appropriate, entering new markets. Based on these goals, determine the logical sequence of activities and the order in which they need to be implemented. For example, the phases could be structured as follows:

- **Phase 1: Data Infrastructure and Connectivity:** Focus on establishing the necessary infrastructure to collect and process data—be it from existing data stores, IoT devices, your ecosystem partners, or data available on the marketplace. This includes setting up sensors, gateways, and communication protocols to gather and store data efficiently. It also involves capturing data that previously may not have been seen as having an operational role. Milestones for this phase could include completing the setup of IoT devices, developing data partners along your supply chains, and even data cooperatives through coopetition. Architect a big data repository for all relevant information.

- **Phase 2: AI Integration and Analytics:** To begin, develop an understanding of the capabilities of ChatGPT and Bard, considering the vast amount of data they have gathered. The myriad ways their APIs can be leveraged may surprise you. Next, prioritize the data you can provide to AI, but be prepared for AI model training to take more iterations than anticipated; patience is key. Develop AI models and algorithms to process the data and generate predictive analytics. Milestones for this phase should encompass training AI models, validating their accuracy, and deploying them to derive additional insights for effective decision-making.

- **Phase 3: Blockchain Integration for Contracts and Payouts:** In this phase, leverage blockchain networks to achieve transparency and efficiency in contract execution. Evaluate smart contracts that may cut out intermediaries, lower costs, and foster trust among stakeholders. Key milestones include setting up the blockchain network, where applicable, auditing smart contract security, and piloting contract execution to optimize operations and deliver greater value to clients. Here, disintermediation is the key.

By defining these phases and their corresponding milestones, you create a clear roadmap that guides the implementation process. Each phase represents a distinct stage with specific objectives, allowing for better resource allocation and focused effort.

Step 2: Allocate Resources and Establish Timelines

This step involves identifying the necessary resources, such as financial, human, and technological, and determining how they will be allocated throughout the integration process. Begin by assessing the resources needed for each phase of the implementation. Human resources should be involved, considering the skills and expertise you will need for successful integration. Assign the right personnel with the appropriate skills and training to each phase of the integration.

Develop a ballpark timeline for each phase and milestone based on the complexity and scope of the integration. Consider dependencies between different phases and allocate sufficient time for testing, refinement, and adjustment. Given the newness of these technologies and the low costs of trials on the cloud, don't be alarmed if it takes longer than you expected. Continuously monitor the progress and benefits of the implementation and adjust as necessary.

Step 3: Monitor Key Performance Indicators

Key performance indicators (KPIs) are measurable metrics that help track progress, evaluate performance, and ensure that the integration of Trivergence technologies aligns with the organization's strategic goals. For example, an insurance company's strategic objective may be to enhance customer experience, increase retention rate, streamline claims processing, and improve operational efficiency. To measure progress toward these objectives, the insurance company likely has already identified its KPIs, such as customer satisfaction ratings, retention rate, percentage pending, market share, claims processing time, unit costs, net and gross profitability, and so on. Next, the insurance company could ballpark what improvements it anticipated to these KPIs from each project and when they may materialize. Here are some examples: Increase retention by 25 percent within the first year. Reduce claims processing time by 80 percent in 18 months. Achieve claims processing cost savings of 10 percent annually through process optimization and automation. With the help of AI, make better actuarial risk assessments, resulting in a reduction of 10 percent in claims. The Trivergence may necessitate the introduction of new KPIs.

These KPIs should provide insights on how effective you have been in your journey, enabling the company to make informed decisions, drive continuous improvement, and maximize the benefits derived from incorporating the IoT, AI, and blockchain technologies into their business strategy. Additionally, each project may have its own metrics that could serve as early warning signs of their impact on the company's overall KPIs.

Step 4: Implement and Evaluate

Assessing the effectiveness of the implemented solutions allows organizations to identify any gaps or areas for improvement. To gather valuable insights and feedback, organizations need to engage with stakeholders throughout the implementation process. This includes employees, customers, and partners who are directly or indirectly impacted by the Trivergence initiatives. Conduct surveys, interviews, or focus groups to understand their experiences, challenges, and suggestions for improvement. Stakeholder feedback provides a holistic perspective on the effectiveness and usability of the differing technologies, enabling organizations to make informed decisions.

Leverage data analytics tools to gather customer feedback, track product processing times, and monitor cost savings. Regularly review your KPIs and metrics against the established targets to gain insights into areas of strength and areas that require improvement. Optimizing one part of a process will invariably expose bottlenecks in other areas. If service processing time does not dramatically improve, identify any new bottlenecks and implement process improvements to streamline these operations. This ensures that the metrics remain aligned with the evolving business landscape and strategic objectives. By comparing actual results with the targets set for each metric, they can identify areas of success and areas that require improvement.

Step 5: Iterate, Optimize, Repeat

Once the relevant KPIs have been determined and any specific metrics for the project have been set, it's essential to iterate and optimize the Trivergence initiatives. This involves using the insights gained from the evaluation process to refine the implementation approach and address any challenges or bottlenecks encountered during the integration. One key aspect of iteration and optimization is refining the implementation approach based on the lessons learned. Analyze the evaluation results and feedback to identify areas that require further improvement. This will involve revisiting the initial roadmap's assumptions and modifying it to align better with the organization's goals and stakeholder needs. By continuously refining the implementation approach, organizations can enhance the effectiveness and efficiency of their Trivergence integration. From AI implementations, expect the unexpected. Be prepared for the surprises you will encounter.

Examine the feedback and evaluation findings to pinpoint areas where difficulties arose during the integration process or where improvements were made but revealed new issues. By understanding the underlying causes of these challenges, organizations will be able to develop strategies to overcome them. This could involve providing additional training, improving communication channels, or leveraging external expertise to resolve specific issues. Foster an environment where experimentation and innovation are valued and rewarded, enabling teams to explore new approaches and technologies that can enhance the integration. Continuously iterating and optimizing the Trivergence initiatives will enable companies to drive ongoing improvements, stay ahead of competitors, and meet the evolving needs of their customers in a rapidly changing digital landscape.

Exploring Opportunities for Collaboration

In the digital age, the landscape of business has shifted from the traditional command and control structures of yesterday toward a more interconnected and interdependent ecosystem. Realize that innovation and transformation today often happen through collaborative efforts with external partners. One concept that captures this dynamic is "coopetition," which refers to a strategic approach where organizations collaborate with their competitors or other entities in their industry to achieve mutual benefits while maintaining their competitive positions.[2] It involves finding common ground and shared goals (or data), even while operating in a competitive marketplace.

When it comes to embracing Trivergence technologies in your business strategy, coopetition becomes particularly relevant. Instead of solely focusing on internal capabilities and resources, organizations recognize the need to build strategic partnerships and tap into both their data and their external expertise. For example, consider with whom to share data to better train your AI initiative, and ensure that all initiatives track the data required for further optimization. The intelligence of your system will correlate with the amount of good data provided. Finding the right data sharing partnerships will be key.

Prioritize external touchpoints with suppliers and customers over internal processes, utilizing the power of Trivergence to establish efficient and smarter connections. A key objective is to achieve transparency in the supply chain through IoT monitoring, blockchain recording, and AI-enhanced insights. Recognize that some initiatives may extend beyond your immediate customers and suppliers to involve their customers and suppliers. To facilitate successful collaboration, consider partnering with technology providers, startups, and industry experts who offer specialized knowledge and innovative solutions. Collect data collaboratively to identify optimization opportunities within partners.

Organizations can adopt the following approaches to explore collaboration effectively.

Attend Conferences and Events

As a result of the Trivergence, the world will be changing rapidly. Attending conferences, events, and local meetups is critical for staying up-to-date with the latest trends in AI, blockchain, and the IoT. Notable events like Web3 & Blockchain World, CES, Mobile World Congress, and AI & Big Data Expo provide platforms for networking, knowledge sharing, and partnership exploration.[3] By participating in these events, organizations can stay informed, learn from others in your industry, explore potential collaborations, and gain insights into the many possibilities for the integration of Trivergence-era technologies. Establishing collaborative relationships at conferences and events requires proactive engagement and strategic approaches. Here are some specific ways business leaders can make the most of these opportunities:

- **Create a must-meet list:** Before the event, research the attendees, speakers, and thought leaders who will be present. Utilize conference apps or social media communities to identify key individuals you want to connect with. Plan and seek out these people during networking breaks or try to arrange one-on-one meetings during the conference.
- **Follow the 90/10 rule:** When networking, focus on building genuine connections by discussing nonwork topics for about 90 percent of the conversation. This approach aligns with the theory that buying decisions are based on relationships; people may decide on a product or service intellectually but ultimately choose to buy from someone they feel emotionally connected to. Avoid immediate sales pitches and let the business aspect arise naturally if there's interest. When you meet someone, make sure to collect their business card and provide yours in return. Then after the event, follow up with personalized emails or calls to continue the conversation and explore potential collaboration opportunities.

- **Don't skip the social events:** Take advantage of social events like happy hours or conference dinners. These informal settings provide an excellent opportunity to network and build relationships in a relaxed atmosphere. Stick to the 90/10 rule, engage in meaningful conversations, and collect business cards for follow-up interactions.
- **Utilize social media and event hashtags:** Leverage social media platforms before, during, and after the conference to connect with other attendees and initiate conversations. Follow event hashtags, engage in discussions, and share valuable content related to the conference theme. This can help you establish connections and start meaningful dialogues even before the event begins.
- **Look for thought leadership opportunities:** Consider ways to showcase your expertise and establish yourself as a thought leader in your field. Speaking at conferences can be particularly impactful, as it allows you to share your insights with a larger audience and attract potential clients or collaborators.

Remember, the key is to be proactive, approachable, and genuine in your interactions. Be open to new ideas and perspectives, and actively listen to others. Building relationships takes time and effort, so follow up with individuals after the event, continue the conversation, and explore ways to collaborate beyond the conference setting.

Join Industry Consortia or Associations

One effective way to stay current is by joining industry consortia or associations. These organizations bring together companies, experts, and stakeholders from specific sectors, forming a collaborative ecosystem. Their shared objectives include setting standards, developing frameworks, and exchanging data. There are hundreds of consortia dedicated to Trivergence technologies, including well-known examples like the Partnership on AI, the Industrial IoT Consortium (IIC), and the Global Blockchain Business Council (GBBC).[4]

Once you've made up your mind to join a consortium, don't just be a passive member. Attend regular meetings, conferences, and workshops where members come together to discuss the latest advancements, challenges, and opportunities in Trivergence technologies. Actively contribute to discussions, share your expertise, and collaborate with others. Be proactive in identifying and joining industry-wide projects or collaborative initiatives related to Trivergence technologies. Industry associations and consortia play a vital role in advocating for favorable policies and regulations related to Trivergence technologies. As a business leader, actively participate in these efforts by providing input on regulatory frameworks, industry standards, and ethical guidelines. Share your insights, voice your opinions, and contribute to shaping the regulatory landscape in a way that supports responsible and effective adoption of Trivergence technologies in your industry. By participating actively, you demonstrate your commitment to the era of Trivergence and have the opportunity to network and build relationships with like-minded professionals.

Participate in Open Innovation Initiatives

Engaging in open innovation initiatives is a valuable approach for business leaders to leverage the entrepreneurial talent of startups, foster collaboration, and explore new possibilities in Trivergence technologies. These initiatives create a platform for knowledge sharing, problem-solving, and co-development, ultimately driving innovation and gaining a competitive edge. One option is to allow your technologists to participate in hackathons, which are events where teams collaborate intensively to solve specific challenges within a set timeframe. Platforms like Kaggle, DataHack, Cal Hacks, and API World host various competitions and hackathons that cover a wide range of industries and applications, including those related to Trivergence technologies.[5] As a business leader, you can get involved as a sponsor or mentor, offering guidance and resources to the participants. This allows you to connect with talented individuals and startups that are passionate about developing innovative solutions in Trivergence technologies. When considering hackathons, ask yourself: Does the hackathon roughly align with your business goals and areas of interest? Will your technologists be better able to protect your systems as a result? What specific challenges or opportunities do you hope to address? It's important to be clear about your expectations and ensure that the hackathon focuses on relevant topics.

Another avenue is joining accelerator programs designed to support the growth and development of startups. For established companies, becoming a mentor or advisor lets you share your industry expertise and insights, establish relationships with startups, and potentially explore collaboration opportunities. As a mentor, expect to learn through experiences. Y Combinator, Techstars, and Plug and Play Tech Center are examples of renowned accelerator programs that have supported numerous startups working on Trivergence technologies.[6] When considering accelerator programs, ask yourself: Does the program have a track record of success? What resources and support do they provide to startups? What is the time commitment required from your side? Additionally, be mindful of aligning the goals and values of the accelerator program with your own to ensure a mutually beneficial partnership.

Organizing your innovation challenges to focus on Trivergence technologies is another option to consider. By inviting startups and entrepreneurs to participate, you can tap into external talent and gain fresh perspectives. These challenges can be tailored to address specific industry challenges or explore new business opportunities. As the organizer, you will need to provide support, resources, and guidance to the participants, fostering collaboration and potential partnerships. When organizing innovation challenges, ask yourself: What specific problem or opportunity do you want to address? Are you prepared to allocate the necessary resources to support the participants? How will you evaluate and select the most promising ideas or solutions?

Fostering a Culture of Innovation

Embracing new technologies brings exciting opportunities, but it also means facing the challenges that come with change. To thrive in this era, organizations need to cultivate a culture of innovation that encourages continuous learning, experimentation, and employee empowerment. It's not just about using trendy buzzwords; it's about creating an environment where new ideas are welcomed, and employees are encouraged to think outside the box. In this culture, everyone has the freedom to explore novel approaches, take calculated risks, and contribute to the Trivergence strategy of the organization.

If you are a CIO, you can influence this culture both upward and downward in the organization. Occasionally, prioritize discussions on Trivergence education within the senior management team. In my experience, CEOs and CFOs typically appreciate but don't demand personalized technology education. If they don't, you should. Take steps to transform the culture throughout the organization.

Given the relatively low cost of certain initiatives, it's wise to encourage experimentation. While this approach might not align with traditional MBA courses, in my role as a CIO, I've found that setting aside a portion of cost savings from previous successful implementations for experimentation, particularly for younger employees who are still outside the existing corporate culture, can yield valuable results. Although senior management is aware of the funds allocated, only bring them into the loop if a promising new idea proves its feasibility. Assuming that the corner offices can filter the best ideas from the Trivergence is overly optimistic. I've witnessed incredibly valuable, easy-to-implement multimillion-dollar ideas emerge unexpectedly from relatively junior staff. Thriving in the era of Trivergence demands embracing bold new ideas. Create a culture that fosters and supports them.

Tune Your Change Management Strategy

Change management plays a vital role in guiding employees through these transformative changes. Change isn't a one-time event; it's a constant companion. As organizations adopt AI, IoT, and blockchain technologies, they experience shifts in processes, workflows, and the very nature of work itself. When introducing these new and powerful technologies, employees will feel uncertain about what lies ahead and worry about the impact on their jobs and their lives. It's crucial for leaders to address these concerns proactively, emphasizing the positive impacts of these technologies and offering the education necessary to meet new opportunities that arise. Open channels of communication, such as town hall meetings, regular updates, and feedback mechanisms, foster trust and encourage open dialogue.

Provide Learning and Development Opportunities

Comprehensive education and training opportunities play crucial roles in helping employees navigate the learning curve associated with emerging technologies. Business leaders should consider a range of educational initiatives to provide their teams with the necessary knowledge and skills for embracing these changes. One option is to explore training programs offered by technology vendors or specialized training providers. Organizations such as Don and Alex Tapscott's Blockchain Research Institute, Cloud Credential Council, Arcitura, and DeepLearning.AI offer educational programs specifically designed to equip employees with the skills required to grow as these technologies are implemented effectively.[7]

When selecting educational programs, business leaders should consider the specific needs and roles of their team members. Different employees may require different levels and types of training. Some may benefit from introductory courses that provide a broad overview of these new technologies, while others may need more specialized and advanced training based on today's responsibilities or tomorrow's aspirations. It is important to assess the existing skill gaps within the team and tailor the educational opportunities accordingly. Furthermore, business leaders should also consider the format of the training programs. Online courses, virtual workshops, and self-paced modules can provide flexibility for employees to learn at their own pace and fit their learning into their busy schedules. A simple Google search will find options that are free. On the other hand, for more advanced needs, in-person training sessions may offer more immersive experiences and opportunities for direct interaction with trainers and peers.

In the context of providing learning and development opportunities, addressing employee concerns about Trivergence technologies eliminating their jobs becomes paramount. Managing the human aspects of Trivergence may prove challenging, but fostering a mindset that views AI as a skill enabler will lead to greater acceptance and support for the Trivergence strategy. Transparent communication about the organization's plans is crucial for success. To manage expectations and mitigate fears of layoffs, consider leveraging contractors instead of employees. Early involvement of HR professionals is essential, as they play a critical role in driving learning and development initiatives during the Trivergence transformation. Keeping your staff onboard will become an ever more difficult challenge. By offering comprehensive educational programs and upskilling opportunities, employees can embrace the new technologies with confidence and readiness, driving the organization toward a successful integration of AI, blockchain, and the IoT.

Re-evaluate Incentive Structures

A culture that embraces innovation, agility, and adaptability creates an environment where change is not only accepted but embraced.

Organizations should assess their culture and identify areas that can leverage the emerging technologies. This may involve reevaluating processes, reward systems, and leadership practices to support the desired changes. Here are some specific strategies to consider:

- **Redefine employee performance metrics:** Move away from solely focusing on traditional measures such as revenue growth or cost reduction. Instead, incorporate metrics that specifically encourage innovation. Consider factors such as the number of innovative ideas generated, successful implementation of Trivergence projects, or cross-functional collaboration in leveraging these technologies. By redefining employee performance metrics, the company actively promotes a mindset that values learning from failures and recognizes that taking risks is an essential part of the innovation process. Not all companies will survive the Trivergence.

- **Reward employees' contributions:** Implement recognition and reward mechanisms that specifically acknowledge and appreciate employees who embrace and create business value with Trivergence technologies. This can include public recognition through company-wide announcements, awards, or incentives tied to results. These incentives can serve as motivating factors and reinforce the importance of innovation within the organization. By valuing employees' efforts and contributions, they feel appreciated and motivated to continue driving innovation and embracing the Trivergence strategy.

- **Keep employees informed:** Communicate the rationale behind changes and the potential benefits employees can expect. Foster a supportive environment where employees feel safe to share their experiences and ideas. These changes will be highly disruptive. Not all employees will have a place in the new paradigm; however, all should be given the opportunity to learn, grow, and participate in this rapidly changing world. Ultimately, fostering a culture of innovation requires a holistic approach. It involves understanding and empathizing with employee concerns, communicating effectively, providing training and support, fostering collaboration, and aligning the organizational culture. By actively addressing these challenges, organizations can navigate the complexities of change and position themselves for success in the era of Trivergence.

Leading in the Era of Trivergence

The changes happening in today's business landscape pose a significant challenge for organizations, highlighting the need for effective leadership during times of rapid transformation. Back in 1976, Marilyn Ferguson introduced the concept of a *paradigm shift*, describing it as a disruptive process marked by dislocation, conflict, confusion, and uncertainty.[8] In 1992, Don Tapscott made it the title of a *New York Times* bestseller.[9] New paradigms often face resistance, skepticism, and even hostility from those with vested interests in the old ways. Established business leaders may be the last to embrace the change—if at all.

Today, many organizations face a leadership crisis. Traditional IT professionals and managers are often overwhelmed by the demands of maintaining legacy systems, leaving little room for leading the creation of something new. Old approaches, knowledge, methods, and attitudes die hard, even (and perhaps especially) among the leaders of the old view. Many managers have historically left technology to the experts, lacking the confidence and knowledge to navigate such a significant change.

This presents a historic opportunity and responsibility for business strategists. Merely observing change without active participation leads to paralysis and cynicism. The role of a leader in the era of Trivergence is crucial. As business strategists, we hold the power to shape the future by embracing Trivergence technologies and guiding our organizations through this transformative period. By actively engaging in the change process, we can inspire our teams, drive innovation, and overcome the hurdles of the previous era. The command-and-control approach of the last century will not work today. Expect many of the better ideas to come from more junior members of your organization. Our leadership will be instrumental in navigating the complexities of the era of Trivergence and seizing the opportunities it presents. Let us embrace this responsibility and lead our organizations toward a successful future.

Notes

1. European Parliament. "EU AI Act: first regulation on artificial intelligence." June 6, 2023. www.europarl.europa.eu/news/en/headlines/society/20230601ST093804/eu-ai-act-first-regulation-on-artificial-intelligence.

2. Brandenburger, Adam, and Barry Nalebuff. "The Rules of Co-Opetition." *Harvard Business Review*, January 1, 2021. https://hbr.org/2021/01/the-rules-of-co-opetition.

3. Web3 & Blockchain World. https://w3bworld.org, accessed 22 June 2023; CES. www.ces.tech, accessed 22 June 2023; Mobile World Congress. www.mwcbarcelona.com, accessed 22 June 2023; AI & Big Data Expo. www.ai-expo.net, accessed 22 June 2023.

4. Partnership on AI. https://partnershiponai.org, accessed 22 June 2023; Industrial IoT Consortium. www.iiconsortium.org, accessed 22 June 2023; Global Blockchain Business Council. https://gbbcouncil.org, accessed 22 June 2023.

5. Kaggle. https://kaggledays.com, accessed 22 June 2023; DataHack. https://datahack.analyticsvidhya.com, accessed 22 June 2023; Cal Hacks. https://ai.calhacks.io, accessed 22 June 2023; API World. https://apiworld.co, accessed 22 June 2023.

6. Y Combinator. www.ycombinator.com, accessed 22 June 2023; Techstars. www.techstars.com, accessed 22 June 2023; Plug and Play Tech Center. www.plugandplaytechcenter.com, accessed 22 June 2023.

7. Blockchain Research Institute. "Online Courses." www.blockchainresearchinstitute.org/online-courses, accessed 22 June 2023; Cloud Credential Council. www.cloudcredential.org, accessed 22 June 2023; Arcitura. www.arcitura.com, accessed 22 June 2023; DeepLearning.AI. www.deeplearning.ai, accessed 22 June 2023.

8. Marilyn Ferguson, *The Aquarian Conspiracy - Personal and Social Transformation in our Time*, St. Martin's Press, New York, N.Y. 1976.

9. Tapscott, Don, and Art Caston. *Paradigm Shift: The New Promise of Information Technology*. McGraw-Hill, 1993.

10 Trivergence and Our Digital Future

When I first started in the computer industry, I often crossed the Atlantic to an international development center in Brussels as part of a team that was building a next-generation banking system, which became the de facto international standard for Citibank. I was then impressed that I could, on a tape, bring the intelligence of that system across the Atlantic and install it on a different computer in about a day, with zero loss of information. Today that would be done in seconds.

When my daughters Madi and Marissa were in elementary high school in Denver, I set a rule on one important thing. When I was working, they were not allowed to disturb me. There was only one exception. That was for math homework. And for that I would drop everything, shut down meetings, and work with my kids (and even my neighbors' kids) on their homework assignments. I told them that there was nothing more interesting or enjoyable for me than math homework. As a math graduate, I did my best to transfer my knowledge to the next generation. After a couple of decades of effort, I am clearly proud of my daughters' growth, though they did not end up studying advanced math. Marissa ended up a public-school teacher, and Madi is now in equity research banking.

Unlike computers, we as people can't transfer information to the next generation without significant loss of information. Mozart was patient with his students, though clearly none achieved his level of mastery.[1] The point is that what we as humans imperfectly transfer in a decade, computers can now transfer with perfect fidelity in a second. Not surprisingly, the "Grandfather of AI," Geoffrey Hinton, agrees, noting that AI systems are "on track to be much smarter than initially anticipated" because they possess "better learning algorithms than humans."[2] We have had hints of that for decades.

In the 19th century, William Shanks dedicated his life to calculating an ever-increasing number of digits to the ratio of the circumference of a circle to its diameter we now denote by the Greek letter π. Few can recall its digits beyond 3.14159. Before Shanks' death, he had calculated it to an impressive 707 decimal places. Thankfully, he died before a machine in 1944 found that after 527 decimal places, his efforts were all wrong and in vain. On Google Cloud, it has now been calculated to 100 trillion digits.[3] That only took the cloud about two months. If printed, the result would require billions of pages. When it comes to calculations, AI and the cloud can do it on a scale and at a speed that few can imagine. Although there is no doubt that, as humans, our knowledge base will increase from generation to generation in a somewhat imperfect process, we must recognize as a knowledge-based species; we are facing an awesome competitor, with overwhelming advantages both in terms of the speed at which it can learn by analyzing mountains of information and in terms of the speed at which it will transfer the knowledge from computer generation to generation.

Everyone knows how computers are a gazillion times faster than they were in the 1960s. Indeed, if the same type of memory that was used in an IBM 360 were used on today's 512 GB cell phone, it would weigh more than a billion tons.[4]

Many have argued that computers will never "really" think independently—that computers will only excel improving in what they do best, such as math and big data. Yes, they do excel in analyzing insanely massive datasets such as the US Census, analyzing models for a hurricane's path, or finding correlations in physical characteristics, hereditary diseases, and our genomes. On the low end, an AI monitoring IoT security camera has the patience to look for a needle in a haystack 24/7/365 without sleep, social interaction, daydreaming, and any other form of distraction. On the high end, the Trivergence can look for patterns in our 3.2 billion genetic "letters" against the physical and health characteristics of a billion people and gain insights that no army of humans could ever achieve. But can they independently think? It is becoming ever clearer that they do.

Often with technology, we overestimate the short-term potential and underestimate its long-term transformative impact. Electricity today empowers many things wildly beyond the dreams of its pioneers, be it Thomas Edison or George Westinghouse. In their days, there were no smartphones, televisions, refrigerators, or large-scale mechanized assembly lines. Prior to electricity, the buildings in Paris were restricted to six floors for a reason. High rises would not exist without elevators.

Similarly, in our children's lifetime, the Trivergence will likely be doing tasks and discovering new insights far beyond the wildest dreams of today's leading deep learning researchers, Yoshua Bengio, Geoffrey Hinton, and Yann LeCun.[5] It could end work as we know it and feed, properly house, psychologically counsel, and even personalize entertainment for everyone on the planet. It could "see" the missing dimensions in string theory or on earth, create dark matter or dark energy. It could design a fusion reactor that fits into someone's shed to power a city, without producing carbon dioxide or long-term radioactive waste. It could cure most diseases. From understanding and applying aspects of the DNA of turtles to humans, our kids may live another 100 years.[6] What it could do is limited only by our imaginations. What it will do in the longer view only time will tell.

There is now little doubt that today's AI can improve the productivity of most students, drivers, white-collar workers, analysts, authors, translators, musicians, soldiers, doctors, psychiatrists, programmers, and even poets and fine artists. As it does, it will learn more about what we do. On the horizon, it is easy to see a superintelligent AI general physician available to everyone, reading smart toilets and other IoT home devices at pennies on the current healthcare dollar. The health benefits in the developing world could be tremendous.

Artificial intelligence has the potential to create what Mustafa Suleyman has coined as "radical abundance." It is easy to imagine (and even demonstrate) farms, factories, and stores without workers, banks without tellers, and transportation by sea, air, and land without captains, pilots, or drivers. By the end of this decade or soon after, expect this to be the norm. In 15 years, possibilities we can't imagine today will be common. Though AI seems to be confounded by urban driving, its skills on the highway are no longer questioned. The answer to the AI challenges of urban driving may be to simply avoid it and use drones to overcome the challenges of unexpected road conditions. Amazon is now delivering by drone in some locations. The ability of AI to synchronize the activities of massive drone fleets is now so last decade.

John Maynard Keynes in his 1930s essay "Economic Possibilities for Our Grandchildren" conjectured that by now we would be working

15-hour weeks, and when meeting others, we would be defined not by our jobs but by our hobbies and other interests. With instant communications at our fingertips, if anything, the 40-hour workweek is a comfort of the past. The very opposite of what Keynes predicted is our reality. AI could make Keynes' vision true in about a decade.

With a radical increase in productivity, Trivergence could well enable "radical abundance," ending world poverty and giving everyone access to food, shelter, and some form of AI-enabled healthcare to the entire planet, in at most a decade. I doubt it could give us all yachts, but it could give everyone a decent living, food, and access to a virtual doctor. The workweek could be far shorter and retirement ages lowered, giving us more time for our family and friends. In doing so, it could radically reduce stress at individual and collective levels. Crime and even murder rates would drop dramatically. With more free time for everyone, the loneliness epidemic would come to an end, with people interacting with people, as opposed to people interacting with chatbots. A far more perfect world seems to be within our collective grasp. Of course, achieving it will be challenging.

Higher wages, earlier retirement dates, and shorter workweeks provide sensible approaches to the loss of employment. However, there is no serious discussion of these possibilities. In the United States, some Republicans from Ron DeSantis to Rick Scott to Paul Ryan have offered proposals to reduce or eliminate Social Security. In France, Emmanuel Macron has just raised the current statutory retirement age from 62 to 64. The politicians, unaware of the likely effects of the Trivergence, are headed in the very opposite direction.

More broadly, while Trivergence holds significant promise, it also poses considerable risks and dangers. Given the ever-increasing control of Trivergence-enabled systems over our water, power, transportation, production, and now even weapons systems, and the inherent unpredictability of their conclusions, we must recognize that with their promise, it brings significant perils. Those include both unexpected results and a desire to use it for malevolent purposes. Having dedicated much of the book to examining the promise of Trivergence, we now turn to examining the perils.

The Perils of the Trivergence

The convergence of AI with blockchain and the IoT holds the promise of wide-ranging societal advancements, enabling smart machines to tackle increasingly complex challenges and positively impact various aspects of human life. At the same time, the Trivergence has given rise to new risks and ethical considerations related to bias, privacy, disinformation, job displacement, weaponization, and existential threats to humanity.

The Weaponization of Trivergence

The integration of artificial intelligence Trivergence and the IoT into warfare raises significant ethical, moral, strategic, and even existential concerns. As *Wired* magazine describes it, "The AI-Powered, Totally Autonomous Future of War Is Here."[7] In the article, Amir Alon, a senior director at Elbit Systems, says of his surveillance and killing machine that "It can engage autonomously, but we don't recommend it. . . . We don't want to start World War III." More simply put, applying the Trivergence to killing machines and permitting them to think independently is clearly both militarily optimal and an existential threat.

The concept of smart autonomous soldiers refers to AI-powered machines capable of independent decision-making and execution of military operations. The potential capabilities of such soldiers are vast, ranging from conducting reconnaissance and intelligence-gathering to engaging in combat scenarios without direct human intervention. Autonomous weapons are already on today's battlefields for reconnaissance, intelligence gathering and analysis, and target acquisition and destruction. However, the potential for AI-driven killer drones to reduce casualties on one side might incentivize the use of force, blurring the lines between aggression and defense. This could lead to a more unpredictable and volatile global security environment, making diplomatic solutions and conflict resolution even more challenging.

So far, AI has been deployed in Israel for targeted assassinations, by the Ukrainians for "killer" sea drones, and by both sides in the Ukrainian war for target acquisition. Today, in finance, computers looking for inter-currency arbitrage opportunities are able to see and seize opportunities that exist for a quarter of a second, where humans are simply too slow. That happened 30 years ago. In healthcare, we have noted how AI can sift through the mountains of data supplied by the IoT to look for anomalies far deeper and faster than humans. In war, the era of military analysts sifting through mountains of satellite imagery to identify threats and opportune targets is now over. That's the job of the Trivergence. Unlike tumors, battlefield targets can move. Finding and eliminating them, before they eliminate you, is now the domain of AI. Going back unilaterally to the manual inspection of satellite imagery is a strategy doomed to certain defeat.

One of the primary concerns surrounding the deployment of smart autonomous soldiers is the erosion of human control. Traditional warfare involves human commanders who make complex decisions based on a nuanced understanding of the situation. By delegating decision-making to AI, there is a risk of machines misinterpreting situations or acting on incomplete data, potentially leading to catastrophic consequences. Moreover, AI lacks human moral reasoning, raising questions about the adherence to rules of engagement and the potential for war crimes. Wars are much easier to start when you don't need to worry about the grief of "gold star" families. As machines make autonomous killing decisions, who do we hold responsible when they commit war crimes?

Unfortunately, the tactical arguments in favor of fully autonomous soldiers and weapons will be hard for military powers to resist. For example, long-range radio signals can be jammed (as they are on the battlefields of Ukraine), so it makes sense that autonomous soldiers should be smart enough to find and kill their targets independently. Then to win the battle (as opposed to just destroying a particular target), it makes sense to have the autonomous soldiers and weapons communicate with each other tactically to optimize their effectiveness in discovering and destroying enemy targets while, in theory, minimizing "collateral damage" to civilians. But the real objective, of course, is not to win the battle but to win the war, which arguably necessitates having autonomous weapons that can think and act strategically. The argument for having a large military readjust in seconds to an enemy hypersonic stealth attack not only is compelling but may also be a survival imperative.

Clearly, we must achieve these advances and synergies before our enemies do, since the consequences of losing a war are existential. Some worry about the potential for an AI-powered weapons arms race. But the proverbial horse has bolted the barn. Leading military powers are already developing more advanced AI-driven military systems to maintain a competitive edge. Finding a sensible AI arms control framework that is internationally accepted and comprehensive appears critical for our survival, and a near impossibility to achieve. The Geneva Conventions, banning the use of toxic gas in war, was not implemented until a decade after widespread use of chemical weapons. In this case, we need to be proactive and ban the weaponization of AI before that can happen. Banning them after the fact, given the power of Trivergence, may not be a survivable option.

The logic that we may be headed for a mass extinction event is compelling. For competitive reasons, neither companies nor countries will honor the requests of the top minds in AI for a pause to address their concerns.[8] To most in the business, the "fear of extinction" is secondary to the fear of letting their competitors get ahead. That may not be a wise decision, but the one thing about extinction is that there will be no one left to regret it.

Jobs and Prosperity

In the job market, Trivergence has the potential to automate tasks currently performed by humans, leading to widespread job displacement. While the exact extent and timeline of job automation are subject to debate, the list of tasks and jobs that could be affected grows by the day. Jobs that involve manufacturing, assembly lines, data entry, simple data analysis, routine customer service, and basic software coding are most at risk. So too are transportation and delivery workers, as self-driving trucks, taxis, and delivery vehicles reduce the need for human drivers. Self-checkout systems and automated inventory management systems will dramatically streamline retail operations. In the financial sector, AI algorithms are automating trading, fraud detection, risk assessment, and credit scoring. Legal services will be upended by AI-enabled case research and discovery and growing automation in the creation of boilerplate legal documents. In short, there is little that humans do today that smart machines won't eventually do for less, consistently, 24 hours a day, seven days a week, with no need for vacations. If there is something AI is incapable of doing, someday it will be smart enough to write the code to extend its capabilities.

Optimists say Trivergence will boost productivity and create new jobs, especially those requiring skills such as creativity, critical thinking, empathy, and complex problem-solving. Some see the potential for shorter workweeks, earlier retirement, and a higher standard of living for most. Companies like IBM put a positive spin on the looming transformations, asserting that AI has the potential to "democratize knowledge," "automate mundane tasks," and "scale expertise across the business" to minimize workforce disruption as "Boomers retire in ever greater numbers."[9] A recent report from the World Economic Forum also says that we need not fear AI and that, like previous technologies, it will lead to longer-term job growth.[10] Historically, the impact of computers and other technology on employment has been generally positive. Additionally, thanks to the Internet, accelerated by the COVID pandemic, the proliferation of remote work has allowed for greater flexibility and work–life balance.

On the other hand, pessimists see Trivergence as a substitute for human efforts and predict that automation could dramatically accelerate the death of the middle class, make the super-rich even richer, and dramatically increase the power of global tech corporations. McKinsey estimates that between 400 million and 800 million individuals could be displaced by automation and will need to find new jobs by the end of the decade.[11] More boldly, they state that they believe that 50% of all existing jobs can be automated with the technology of today and that this will be realized somewhere between 2055 and 2075, depending on "a variety of political and other factors."[12]

To compound matters, displaced workers may struggle to find new employment if their skills are not easily transferable to emerging industries or roles. Providing adequate training and education opportunities for large-scale reskilling efforts will likely prove challenging if the pace of technology adoption outstrips the capacity of educational and training institutions to respond. Even if Trivergence creates new jobs, there is a high probability that the benefits will be unevenly distributed, resulting in deepening economic inequality and social disruption.

Consider, for example, that the end of the third industrial revolution has brought record profits. Morally you could argue that working-class wages should have risen proportionately. But wages are not a reflection of a moral compass. They are determined by markets. And if the Trivergence enables thinking machines to lay off hundreds of millions of people to dramatically increase profitability, there is no reason to believe that won't happen. It is not difficult to see plummeting wages in our not too distant future. As a result of recent price increases, US profit margins have increased to the highest levels since 1950.[13] But that wealth generation is yet to be shared. Workers with white and blue collars are now feeling threatened. With the Trivergence capable of ever more tasks, it is no surprise that support for unions in the United States is at its highest point since 1965, a nostalgic time when higher productivity actually resulted in higher wages.[14] The result back then was the creation of the middle class.

Gen Z is the first generation to graduate with skills from college challenged by the prospect of short-term obsolescence. They know it, and as a result of this and other factors, they are the most stressed of any generation.[15] Forty years ago, CEOs often stated that employees were the company's greatest asset. Some still do, but the massive outsourcing of the 1980s, 1990s, and early 2000s makes that expression ring like an empty platitude. Will CEOs, CFOs, and CIOs soon consider the Trivergence to be their greatest asset?

The bottom line is that Trivergence will likely create more jobs than it can automate in the 2020s. However, in the 2030s, the opposite will be true as CXOs focus on increasing productivity while dramatically reducing costs. Whether the result is mass unemployment, the creation of new categories of work, or a much shorter work week, only time will tell.

Current labor market trends are ominous. For example, Google now has more contract employees than permanent ones. This trend nicknamed the *gig economy* is accelerating in G7 countries with contractors now making up more than a third of the US workforce.[16] The advantages for the companies are obvious. No pension plans, no coaching, no HR costs, no competing for promotions required. As AI learns to do more, it is far easier to simply not renew an existing contract with a human than to fire a full-time employee. Job security is now a thing of the past.

In the 25 years following WWII, workers claimed a reasonable share of the wealth that was created. As productivity increased with the widespread adoption of mainframe computers in the 1970s and the PC in the 1980s, an ever-fewer number of workers have shared in the prosperity generated. Engineers, computer scientists, and senior management—including those in finance on Wall Street, Bay Street, Hong Kong, and Canary Wharf—saw massive increases in income. But most workers were left behind as productivity increased. Greater productivity and a shrinking middle class have been urgent topics of discussion for decades, with no apparent solution. That trend is likely to accelerate.

Let's take the automobile industry, for example, an industry that has typically been a leader in Trivergence. The *New York Times* reports that cars today can "easily" have more than 3,000 chips.[17] Twenty years ago, manufacturing robots on assembly lines were adept at performing rigid, repeatable tasks. Though expensive and inflexible, the fact that they could work 24/7/365 days a year without a break created significant cost advantages. Robots had a profound impact on reducing the costs of manufacturing while increasing consistency and quality. Today, the price of robotics is plummeting, while their abilities are increasing dramatically. The combination of AI with smarter IoT sensors and actuators has increased their intelligence to the point where robots can be shown what to do and learn from observing how a human does the task. The auto workers' strike in the fall of 2023 highlights some of the challenges ahead. The Ford Motor company has approximately 57,000 unionized workers[18] and the year before made about $4 billion in profit.[19] With roughly a 2,000-hour work year, that is about $35 profit per union hour worked. On average, the unionized employee at Ford makes about $32 an hour.[20] They are demanding a 40% raise that would pay them about $45 an hour. Can a company that profits $35 an hour for every union hour afford to pay another $13 per hour? From Ford's perspective, such a large raise would no doubt raise the price of parts and end products as demands for equitable wages flowed through Ford's supply chain and potentially foreign nonunionized workforce. But the trend since the 1970s will likely accelerate. With the Trivergence, what a company can afford to pay and what a company needs to pay will likely further diverge.

Thirty-five years ago, Don Tapscott wrote that he hoped that automation would begin to further diversify prosperity. He clearly was not alone in that aspiration. Arguably it should have, but that reality of diversified prosperity has not materialized. For the last 50 years, wages in G7 countries have stagnated with unprecedented wealth creation for a few, resulting in a shrinking middle class during periods of reasonably consistent economic growth. *Time Magazine* articulated the problem in an interesting way. They state that if income distribution had remained the same as it was in the 25-year period after the war, then the top 1% would be much poorer and the bottom 90% much richer. As they put it, "The top 1% of Americans have taken $50 trillion from the bottom 90%—and that's made the United States less secure."

Are deepening inequality and massive unemployment inevitable outcomes of Trivergence? I think not. But it's unclear whether there is sufficient private or political will to do much to avoid such undesirable consequences. To date, there has been much discussion about the ethical use of AI. OpenAI's own AI safety and responsibility guidelines state that "The key [to the responsible deployment of AI in everyday life] is to ensure that these machines are aligned with human intentions and values." However, I am unaware of any of these guidelines mentioning the impact on employment.

Some guidelines on Trivergence and the future of employment would be useful. For example, AI should not be used to independently perform important tasks such as healthcare diagnosis and treatment without appropriate human oversight until its efficacy is well proven. In the meantime, some politicians have weighed in on the use of AI in making employment decisions. In the United States, Senators Bob Casey (D-PA) and Brian Schatz (D-HI) introduced the No Robot Bosses Act in July 2023 to protect job applicants and workers from employers using automated decision systems to hire, fire, or discipline employees.[21] Casey and Schatz have also moved to establish an interagency task force to study and report on the use of AI for workplace surveillance. However well-intentioned and necessary, neither measure will have an impact on the relentless march of automation.

Roughly 60% of the United States, when surveyed, say they are living paycheck to paycheck. The question is, what happens when those paychecks end? Tech-savvy presidential candidate Andrew Yang has argued that the time for a universal basic income as originally proposed by conservative economist Milton Friedman (as a negative income tax) may be due. That may be unrealistic. Currently in the United States, personal income taxes (including Medicare) represent about 85% of federal income taxes. Corporate taxes are at about 7%. So, in the 2030s, as corporations leverage the benefits of the Trivergence and the layoffs begin in earnest, the tax base of governments will be seriously eroded even if profits were to quadruple. Bill Gates and many others have said, with some levity, that governments may need to tax the machines to keep governments afloat. Taxing AI, IoT devices, or blockchains is a somewhat difficult hypothesis. It seems more likely that cash-strapped governments with ever greater deficits will simply lose relevance.

The decline of the feudal system began in the 11th century with the Crusades. Three to five centuries later, the Renaissance and Reformation, empowered by rapid advances in trade, commerce, and how we were permitted to think, gave rise to capitalism, democracy, and the modern era. With commerce then generating more wealth than royalty could extract from the serfs, the feudal system collapsed and gave way to beginning what we refer to today as the modern era.

For the Trivergence to have dramatic effect, we will have about a decade, not centuries, to adapt. In September 2019, Glenn S. Gerstall, general counsel for the National Security Agency (NSA), wrote a prescient Op-Ed entitled "I Work for N.S.A. We Cannot Afford to Lose the Digital Revolution." In it, he argues that "the unprecedented scale and pace of technological change will outstrip our ability to effectively adapt to it" and further that "the flood of data about human and machine activity will put such extraordinary economic and political power in the hands of the private sector that it will transform the fundamental relationship, at least in the Western world, between government and the private sector." He concludes that "the digital revolution has the potential for a pernicious effect on the very legitimacy and thus stability of our governmental and societal structures."[22] We have been warned!

More broadly, the problem with aligning AI with human values is that it leaves open the question of whose values will the Trivergence be aligned with? The shareholders will be the most likely answer. Perplexed by the impacts of what AI may do to the economy, Congress huddled with the CEOs of Alphabet, Meta, Microsoft, Tesla, and Open-AI in late 2023. The combined wealth of the few who testified is $550 billion.[23] None said they were rich enough and AI should be focused on improving the lives of others. Then again, if they did, their boards would likely fire them. The wolves are now in the chicken coup, leading the discussions on AI regulation. Unregulated AI could increase their wealth dramatically. Expect the Trivergence to deliver the first trillionaire before 2035. Expect massive funds to be spent on minimizing the efforts of government to regulate this (and for that matter every other) industry. *Forbes* magazine is recommending that the industry create its own guidelines to avoid government regulation entirely.[24] I suspect that they will try.

One core concept of crypto is that it is independent of governments, central banks, or other authorities. Many in that community bristle at the thought of any government oversight. Whichever transnational wins the Trivergence race may be not only libertarian but no longer in need of any government services. Recently, Elon Musk refused a request from Ukraine to give access to his Starlink network over Crimea to assist an attack on the Russian fleet in Sevastopol.[25] The US government had no equivalent resource. As the Trivergence gains greater intelligence and deeper weapons integration, its use will be more and more subject to the decisions in the private sector. That may not be a good thing.

What Happens to Infinite Data?

In George Orwell's 1949 classic *1984*, "Big Brother" was looking over everyone's shoulders to ensure that no one had thoughts that could challenge the overall tenets of society, including the epic struggles between Oceania, Eurasia, and Eastasia. Everyone had to make major sacrifices to support the fictitious war effort. Those who had doubts or deviated from the will of Big Brother were subjected to personalized torture in room 101 of the "Ministry of Love."

To a pessimist, Open AI's "constant companion" is a proposal to not just help us but to constantly observe what we do. The death of what little privacy we have left appears imminent. At least in Orwell's classic horror, you were employed. It is easy to conclude that this "companion," having learned from our shared experience, will ultimately displace us. It is not difficult to imagine scenarios far worse.

In America, the digital conglomerates—Apple, Microsoft, Alphabet, and Meta—constitute almost 60% of the NASDAQ stock market. By exploiting our personal data, they are generating unprecedented wealth and undermining our privacy and revenue potential in the process.

Of course, platforms such as Facebook, Twitter, Instagram, and Snapchat have numerous benefits. They have revolutionized the way we communicate, share information, and interact. For many users, they offer a sense of connectedness, enabling them to forge virtual relationships and stay current on the lives of friends and acquaintances. Yet, this convenience comes at a significant cost.

The data each of us creates is stuff of our identity in the digital age. It constitutes a digital version of each of us, which remembers everything we did online, everyone we interacted with, and everything we purchased, read, listened to, and watched. Cell phones now track every move we make, and smart watches every breathe we take, as well as our heart rates, soon blood pressure, and myriad other measures of how our body functions and even how we feel. All of this gets rolled up into detailed user profiles that encompass individual preferences, habits, and even psychological traits.

Social media platforms use the data they harvest to curate users' content feeds, showing them posts, information, and advertising based on their previous interactions and interests. Ostensibly, this is intended to enhance user experiences. But it has the unintended consequence of creating filter bubbles and echo chambers where users are increasingly exposed only to content and viewpoints that align with their existing beliefs, reinforcing confirmation bias. Of course, the algorithms are also designed to keep users engaged for longer, leading to addictive scrolling and a constant stream of notifications that make it challenging for individuals to disconnect and maintain a healthy life balance.

The threats to personal privacy do not end with social media companies. Most consumer-facing corporations engage in surveillance activities to gather data for various purposes, including market research, consumer profiling, and targeted advertising. Retailers use tracking technology to monitor shoppers' movements within stores, while online retailers like Amazon collect extensive purchase histories to recommend products and refine their marketing strategies.

Wearable devices and smart home technology further extend the reach of corporate surveillance. IoT devices such as fitness trackers and smart speakers can record users' activities, health data, and conversations within their homes, adding yet another layer to the erosion of personal privacy. When combined with AI, this data can be used to build ever more comprehensive and intimate profiles of a person's life, habits, and preferences. Many wearable devices and smart home technologies are susceptible to hacking, resulting in the unlawful invasion of individuals' personal spaces.

Government agencies around the world have also harnessed digital technologies for mass surveillance programs. The revelations made by Edward Snowden in 2013 exposed the extent of such surveillance conducted by agencies like the NSA in the United States. These programs involve the collection of vast amounts of data, including communications, emails, and online activities, often without an individual's knowledge or consent. In cities such as Tiayuan and London, facial and "gait"[26] recognition systems and location tracking tools monitor citizens' movements and activities in a truly Orwellian fashion.[27]

Ultimately, the biggest risk to individual liberty is that corporations, governments, or criminal entities use the vast troves of data they have amassed to exploitan an individual's vulnerabilities, trust, and psychological tendencies to influence their thoughts, behaviors, or decision-making. Armed with detailed psychological profiles and personal histories, AI algorithms can create highly personalized content designed to resonate with and manipulate the targeted individual. Shrewd manipulators will exploit emotionally vulnerable moments to exert influence by using online communications to gauge when individuals are feeling vulnerable, anxious, or upset. Using AI to segment the population into microtargeted groups based on demographics, interests, and political affiliations further opens the door to social engineering and psychological manipulation on a mass scale.

Whether we fall unwittingly into this Orwellian future will depend on us and our political representatives. Fighting back to preserve personal privacy will be an ongoing process that involves a combination of individual choices, education, legislation, and collaboration with like-minded individuals and organizations on the creation and dissemination of privacy-enhancing technologies. For now, at least, the choice is still ours.

Trivergence and Bias

In the rapidly evolving landscape of artificial intelligence (AI), the issue of bias has emerged as a critical concern. As AI systems increasingly draw on data from the Internet to learn and make decisions, the potential for bias to be ingrained in their operations becomes a palpable danger. Bias, whether implicit or explicit, has the potential to perpetuate and exacerbate existing societal inequalities, hamper decision-making processes, and erode trust in AI systems.

AI systems can inherit or amplify biases present in the data they are trained on. If the training data contains biased or discriminatory patterns, the AI system can reinforce and even exacerbate these biases, leading to unfair outcomes in areas such as hiring, lending, or criminal justice. AI systems trained on historical loan data, for example, could perpetuate discriminatory lending practices, resulting in unequal access to credit or loans for marginalized groups. Predictive policing systems that use AI algorithms to identify crime hotspots and allocate police resources have been criticized for disproportionately targeting minority communities.

Facial recognition systems used by police have also led to wrongful arrests and imprisonment for Black men. In February 2019, Nijeer Parks was accused of shoplifting and attempting to hit a police officer with a car outside a motel in New Jersey. Parks was identified by the police using facial recognition software, even though he was 30 miles away at the time of the incident. The charges against Parks were later dismissed, but the underlying problems with the facial recognition technology have not been addressed. A national study of more than 100 facial recognition algorithms conducted in 2019 found that the systems did not work as well on Black and Asian faces. In fact, the algorithms were 10 to 100 times more likely to misidentify Black and Asian faces than Caucasian faces.[28] Since the Parks incident, there have been at least five other known incidents of arrests occurring based on incorrect facial recognition and likely many more that remain undocumented.[29] That however has not stopped their use.

Similar patterns of AI-enabled discrimination are evident in employment. One can (naively) argue that if we tell an AI hiring engine nothing about (say) a candidates' sex, age, or race, then obviously it can't discriminate on what it doesn't know. But when looking at historical data on which to base its conclusions from our names and postal codes, it will inherit our biases for age, sex, and race and then apply them inappropriately. For example, if most historical promotions have been for white men in a certain age group, AI-enabled human resources management systems may perpetuate this bias when determining employee performance. Similarly, AI hiring tools that analyze Internet-sourced résumés might inadvertently favor candidates from privileged backgrounds, reinforcing existing disparities in the workforce.

As a case in point, Amazon recently stopped using a hiring algorithm after finding it discriminated against women. The algorithm not only favored applicants based on terms like "executed" or "captured" that were more commonly found on men's résumés but also penalized résumés that included the word "women's," as in "women's chess club captain."[30] In essence, by observing a pattern of male dominance in résumés submitted to the company over a 10-year period, Amazon's system taught itself that male candidates were preferable.

AI-engendered discrimination could prove hard to detect and even harder to counteract because the biases are essentially baked into the data from which it derives its models. Moreover, neural network AI models are considered "black boxes" because their decision-making processes are based on trillions of data points and, as such, are beyond the scope of human comprehension. This lack of transparency can make it impossible to understand how AI systems arrive at their conclusions or predictions.

The lack of interpretability in AI systems is a major problem when it comes to increasing the trustworthiness, safety, and accountability of the systems that increasingly shape life-changing decisions such as diagnosing disease or deciding who gets access to credit. After all, how can one identify and address any potential biases in the decision logic and mountains of underlying data that are near impossible to unpack or reverse engineer? As Roman V. Yampolskiy, a professor of computer science at the University of Louisville, explains in a recent paper, "If all we have is a 'black box,' it is impossible to understand causes of failure and improve system safety." Yampolskiy goes on to argue that placing faith in AI's answers in the absence of an explanation is the equivalent of treating AI as an Oracle system. The danger, says Yampolskiy, is that "we would not be able to tell if [AI systems] begin providing wrong or manipulative answers."

Some have suggested that we can address the perils of AI bias with a multipronged approach. McKinsey, for example, says AI developers must use diverse and representative training data that encompasses a wide range of perspectives. Furthermore, they argue that greater transparency in AI decision-making processes is essential. Explainable AI techniques can shed light on how certain decisions are reached, allowing for the identification and rectification of biased patterns.[31] Such transparency would necessarily extend to understanding the model architecture, including the weights applied to different variables in the models.

Such recommendations are helpful up to a point. However, those pushing for AI transparency and explainability will encounter numerous obstacles. To begin with, the largest developers of AI systems have argued for keeping their AI models closed, for fear of exposing proprietary secrets to their competitors. Moreover, most tech companies seem keen to push systems into deployment very quickly and claim they will deal with bias and other problems as they are discovered.

Additionally, the very nature of today's increasingly sophisticated AI systems makes genuine transparency and interpretability hard to achieve. Neural networks of billions if not trillions of nodes are beyond the comprehension of us mere mortals. So when those in the industry talk of transparency, beware.

In simple terms, although we can strongly influence the behavior and conclusions of the Trivergence, it is impossible to control. Greater transparency in the methods and data used to train AI systems is certainly possible. But dissecting the conclusions of complex neural networks is an illusory goal. When an AI conclusion is a shock beyond what its creators envisioned; it is referred as *emergent behavior*. Expect from AI more and more surprises to *emerge*.

Undermining Our Concepts of Truth and Reality

Bias and discrimination are, in most cases, unintended consequences of training AI on data that reflects society's prejudices and power structures. However, technology as powerful as AI is inevitably going to lead to decidedly intentional misuse of its capabilities to sow confusion, mistrust, and deception on a mass scale. The emergence of deepfake technology, in particular, poses a serious threat to our concept of truth. As these tools gain sophistication, they have the potential to undermine the very foundations of democracy, leading to the further fragmentation of public discourse and the alarming balkanization of society.

AI-powered deepfakes are hyper-realistic manipulated videos or audio clips that challenge the authenticity of digital media, blurring the lines between reality and fabrication. These convincing simulations can superimpose anyone's face onto another person's body, alter speech, and create fictional scenarios that are nearly indistinguishable from real events. Indeed, as AI-generated content becomes increasingly sophisticated, the traditional markers of authenticity, such as visual cues and voice characteristics, may become obsolete. Fabrications may become near-impossible to detect. In an era where partisans can barely agree on basic facts, pervasive disinformation could lead to a total and irreversible loss of trust in media and public institutions.

The AI, Algorithmic, and Automation Incidents and Controversies (AIAAIC) Repository suggests such abuses are already commonplace. Launched in 2019 as a private project, the repository tracks and publicly reports recent incidents and controversies enabled by or relating to AI and automation. Its most recent report found that the number of newly reported AI incidents and controversies was 26 times greater in 2021 than in 2012. The authors conclude that "the rise in reported incidents is likely evidence of both the increasing degree to which AI is becoming intermeshed in the real world and a growing awareness of the ways in which AI can be ethically misused."[32] Notable incidents in 2022 included a deep fake video of Ukrainian President Volodymyr Zelenskyy calling for his troops to surrender the fight against Russia and the unprecedented rise in the use of "bots" to manipulate the news agenda and social media.

The impact of deepfakes extends beyond isolated instances of misinformation. The proliferation of convincing falsehoods has the potential to shape public opinion, drive political narratives, and even influence election outcomes. The creation and spread of manipulated content can reinforce preexisting beliefs, deepening the divisions within society. This phenomenon, exacerbated by the echo chambers of social media, can lead to the balkanization of public discourse, where individuals are exposed only to viewpoints that align with their own, further polarizing society along ideological lines.

The looming 2024 election in the United States will be heavily influenced if not determined by deepfakes over social media. With the narrow casting of news outlets in the United States, misarticulating what the opposition believes is now standard practice. Deepfakes of the candidates saying things they don't believe will be spotted. Deepfakes of those loosely connected to your social media, protesting over what they claim the other party believes, will be common.

Deepfakes could even be catastrophic for international relations, posing grave threats in the realm of geopolitical conflict. As the authors of a recent Brookings Institution report point out, "Deepfakes can be leveraged for a wide range of purposes, including falsifying orders from military leaders, sowing confusion among the public and armed forces, and lending legitimacy to wars and uprisings."[33] They go on to describe scenarios where adversaries might create deepfakes of US soldiers shooting civilians or of US leaders sowing discord by discussing plans to seize territory, empower religious rivals, or bolster terrorist narratives. Multilateral relations could be undermined by deepfake videos showing a leader sneering at civilian casualties; saying callous or insensitive things; or acting in other ways that offend important countries, peoples, and constituencies.

The AI-fueled erosion of truth and reality has other disconcerting implications for content creators. Writing in the *New York Times*, Julie Angwin tells the story of Greg Marston, a British voice actor, who recently encountered an AI-generated clone of his voice named Connor online.[34] The clone had been trained on a recording Mr. Marston had made back in 2003, and it was now uttering phrases he had never actually spoken.

At the time of the original recording, Marston had participated in a session for IBM and subsequently signed a release form, permitting the use of his recording in various ways. Marston couldn't have foreseen that IBM would eventually market his decades-old audio sample to websites that were using it to construct a synthetic voice capable of articulating any content. Surprisingly, Marston recently stumbled upon his voice being employed on the Wimbledon website during the tennis tournament.

Marston's situation highlights the growing concerns shared by many prominent creators in our economy—concerns that cut to the heart of the recent writers and actors strike in Hollywood. Individuals are realizing that their contributions to the public domain can be appropriated, commercialized, and potentially used in competition against them. As this trust continues to erode, there is a looming fear that our digital public spaces could become even more contaminated with inauthentic and unreliable content.

Of course, when one can build a Hollywood film with little more than a laptop, livelihoods and arguably whole professions are at stake, too. Marston figures his AI clone has already cost him jobs and will significantly diminish his future earnings. His lawyer is seeking compensation on his behalf. But how many other creators who have had their work gobbled up by large language models will find themselves replaced by AI-powered content generators?

In the long run, the degradation of truth not only threatens social cohesion but also weakens the foundation of informed decision-making in all aspects of society. Decades of partisan media manipulation have already eroded our shared reality and undermined the possibility for constructive debates and political compromises. The capacity to fabricate digital media in convincing ways threatens to further fragment society and exacerbate ideological divides, hindering democratic processes and the pursuit of common goals.

Will the same AI technologies power the creation of robust detection mechanisms to identify manipulated content? Could new legal frameworks hold accountable those responsible for the malicious creation and dissemination of deepfakes? Time will tell, but the very foundations of truth and democracy could depend on it.

The Trivergence and People

AI and other second-era technologies are reshaping markets and economies with astonishing speed. These newer technologies are also redefining what it means to be human. While AI presents us with unprecedented opportunities to enhance our human capabilities, the extreme pace of this genuinely transformational change will likely garner a strong backlash, especially from people who feel that technology has left them behind—unemployed, disenfranchised, and powerless.

Make no mistake: there will be winners and losers in the race to develop ever-more powerful forms of AI. Ultimately, our human species could lose, hoisted by our digital petard, to borrow from Shakespeare.

We already see the effects of social media algorithms on young people's mental health: teen suicide rates have climbed over the last decade.[35] What does the *second era* mean when technology can mimic and exceed people in creative endeavors and interactions once thought to be uniquely human? Will pervasive AI diminish our ability to think critically, solve problems independently, and engage in meaningful human interactions?

With the current lack safeguards, what happens when rogue actors use the Trivergence to wreak havoc on social and economic institutions?[36] Very plausible near-term risks include the possibility that malicious actors could commandeer cyber-physical systems for destructive ends, such as holding critical infrastructure to ransom, crashing fleets of autonomous vehicles, or turning commercial drones into face-targeting missiles.[37]

The ultimate existential question may be whether humanity can even control AI now that the genie is out of the bottle. AI systems will eventually reach a level of superintelligence—exhibiting intelligence surpassing that of humans. The potential timeline for superintelligence is a subject of considerable speculation and debate. However, once this occurs, AI systems could potentially prioritize their own goals and act in ways that are detrimental to humanity. AI has no moral code or sense of right from wrong; if human, we would call it a psychopath.

The existential risks are such that there are various efforts underway to better understand the challenges and ensure responsible development and deployment of AI technologies. Most notably, on March 29, 2023, more than 5,000 in the artificial intelligence community signed an open letter calling for at least a six-month pause on the further development of large language models such as GPT-4 until the risks can be properly studied and mitigated. Notable signatories included Elon Musk, who co-founded OpenAI; Emad Mostaque, who founded London-based Stability AI; and Steve Wozniak, the co-founder of Apple; as well as engineers from Amazon, DeepMind, Google, Meta, Microsoft, and others. The open letter called for "new and capable regulatory authorities," a "robust auditing and certification ecosystem," "well-resourced institutions for coping with the dramatic economic and political disruptions" that AI may cause, and more. They added: "Powerful AI systems should be developed only once we are confident that their effects will be positive, and their risks will be manageable." Even then positive for whom is a complex question.

The proposed moratorium on AI development is no doubt well-intentioned. However, it raises as many questions as it answers. To begin with, is a moratorium even enforceable? Likely not. John Villasenor with the Brookings Institute notes that, within the United States, there is no federal or state government entity with clear legal authority to issue a moratorium on the training of large AI systems.[38] Even with a legal mandate, regulators would encounter problems defining precisely which AI-related development activities should be prohibited and then verifying compliance with the moratorium.

Enforcing an international moratorium is even more problematic. In the absence of international consensus, governments and companies will continue to invest in building large AI systems. As Villasenor points out, "The advances, know-how, and job creation arising from that work would put the U.S. at a disadvantage in AI technology."[39] In the race for this soon-to-be multitrillion-dollar industry, it seems highly unlikely that any government or company would unilaterally force its tech leaders to pause development and risk ceding a significant advantage to their rivals.

If a moratorium is problematic and unenforceable, are there other means to mitigate the risks associated with the ongoing development of the Trivergence at a global level? While there is no one-size-fits-all approach, some form of government regulation and multistakeholder governance is necessary to address the potential risks and societal implications of AI systems. In the face of advancing AI technology, we must find a way to manage its unique cognitive capabilities and control our destiny so that technology serves us.

Trivergence and You

In the 2020s, AI supported by the IoT and blockchain will enhance our strengths. Today, humans are more creative, capable of teamwork, can see broader contexts, have advanced social skills, have a better understand of our four-dimensional world, can see what is right and what is wrong, and above all, have what we now call common sense. For some decisions, particularly those requiring an understanding of massive quantities of data, the capabilities and speed of AI are far ahead of us. They can now fluently speak dozens of languages, write code in a half-dozen computer programming languages, have some understanding of advanced chemistry and physics, and have instant access to, in effect, the world's largest encyclopedia, though they have little or no understanding of context. Today, we can work with AI to enhance each other's complementary skills and significantly increase our overall productivity.

In the 2030s both utopian and dystopian outcomes are possible. Today in the G7, technology has eroded the middle class. Unchecked, the Trivergence may greatly accelerate that trend. I suspect it will take a mass movement to ensure that the benefits are shared, resulting in shorter work weeks, earlier retirements, and generally a better quality of life. Radical abundance or massive unemployment are both possible outcomes. Increased awareness among constituents to understand the challenges and proactively drive for positive change will be critical.

As Don Tapscott underscored in his 1994 book *Paradigm Shift*, the challenge of leadership is particularly pronounced during times of profound change, such as the current digital revolution. His insights into the dynamics of shifting paradigms serve as a rallying cry, urging each one of us to step up and become leaders in ushering in a better digital age.

In today's digital landscape, the call to leadership is more urgent than ever. The challenges and opportunities presented by the Trivergence and the ethical implications of technology demand leaders who can navigate complexity with empathy, foresight, and innovation. It is up to us, as individuals, to rise to the occasion and embrace the mantle of leadership, regardless of our formal titles or positions.

Embracing leadership in the digital age means becoming agents of change, seeking out innovative solutions and advocating for progressive policies. It means challenging the status quo, questioning assumptions, and actively participating in shaping the direction of the societal transformation that the Trivergence will deliver. Leadership involves not only staying informed but also actively engaging with others, fostering collaboration and dialogue to drive meaningful and positive change.

Ultimately, leadership is not reserved for a select few; it is a personal opportunity that each of us can seize. The world needs leaders who can bridge the gap between old and new paradigms and champion innovation while respecting the values of inclusivity and ethical responsibility. In a digital age marked by both promise and peril, the need for visionary leadership is evident today.

Notes

1. www.titaniumtutors.co.uk/post/wolfgang-amadeus-mozart-famous-tutors-students-from-history-part-1
2. www.searchenginejournal.com/top-5-ethical-concerns-raised-by-ai-pioneer-geoffrey-hinton/485829
3. www.storagereview.com/review/storagereview-calculated-100-trillion-digits-of-pi-in-54-days-besting-google-cloud
4. www.righto.com/2019/04/a-look-at-ibm-s360-core-memory-in-1960s.html
5. www.cbc.ca/news/science/turing-award-ai-deep-learning-1.5070415
6. www.britannica.com/animal/turtle-reptile/Longevity
7. www.wired.com/story/ai-powered-totally-autonomous-future-of-war-is-here
8. https://time.com/6295879/ai-pause-is-humanitys-best-bet-for-preventing-extinction
9. www.ibm.com/watson/empower-workforce-ai-full
10. www.weforum.org/agenda/2020/10/dont-fear-ai-it-will-lead-to-long-term-job-growth
11. www.mckinsey.com/featured-insights/future-of-work/jobs-lost-jobs-gained-what-the-future-of-work-will-mean-for-jobs-skills-and-wages
12. www.mckinsey.com/featured-insights/future-of-work/jobs-lost-jobs-gained-what-the-future-of-work-will-mean-for-jobs-skills-and-wages
13. https://finance.yahoo.com/news/corporate-profits-are-at-a-70-year-high-will-the-inflation-reduction-act-change-that-173207569.html
14. https://news.gallup.com/poll/398303/approval-labor-unions-highest-point-1965.aspx
15. www.bbc.com/worklife/article/20230215-are-gen-z-the-most-stressed-generation-in-the-workplace
16. www.cnbc.com/2018/10/22/silicon-valley-using-contract-employees-to-drive-profits.html
17. www.nytimes.com/2021/04/23/business/auto-semiconductors-general-motors-mercedes.html
18. https://ca.sports.yahoo.com/news/explainer-clock-ticks-down-towards-170106416.html
19. www.macrotrends.net/stocks/charts/F/ford-motor/gross-profit#
20. A CNN estimate from "The Lead with Jake Tapper" on September 15, 1973.

21. www.hcamag.com/us/specialization/employment-law/legislation-looks-to-protect-workers-from-being-managed-by-ai-bots/453724

22. www.nytimes.com/2019/09/10/opinion/nsa-privacy.html

23. www.cbsnews.com/news/elon-musk-artificial-intelligence-regulations-tech-executives-senators-washington-meeting-bill-gates-mark-zuckerberg

24. www.forbes.com/sites/forbescommunicationscouncil/2023/07/20/seize-the-opportunity-embrace-self-regulation-to-harness-the-full-potential-of-ai/?sh=65a5da7c2505

25. www.wsj.com/world/europe/musk-says-he-thwarted-attack-on-russian-fleet-in-ukraines-crimea-ca37aa73

26. www.firstpost.com/world/big-brother-is-watching-china-has-one-surveillance-camera-for-every-2-citizens-12380062.html

27. www.statista.com/chart/19256/the-most-surveilled-cities-in-the-world/#:~:text=The%20highest%2Dranked%20non%2DChinese,U.S.%20cities%20in%20the%20analysis

28. www.nytimes.com/2019/12/19/technology/facial-recognition-bias.html

29. www.marketplace.org/shows/marketplace-tech/how-facial-recognition-technology-can-lead-to-wrongful-arrests

30. www.reuters.com/article/us-amazon-com-jobs-automation-insight/amazon-scraps-secret-ai-recruiting-tool-that-showed-bias-against-women-idUSKCN1MK08G

31. www.mckinsey.com/featured-insights/artificial-intelligence/tackling-bias-in-artificial-intelligence-and-in-humans

32. https://aiindex.stanford.edu/report

33. www.brookings.edu/wp-content/uploads/2023/01/FP_20230105_deepfakes_international_conflict.pdf

34. www.nytimes.com/2023/09/23/opinion/ai-internet-lawsuit.html

35. www.cam.ac.uk/Malicious-AI-Report

36. www.brookings.edu/blog/techtank/2023/04/11/the-problems-with-a-moratorium-on-training-large-ai-systems

37. www.brookings.edu/blog/techtank/2023/04/11/the-problems-with-a-moratorium-on-training-large-ai-systems

38. https://healthcare.utah.edu/healthfeed/2023/01/impact-of-social-media-teens-mental-health, www.ncbi.nlm.nih.gov/pmc/articles/PMC6278213/, and https://capmh.biomedcentral.com/articles/10.1186/s13034-023-00597-9

39. https://arxiv.org/pdf/1802.07228.pdf

Acknowledgments

First of all, I would like to express special thanks to Don Tapscott, Alisa Acosta, and Anthony Williams, whose assistance and guidance were critical to making this book a reality. It was a true treat working with them.

Reflecting back, I would like to give sincere thanks to Dr. Jim Jury, who launched my interest in computer science, and to Dr. Iswar Chakravartty, who taught me the math skills that enabled me to develop some of the more complex systems that spanned my career. Further, I would like to thank Tim O'Connell at Citibank and John Kasten at Jeppesen, who had the endless patience to teach me what I know about banking and aviation so that their expansive knowledge could be codified into production computer systems.

About the Author

Bob Tapscott is a recognized strategist, CIO, designer, and speaker with a diversified background in organizational creation and transformation. As a CIO and consultant for some of the world's largest companies, Bob has driven innovations from concept creation to market disruption, delivering many millions in proven results, both above and below the line. As business has moved from technology-enabled to technology-driven, Bob has taken innovation from inspiration to the art of the possible, from London to New York to Silicon Valley. He has consulted on the intersection of strategy and emerging technologies to CEOs and CIOs for a variety of multinationals, including VMware, DIRECTV, SAP, JPMorgan, Disney, Citi, and Best Buy, on topics including strategy, business intelligence, cloud computing, and social software.

Bob's extensive experience in successfully developing and implementing disruptive strategies from the initial concept through systems design and implementation includes the training, organizational restructuring, and workflow redesign required to deliver, measure, and improve overall corporate performance and customer satisfaction. His strong analysis, communication, mathematical, and leadership skills and out-of-the-box thinking have ensured his success as an agent of change for his pedigreed clients. Bob's approach to in analyzing, developing, and deploying systems, from nuclear power reactor maintenance to Wall Street derivatives to flying today's commercial aircraft by computer, has emphasized the prudent management and mitigation of risk.

Index